'... the most thorough and detailed book on the Pakistani Taliban—a phenomena that, like ISIS, is wrapped in secrecy, subterfuge, and a reluctance to bare themselves to outsiders. Sheikh has broken those boundaries and penetrated the mindset, traditions, religiosity, and ideological beliefs of their leaders and foot soldiers.... Her book combines journalists' hunger for facts and interviews with a sociological and anthropological analysis of what motivates the Pakistani Taliban.'

—Ahmed Rashid, Pakistani journalist and
the author of *Taliban: Militant Islam,
Oil and Fundamentalism in Central Asia*

'This remarkable and timely book enters the minds and the mindset of the Pakistani Taliban, exploring motivations that are both religious and sociopolitical.... [I]t views the movement from inside, establishing a fresh approach to the study of activist religious organizations. This should be required reading for anyone concerned about the cultural politics of the region and the global rise of strident new movements of religious violence.'

—Mark Juergensmeyer, professor of sociology and
global studies, University of California,
Santa Barbara, USA, and the author of
Terror in the Mind of God

'A unique glimpse into the birth and operation of one of the most important new millenarian groups, the Pakistan Taliban. Sheikh shows that while religion is an organizing principle, it is paradoxically the fear that Islam is the target, which is part of the problem. This reversal of the Western narrative of Islamic extremists does not make the Pakistan Taliban easier to deal with; as she shows, it is highly secretive and might be with us for a long time. Her study has implications for the policy community in Pakistan and the West which must grapple with this latest variety of millenarianism.

—Stephen P. Cohen, South Asia expert at
Brookings Institution, Washington, DC, USA,
and the author of *Shooting for a Century:
The India–Pakistan Conundrum*

T0346726

guardians of god

guardians of god

Inside the Religious Mind
of the
Pakistani Taliban

Mona Kanwal Sheikh

OXFORD
UNIVERSITY PRESS

OXFORD
UNIVERSITY PRESS

Oxford University Press is a department of the University of Oxford.
It furthers the University's objective of excellence in research, scholarship,
and education by publishing worldwide. Oxford is a registered trademark of
Oxford University Press in the UK and in certain other countries.

Published in India by
Oxford University Press
22 Workspace, 2nd Floor, 1/22 Asaf Ali Road, New Delhi 110002, India

© Oxford University Press 2016

First Edition published in 2016
Third impression 2021

ISBN-13: 978-0-19-946824-9
ISBN-10: 0-19-946824-9

Typeset in Berling LT Std 10.5/14
by Tranistics Data Technologies, New Delhi 110044
Printed in India by Replika Press Pvt. Ltd.

To those who suffer from war and violence,
whether in the East or West

Table of Contents

List of Illustrations

Acknowledgements

Many people facilitated the journey that led to this book. First and foremost, I owe a special thanks to Mark Juergensmeyer for encouraging me to write an account of my encounters with the Taliban adherents, literally moments after the satisfaction of having submitted my PhD dissertation began to fade. During my research, Professor Juergensmeyer's encouragement was priceless, and I am forever thankful for the mentoring he provided during my two research stays at the Orfalea Center for Global and International Studies at the University of California, Santa Barbara.

I also owe a great deal to Ole Wæver, who supervised me during the process of writing both my MA thesis and PhD dissertation. His encouragement pushed me towards investigating the nexus between religion and violence. Ever since I attended his class on international relations and security studies as a student of political science, Professor Wæver's conceptualization of security as a speech act has left a great impression on me, and it has had a strong influence on the way I chose to study the Taliban movement in Pakistan. For this, and also for his candid support, critique, and encouragement, I will always remain very thankful.

The third of my top three heroes during my years of research is Victor Faessel, the programme director at the Orfalea Center for Global and International Studies. It is truly rare to meet a person who embodies such a sense of integrity and open-mindedness. I am profoundly thankful for all the practical assistance he provided me and my family and for his warmth and support throughout my research visits.

For assistance with data collection in Pakistan, I am indebted to the extraordinarily helpful and supportive Rahimullah Yusufzai, the executive editor at the *News International* in Peshawar. My heartfelt thanks go to him for his assistance, practical support, and guidance. I am also thankful to Delawar Jan, who assisted me with interviews in Peshawar. The driver who took me from place to place, made sure that every meeting proceeded as comfortably as possible, and intervened with helpful advice when I felt insecure also deserves a thousand thanks, though I doubt he will ever read this.

My three research assistants have been priceless assets: Kamran Khan Yusufzai in Peshawar assisted me in translating and interpreting data down to the last punctuation mark, Maja Greenwood in Copenhagen helped me create the landmark database of Taliban recruitment material available through the library at the Danish Institute for International Studies, and Daniel Zorub in Santa Barbara assisted me during the last phases of completing the draft of the book. I also owe a big thanks to Erika Bűky for helping with giving the book a final shape.

I am also grateful to Amir Rana, the director at the Pak Institute for Peace Studies in Islamabad, for his amazing hospitality and helpful attitude. And while many others facilitated my research in Pakistan, I must extend special thanks to Laila Bokhari, Mujtaba Rathore, Safdar Hussain, and Sajjad Azhar. I hope to be able to return their kindness some day.

I am also thankful to Scott Appleby, who took time out of his busy schedule to host my visits to the Kroc Institute for International Peace Studies, University of Notre Dame. His work on religion, violence, and peace building has been truly inspiring for me, and his diplomatic abilities and efforts to bridge differences are most admirable. Other inspiring scholars who have influenced me through their conversations or comments on my work are Cynthia Mahmood, Cecelia Lynch, and Daniel Philpott. I also owe thanks to the Institute for South Asia Studies at the University of California, Berkeley, and its staff, who hosted me as a visiting scholar while I was finishing my book.

In addition, I am grateful to the activists who agreed to become part of my research project. I suspect that some of my perspectives and conclusions are different from what they might have hoped for, but I hope I have not abused their trust. To take in a foreigner as they did is not an easy task, and I thank them for giving me the chance to hear and understand their views of the world.

The last category of people to whom I owe acknowledgments is my family—especially my father, who was so worried about my safety in Pakistan that he decided to accompany me to every meeting, though he surely had better things to do. I am thankful that he agreed to sit and wait in the car until I was finished with an interview that could easily take an hour or two. All these years, my mother also safeguarded me by making sure that my and my family's energy supplies were refilled at least once a week with proper desi foods. My mother-in-law has been yet another backbone of family health and well-being, and has always been willing to lift burdens off our shoulders in stressful and busy times. I am thankful to her as well for raising that son of hers who has become my rock and always supports every aspect of my work process. Thank God for him, and for my three twinkling gems, Zahra, Ismael, and little Isak.

☙

Abbreviations and Acronyms

ANP	Awami National Party
ETIM	East Turkestan Islamic Movement
FATA	Federally Administered Tribal Areas
HM	Hizbul Mujahideen
IDA	Islamic Democratic Alliance
IDPs	Internally Displaced Persons
IJU	Islamic Jihad Union
IMU	Islamic Movement of Uzbekistan
IRA	Irish Republican Army
ISI	Inter-Services Intelligence (Pakistan)
JeM	Jaishe Mohammad
JI	Jamaate Islami
JuD	Jamaat ud Dawa
JUI	Jamiat Ulamae Islam
JUI-F	Jamiate Ulamae Islam (Fazlur Rehman faction)
JUI-S	Jamiate Ulamae Islam (Sami ul Haq faction)
KPP	Khyber Pakhtunkhwa Province
LeJ	Lashkare Jhangvi
LeT	Lashkare Tayba
MEMRI	Middle East Media Research Institute
MMA	Muttahida Majlise Amal
MTT	Muqami Tehrike Taliban

NATO	North Atlantic Treaty Organization
NGO	Non-governmental organization
PA	Political Agent
PATA	Provincially Administered Tribal Areas
PPP	Pakistan People's Party
PTV	Pakistan Television Corporation
SSP	Sipahe Sahaba Pakistan
TJP	Tehrike Jaferia Pakistan
TNSM	Tehrike Nifaze Shariate Muhammadi
TTP	Tehrike Taliban Pakistan
UJC	United Jihad Council
WHO	World Health Organization

Prologue

A few weeks after my return from a research trip to Pakistan in 2008, a suicide attack occurred on the exact spot in the city of Islamabad where I had been standing with my notebook. I had been writing down the slogans shouted out at a large demonstration against the government of Pakistan and what the demonstrators saw as its submission to the American government. A 30-year-old suicide bomber affiliated to the Taliban blew himself up near the Red Mosque (Lal Masjid), killing 19 people and wounding approximately twice as many. The attack was seemingly aimed at the members of the Pakistani police force, and occurred exactly one year after Pakistani security forces stormed the mosque—it was accused of being a terrorist factory. The suicide attack showed that the government's crackdown on the Red Mosque in 2007 remained a symbol of the confrontation between the Pakistani government and army on the one hand and the Pakistani Taliban on the other.

In 2008, another suicide attack destroyed the Marriott Hotel in Islamabad, creating headlines that described the tragedy as the 9/11 of Pakistan. According to Reuters, 53 people were killed and another 266 wounded. Shortly before the attack, the Marriott was suggested as a meeting place by an activist from the militant movement Lashkare Tayba (LeT) with whom I had set up an appointment. I declined to meet there because I remembered the advice of veteran colleagues who had the experience of interviewing militants in South Asia: to avoid positioning myself as a foreigner by meeting at a hotel that was a symbol of American dominance. However, had I taken the wrong decision, I might have been there when the attack took place.

When I first travelled to Pakistan with the ambition of interviewing militants affiliated with the Pakistani Taliban movement, I did not know what to expect or what kind of challenges I would face in the process of setting up meetings. I was, however, very conscious about how I presented my research and myself in order to avoid creating psychological barriers. I wanted honest answers. I wanted to break down barriers. And I was seeking to create an atmosphere of mutual trust. However, I found myself engaging in evasions: I preferred to present myself as affiliated with a university in Scandinavia rather than in Denmark, due to the tarnished reputation of Denmark after the Cartoon Crisis (the controversy in 2005 over a Danish newspaper's publication of 12 satirical cartoons depicting the Prophet Muhammad). When accounting for my research stay in the United States (US), I felt more comfortable describing myself as being affiliated with a university in California rather than in the US, hoping my interlocutors' sense of geography was as weak as my own.

What I did during my quest to interview affiliates to the Pakistani Taliban seems more daunting in retrospect than it felt while I was in the midst of it. My images of Pakistan at that point were formed from childhood memories of the summer vacations we used to spend there—attending huge wedding parties, eating loads of *chatpattey* dishes, visiting family, and seeing many friendly faces. I had never before experienced the side of Pakistan that I came to explore as an academic researcher. Through my research travels, my image of Pakistan has become rather more complex (perhaps unsurprising for a densely populated country housing more than 180 million people), and my travels have added new perspectives to the impressions contained in my narrow childhood memories.

I was surprised to find that I could meet with, and interview, a considerable number of the militants who are depicted in news reports as secretive and unapproachable. I initially did not have a clear idea about how to establish contact with them. I assumed that I couldn't simply call a Taliban militant engaged in illegal and violent acts and agree on a time for an interview. I found out, however, that I could do exactly that, provided someone gave me a phone number.

In many situations I had to make quick and intuitive decisions that might have proved wrong. Among these decisions were choices about the meeting places. Often my interview subjects chose the place, sometimes taking me to their private, guarded houses. In some situations my driver accompanied me and introduced me. By pure coincidence, he was from Dera Ismail Khan, a city in northwestern Pakistan, spoke Pashto, and knew the Pashtun cultural codes. His introductions made some of the interviewees more comfortable speaking with me.

One of the aspects of my research for which I was least prepared was my surveillance by the intelligence services. I have no idea whether they kept track of every meeting I had in Pakistan. I only know that an agent of the military intelligence service, Inter-Services Intelligence (ISI), shadowed me during my stay in the Khyber Pakhtunkhwa Province (KPP) and that somewhere in an ISI drawer there is a file with my name and the picture he took of me. My meeting with the agent, whom I found sitting in the lobby of my hotel in Peshawar one morning, was one of the experiences I was not prepared for. Since I was continuously warned against 'the agencies', the sudden appearance of the agent at my hotel was intensely nerve-racking. It happened the morning after one of my journalist acquaintances had invited a leading figure of the governing secular Pashtun Awami National Party (ANP) of the KPP to the hotel where I was staying. The journalist had insisted that I should listen not only to the Taliban activists but also to someone with a completely different view in order to avoid bias in my writing. The situation caused me a lot of unease, since on the arrival of the ANP member, with very visibly armed bodyguards, I was told that activists affiliated with the Taliban had killed some of his family members and had recently launched a couple of attacks against him.

While I was somewhat nervously preparing to leave the hotel the next morning, the intelligence agent introduced himself, letting me know that he had received orders to keep an eye on me. He asked me about the purpose of my visit, whom I had been meeting with, what sort of questions I was asking, and so on. When I asked for his identification, he turned his back to me to lift up his kameez (without pockets) and reach into his elastic belt. It so much resembled a move I had often seen in American action movies that I leapt and hid behind the nearest pillar in the hotel lobby. Peeking from behind the pillar, I realized, to my great relief and embarrassment, that he had been reaching for his ID and not his gun.

However, my unease never disappeared completely during my research visits to Pakistan. I had heard many stories about the unpleasant actions of intelligence services—Pakistani, American, and Indian. Indeed, this was one reason I was careful not to ask the militant activists any questions to which I did not want to know the answers. I was not interested in knowing any concrete details that could be of intelligence interest, which in any case were beyond the scope of my research. On one occasion, while having lunch at an open-air restaurant in Islamabad, one of the journalists I was meeting with pointed at a food stand and told me a story about a young bearded boy who used to stand there every day. One day the boy disappeared, he said, and according to the journalist's sources, he had been 'taken' by one of the intelligence agencies. While he was in their custody a terrorist attack took place, and the boy was charged with perpetrating it.

Another story about questionable intelligence behaviour created big headlines in Pakistan in 2008 when the local *Daily Times* published a story about the terrorism suspect Aafia Siddiqui, who had reportedly lost her mind after being mistreated for five years in the US custody. The story was debated fiercely and emotionally in every newspaper and every big Pakistani news channel. It caused public outrage because interviews with Siddiqui's family revealed that they had had no contact with her since her mysterious disappearance from the streets of Karachi some five years earlier. The family also claimed that they did not know the whereabouts of her three young children, who were supposedly with her when she was arrested.

In retrospect, I believe that I could not have fully prepared myself for many of the situations I faced, since conflict arenas are inherently unpredictable and chaotic places to conduct research. Within my field of political science, very little has been written about how to conduct field research in dangerous sites where highly polarized conflicts prevail. This topic is also largely neglected in the political science literature on qualitative field research. Most of the literature on field research in violence-prone areas comes from social anthropology.[1] Even there, little has been published on the practical implications and challenges of conducting field research in a conflict setting.[2]

In order to get close to Taliban activists and affiliates, I found it important to develop an atmosphere of trust and honesty. This approach obviously contains an ethical and methodological dilemma. Anthropologists are often trained to face such difficulties through the discipline's ethos of suspending all a priori judgements and concentrating on listening and observing. For political scientists, the question has largely been neglected. Suspending judgement is a valuable ideal, but how is it possible to behave with complete honesty towards people carrying out or praising morally condemnable acts?

Once when I was interviewing a female activist, I joined her in one of the five daily Muslim prayers. This action made her speak more openly to me, giving me the impression that she now perceived me as 'one of them'. Later, when we were sitting on her bed as we chatted, she became very excited, showing me pictures of a 'martyred' family member. While talking, she looked at me several times, apparently seeking some sort of affirmation. Then she asked me directly, 'Doesn't he look peaceful? You can see from the expression on his face that he is one of Allah's special friends, right?' I nodded politely, but on my way back from this visit, I felt tense. In no way had the dead body of her relative, with blood still running from the corner of his mouth and a face full of wounds, looked peaceful to me. On the contrary, I found the glorification of blood and death repelling. In that situation I did not react honestly because I did not want my informant to stop being honest, and as a result, I felt my own honesty compromised.

Although this sort of dilemma was recurrent for me, I did not see my role as that of a critical journalist. I believed that for the most part, behaving like an uncritical microphone holder would best facilitate the sort of insights I was seeking. I wanted to hear these people's stories and understand their mindset.

I was allowed to record almost all my interviews, though I promised anonymity to some of my informants. The recordings were made for temporary purposes, so that I did not have to divide my attention between taking notes and engaging fully in the conversation. For this reason, I have chosen not to make the recordings publicly available.

Another ethical concern was finding a balance between transparency and respecting the confidences of my interviewees. Some of them were not fully aware of the consequences a few of their statements might have. I have dealt with this dilemma by translating and including only selections from our conversations that I find illustrative and relevant. I have attributed quotations only to activists who chose not to remain anonymous, and then included only the messages that they clearly wanted to convey to a larger audience. By not making the complete conversations publicly available, I have also chosen to avoid exposing the interviewees to the possibility of political reprisals or other risks or compromising the agreements I made with them.

Before leaving for Islamabad, my first destination, I prepared an initial list of the leading figures within the different

Taliban-affiliated movements, derived from researching international and Pakistani newspapers. I also established contact with Pakistani journalists, editors, and field researchers who could help put me in touch with the activists I wanted to meet. Over time I developed a sizeable network of my own contacts, thanks to the snowball effect of becoming acquainted with a number of very helpful and hospitable journalists and local researchers. When I could not meet Taliban activists in person because of my safety concerns, logistical barriers, or the fact that the people concerned had gone underground, I was sometimes able to conduct telephonic interviews. The conversations took place mainly in Islamabad and the KPP and typically lasted one to two hours, though some were shorter and more structured. How these conversations developed depended on, among other things, how foreign the interviewees perceived me to be.

Before leaving for Pakistan I was uncertain whether being a female would be an obstacle to my research—whether the activists would take me seriously or even consent to talk to me. However, being a female did not cause me any trouble: on the contrary, it appears to have been an advantage, perhaps because cultural codes might have made me appear unthreatening. On one occasion, a militant refused to speak to me, even on telephone, because of his conviction that it was inappropriate to speak directly to a woman outside his family. Through the male journalist who had helped me set up the interview, the militant proposed a peculiar but pragmatic solution: he suggested that we use the loudspeaker feature of the phone. I would ask the questions (which he could hear), the male journalist would repeat them, and the interviewee would answer.

On another occasion, I was asked to cover myself more before meeting the interviewee. Generally, I always followed local customs and dress codes, but this time my clothes were scrutinized by some of his followers and family before I was allowed to meet him. For some reason that went beyond modesty, I needed to put on a double layer of headscarves before my outfit was considered appropriate.

My impression was that the Taliban adherents wanted to talk to me because they expected a sympathetic portrayal. Although they seemed eager to get their viewpoint across, many of them refused to speak to Western journalists or researchers, either on principle or as a result of bad experiences. One of my interviewees told me how he had once warmly welcomed a BBC journalist, provided her with food and shelter in his own house, and allowed her to make uncensored recordings in a religious seminary over some days. However, the only image that made it into the TV story, he said, was a picture of two young boys fighting over a plate of food. Another newspaper journalist who had interviewed him for several hours had begun his article focusing on what was described as his 'unhygienic' toenail—the result, as he explained to me, of a microphone that had once fallen on his foot and broken the toenail. Obviously, he told me, this particular journalist wanted to humiliate Taliban-affiliated activists by portraying them as aggressive and dirty people instead of paying attention to their point of view.

The people I spoke with were often bitter not only about trivializations and humiliations of this kind but also about Western ignorance of Islam. One of the moments I remember most clearly from my travels was during my meeting with Sami ul Haq in the KPP, one of the strongholds of the Pakistani Taliban. Sami ul Haq, who is often referred to as 'the Father of the Taliban', runs the Darul Uloom Haqqania, the largest and one of the most popular religious seminaries, attended by both Pakistani and Afghan students. Shortly after he welcomed me, he said, 'In the West, fatwa means bomb!' and burst into laughter. His mirth was nevertheless quickly controlled and replaced with a serious and somewhat tense facial expression. Raising his eyebrows and opening his eyes wide, he continued: 'A journalist once wrote that *fatwas* are *produced* in religious seminaries.' He shook his head, indicating that this was about as hopeless as it gets. For him, it was incredible that a word that typically denotes the jurisprudential opinion of a religious scholar was interpreted as referring to bombs and weaponry.

From my own upbringing in the West and my encounter with public stereotypes of Muslims, I recognize the frustration of being portrayed in a certain light. I, therefore, hope that I can fulfil my ambition providing a nuanced portrayal of who the Pakistani Taliban are and how they justify their embrace of violence. In contrast to the movement that arose in the 1990s and took over large parts of Afghanistan, the Taliban is no longer a monolithic phenomenon but a term that covers a broad range of Afghan and Pakistani movements with varying political and religious agendas.[3]

I was sleepless for many nights after I came back from my first research trip to Pakistan, trying to reconcile, on the one hand, horrifying calls for violence, with anger and feelings of violation, and on the other the longing for justice, peace, order, and legitimate rights. I struggled with images of young boys who asked me what I would do if I saw my family members being killed, or if I had to live with the buzzing sound of drones over my roof; the young boys who said that if they had a choice, they would want a decent employment or take an education. With all the ambiguities I met on my way into the mindset of the Taliban and their adherents, I cannot say I ever encountered pure evil: in some ways that would have been less troubling for me and for others who are trying to comprehend how to respond to an escalating cycle of violence in Pakistan.

⤫

Notes and References

1. Ethical issues in conducting field research in violently divided societies are discussed by several authors, although their research topics and approaches vary greatly. See Philippe Bourgois, 1990,

'Confronting Anthropological Ethics: Ethnographic Lessons from Central America', *Journal of Peace Research*, 27(1): 43–54; Hannah E. Gill, 2004, 'Finding a Middle Ground between Extremes: Notes on Researching Transnational Crime and Violence', *Anthropology Matters Journal*, 6(2): 1–9; Raymond M. Lee, *Dangerous Fieldwork* (Thousand Oaks, CA: SAGE, 1995); Richard Mitchell, *Secrecy and Fieldwork: Revelation and Concealment in Post-Modern Ethnography* (Beverly Hills, CA: SAGE, 1993); Maria B. Olujic, 'Coming Home: The Croatian War Experience', in Carolyn Nordstrom and Antonius C.G.M. Robben (eds), *Fieldwork under Fire: Contemporary Studies of Violence and Survival* (Berkeley: University of California Press, 1995), pp. 186–204; Frank N. Pieke, 'Accidental Anthropology: Witnessing the 1989 Chinese People's Movement', in *Fieldwork under Fire*, pp. 62–79; Jeffrey A. Sluka, 'Reflections on Managing Danger in Fieldwork: Dangerous Anthropology in Belfast', in *Fieldwork under Fire*, pp. 276–92; Joseba Zulaika, 'Face: The Anthropologist as a Terrorist', in *Fieldwork under Fire*, pp. 206–22; Nancy Scheper-Hughes, 1995, 'The Primacy of the Ethical: Propositions for a Militant Anthropology', *Current Anthropology*, 36(3): 409–40. See also Kevin Avruch, 2011, 'Notes toward Ethnographies of Conflict and Violence', *Journal of Contemporary Ethnography*, 30(5): 637–48; Christopher J. Kovats-Bernat, 2002, 'Negotiating Dangerous Fields: Pragmatic Strategies for Fieldwork amid Violence and Terror', *American Anthropologist*, 104(1): 208–22.

2. Ethnographic studies of violence typically study the victims or subjects of violence but rarely the perpetrators of violence. Anthropologists have more often tended to investigate violence with an agenda, looking for positions from which to speak against it; for obvious reasons, this is easier to do when writing from the perspective of the victims. This tendency has been criticized by Dennis Rodgers, who argues that a critical bias towards the victims of violence leads to an under-theorization of the experiences behind the perpetration of violence. See Dennis Rodgers, 2010, 'Making Danger a Calling: Anthropology, Violence and the Dilemmas of Participant Observation', Working Paper 6, Crisis States Programme, DESTIN Development Research Centre, London.

3. There is little literature on the Pakistani Taliban movement. Those who have studied the Taliban movement (notably the Pakistani journalist Ahmed Rashid and also, more recently, Antonio Giustozzi) have focused on the Afghan Taliban and have not treated the Pakistani Taliban as a separate movement. Of the very few books that have the Pakistani Taliban at their centre, none looks at how the Pakistani Taliban justify violence. See Amir Mir, *Talibanisation of Pakistan: From 9/11 to 26/11* (New Delhi: Pentagon Press, 2009); Mujahid Hussain, *Punjabi Taliban: Driving Extremism in Pakistan* (New Delhi: Pentagon Press, 2012). Hussain's work on the Punjabi Taliban profiles only that movement, whereas Mir's book focuses on the major events during the past decade involving the Pakistani Taliban. Most of the existing work on the Pakistani Taliban and their rationales for violence, other than short articles by Pakistani journalists, are found in reports from think tanks that are connected to political positions. These are typically published by the US intelligence community and are born out of strategic questions about how to win the war in Afghanistan.

Introduction: Worlds Apart

This book portrays the new generation of Taliban militants in Pakistan, which arose in response to the invasion of Afghanistan by the US and the North Atlantic Treaty Organization (NATO) in 2001. Before the invasion, the Pakistani Taliban did not exist as a noteworthy phenomenon—as the threat to local and international stability it has now become. In spite of the increased level of global public attention, no comprehensive accounts have yet been offered about the rise of the Pakistani Taliban, their grievances, and the justifications they offer for violence. This book, based on several years of first-hand research, attempts to fill this gap.

I have had hours of conversation with Pakistani Taliban militants and their supporters, eaten mangoes with them, joined them in prayers, looked at pictures of their martyrs, and listened to their emotional anthems about the need for jihad. The portrayal of the Pakistani Taliban is based on my personal meetings with adherents of the movement and my examination of other genres of communication disseminated by the Pakistani Taliban, including recruitment materials such as speeches, leaflets, press releases, videos, and jihadi anthems. The overall objective of this book is to open a window to the narratives that flourished among the Pakistani Taliban adherents when the movement was established, and the narratives that have continued to strengthen the existence of Taliban-affiliated movements in the years after its establishment.

In dominant Western discourses after 2001, the Taliban was portrayed as a purely destructive force operating according to a medieval, fanatically religious world view. And a common political reading was that the invasion of Afghanistan was a defensive response provoked by the 9/11 attacks on the US—a *reaction*. In many Western countries, especially those that joined the Coalition and the NATO forces in the invasion of Afghanistan in 2001, this depiction persists more than a dozen years later.

What initially puzzled me and made me pursue the line of inquiry taken up in this book was the fact that Osama bin Laden expressed a similar view in his justifications for 9/11. He stressed, as many Islamist militants have subsequently echoed, that the world was *already* at war. In his view, the perpetrators of the 9/11 attacks and their sympathizers were acting defensively: they had been provoked to *react* against the US expansion of military bases in the Middle East, its imperialist policies, and militarist behaviour towards the Muslim world.[1] Seemingly, both sides believed that their actions were provoked by attacks from the other side. This book demonstrates how the Pakistani Taliban, too, frame their violence as a *reaction*. They are acting not only according to their religious views but also according to their political grievances and to the perception of being under attack.

One of the most profound lessons I have learnt from my research and, in particular, from conversations with Taliban activists in Pakistan is what it really means when people are 'worlds apart' conceptually: how devastating the consequences can be when people have completely different readings of the very same event or war. This concern preoccupied me not only intellectually but also as a strongly felt, almost paralysing frustration for a long time after my return from Pakistan. I realized that a significant part of this conflict was, and is, about the very nature of the war— that is, the two sides have very different readings of what the war is about, in the first place, and who the aggressor is. This lesson, I believe, is valuable in understanding the conflict dynamics upholding the contemporary terrorism threat to both the US and Europe.

By listening to the perspectives of the 'other side', I learnt that they were never particularly concerned about whether the 9/11 attacks were justifiable. Strikingly, a few defended that particular act and no one really criticized it. Rather, they regarded the war they were fighting as a defence of their religion, and for them the attacks on their religion had their inception much earlier than 2001. Many of those I talked to had noted George W. Bush's use of the term 'crusade' in his speech launching the 'War on Terrorism'.[2] They regarded it as proof that their enemies were engaging in a religious war.

Jonathan Z. Smith writes that a typical dilemma confronting students of religion (including myself) is whether to focus on those things that 'excite horror and make men stare' or to concentrate on common stories.[3] In this book, I employ both lenses, on the one hand by focusing on potentially horrifying rationalizations of violence, and on the other, by showing the extent to which the narratives of the Pakistani Taliban reflect universally valid and familiar dynamics of security and claims of defence—thus, common stories. While some of the Talibani justifications of violence are rooted in particular religious imagery and, therefore, appear to be more offensive and aggressive than defensive, some of these are also rooted in a concern about the security of their religion, their lives, and the territorial integrity and autonomy of the areas they hail from or are defending. I hope to bring out this complexity, and my findings are, therefore, a response both to those who would argue that religion is the main driving force behind the Taliban violence and to those who would argue that it is just rhetoric that disguises their 'true', worldly motivations.

My intellectual upbringing in a critical branch of security studies known as the Copenhagen School of security studies has made me instinctively critical of claims about security threats, regardless of who makes them.[4] The lack of consensus over what *security* implies means that it is helpful to understand security as a speech act: as a process by which a powerful actor successfully makes a claim about an existential threat and simultaneously identifies the appropriate response—very often one that involves uncompromising violence. The successful naming of threats almost always has a contextual background that can help explain why some issues gain urgency over others. We, as observers, need to step back and critically assess how it becomes possible for powerful security actors to elevate a situation from a matter of politics to one of security, where the central claim is that the threat cannot be defused by negotiation or diplomacy. This point applies to both state and non-state actors, and thus movements like the Taliban can be seen through the lens of security politics.

A central trait of religious movements that embrace violence is that they perceive their own actions as acts of defence to secure something of vital importance that would otherwise be wiped out by evil forces. In the period since 9/11, both the US on the one hand and the Al-Qaeda and the Taliban on the other have made similar claims about an existential threat to some central value or ideology and devised a (violent) way to deal with it. The similarity in these dynamics forces us to evaluate the context from which the defensive claims are made. We surely understand our own viewpoint, but we often fail to understand where our opponents are coming from. This seems to be the tragedy not only of this conflict but also of most conflicts in human history.

Why Listen to the Pakistani Taliban?

Pakistan has been severely affected by the decade-long war in the neighbouring Afghanistan. The high numbers of civilian and military casualties and the escalation of violence throughout Pakistan indicate the impact of this war. Figures from 2014, when the US was supposed to withdraw from Afghanistan, show that the total number of civilians killed in Pakistan between 2001 and 2014 is close to the toll in Afghanistan. In Afghanistan, 26,270 civilians have been killed by direct war-related violence, whereas in Pakistan about 21,500 civilians have been killed as a result of the war in Afghanistan spilling into Pakistan. Adding to this, 6,000 Pakistani security personnel have been killed.[5]

The rise of the Pakistani Taliban movement since 2001 has challenged the internal stability of the country to a degree that is arguably affecting the government's security and political priorities. The past decade has been full of traumatic events for a country whose prime security concerns used to be linked to either separatist demands (from the Pashtun areas, Baluchistan, or Sindh) or the enduring rivalry with India. These events include the Pakistani army's intrusion into the semi-autonomous tribal areas of Pakistan during 2002–4, the launch of the US drone programme in northwestern Pakistan in 2004, the Pakistani army's operation against the Red Mosque in Islamabad in 2007, the Pakistani Taliban's takeover of the Swat valley and its adjacent areas in 2008–9 as well as the subsequent army raids and refugee crisis, the Taliban attack on the schoolgirl Malala Yousafzai, and the rapid expansion of the Taliban movement from the tribal areas into the urban centres of Punjab and Sindh. These events raise the questions of what Pakistan and the Western world should expect in the future and what measures might be helpful in transforming the conflict dynamics in Pakistan.

The Pakistani Taliban became front-page material all over the Western media in October 2012, when the news broke that a 15-year-old schoolgirl and activist, Malala Yousafzai, had been cold-bloodedly shot in the head by a Taliban militant. Fortunately, she survived, but the attack confirmed the beliefs of many that the Taliban is a purely evil force without any legitimate motivation, and that there is no other solution to Taliban violence than eliminating the movement through military force. With the Malala incident, many in the West also became aware of the fact that a separate Taliban movement had been growing within Pakistan, a movement that had bonds to, and similarities with, the Afghan Taliban, but also had its own nationally oriented political agenda.

The attack on Malala displayed the most brutal side of Taliban violence. Yet it provoked immediate disagreement within the Taliban as to whether it was justified. This controversy illustrated elements of how the Pakistani Taliban justifies acts of violence and their rationale for rebellion. For example, Adnan Rasheed, the leader of a Taliban unit in the tribal areas, wrote an open letter to Malala in the summer of 2013. Although he said that he wished the attack had never happened, he also tried to express the Taliban's frustration over the West's lack of consistency in placing a value on human lives. Addressing Malala in the wake of a speech she delivered at the United Nations (UN) headquarters after recovering from the incident, he wrote:

> You say Malala day is not your day; it is the day of every person who has raised voice for their rights, I ask you why … ? [I]f you were shot by the Americans in a drone attack, would the world have received updates on your medical status? Would you be called 'daughter of the nation'? Would the media make a fuss about you? Would General Kiyani have come to visit you and would the world media be constantly reporting on you? Would you be invited to the UN? Would a Malala day be announced?[6]

With their present policies, it seems that both Pakistan and the US, with its drone attacks in the tribal areas, are reinforcing and playing into the grievances of the Taliban. These policies can only encourage resistance towards the West and the Pakistani government and security forces. In June 2014, the Pakistani military launched a large-scale operation (Operation Zarb-e-Azb) in North Waziristan. This was described as a death blow to the negotiation attempts initiated by Nawaz Sharif's government in the beginning of 2014. In the wake of the operation, as of July 2014, more than 800,000 internally displaced persons (IDPs) were registered. The suffering of refugees has been one of the most powerful forces increasing the mobilization capacity of the Pakistani Taliban. Yet many people in Pakistan saw the military operation as the only solution.

Looking back at the history of the Pakistani Taliban, the launch of the military operation appears to be simply a repetition of the mistake that led to the establishment of the Pakistani Taliban in the first place. The invasion of Afghanistan and the Pakistani army's deployment of approximately 70,000 troops in the frontier areas during 2002–4 were the primary reasons why the Pakistani Taliban took up arms. The Pakistani army's intrusion into tribal areas, in particular, was seen as an insult to tribal autonomy and the right to self-determination.

While the Coalition forces have predominantly focused their attention on Afghanistan, the Pakistani Taliban have risen to become a phenomenon that not only may pose a severe challenge to stability in Pakistan and Afghanistan in the years to come, but also has the potential to turn more forcefully against the West. Although the Pakistani Taliban have generally restricted their activities to Afghanistan and Pakistan thus far, its narratives draw the contours of a global war between Islam and the West.

The US policies towards Afghanistan and Pakistan have suffered from the same lack of insight into the drivers of violence and the factors that contribute to the mobilization capacities of the Taliban. Ten years after the invasion of Afghanistan, the former leader of the Coalition forces, Stanley McChrystal, admitted in a speech delivered at the Council on Foreign Relations that we still did not have the knowledge that would bring an end to the conflict in Afghanistan.[7] The enemy that the Coalition forces met in Afghanistan and Pakistan has indeed been challenging because it proved not to be organized according to the principles that characterize modern Western institutions and thus not amenable to our dominant schemes for making sense of institutions. With the contemporary fragmented and decentralized structure of the Taliban and shifting alliances between the Afghan and Pakistani Taliban movements, the strategy of 'cutting off the head of the snake' by killing those at the top of the organizational hierarchy through drone attacks has turned out to be an ineffective approach.

If we do not understand what drives the resistance and keeps the conflict alive, we can expect further destabilization not only of Pakistan and Afghanistan but ultimately of global security. The conflict between Islam and the West is hardly an inevitable battle between two contending sets of values or civilizations, but the fact that we are increasingly seeing forces both in the West and in movements like the Pakistani Taliban drawing on the imagery of a fundamental clash illustrates the risk that the conflict will keep on reproducing itself and that the clash will become a self-fulfilling prophecy.

Taliban Communications

This book is based on an exploration of various forms of Taliban communications. These include not only field interviews with Taliban-affiliated activists and leaders but also recruitment videos and recorded speeches, leaflets and pamphlets (*shabnamen*), jihadi anthems (*taranay*), and press releases to the local media.[8] These communications are of interest because they often explain the rationale behind different operations undertaken by the Taliban or attempt to explain the Taliban side of the picture to a larger Pakistani audience.

I have collected some of this material myself. Other material, especially the recruitment pamphlets, some videos, and press releases issued to the Pakistani media, I was able to gather thanks to considerable assistance from Pakistani journalists. Some material is available on the Internet, but many potential recruits in the tribal and frontier areas do not use the Internet or have easy access to it. This means that much of the material I have gathered is original and has not yet come under scholarly scrutiny. Most Taliban material is issued in both Urdu and Pashto, but in cases where I could not find illustrative material in Urdu, which is my mother tongue, I have included the Pashto material. Most of the Pakistani Taliban's communication materials are directed towards a Muslim audience, unlike those of the Al-Qaeda, which often also address the West or 'wayward' Muslims. My approach to the interviews and the various other communication materials has been to look for the ways religion appears in justifications of violence and to detect the Taliban rationales for embracing violence.

The interviews cited here represent only a selection of the ones I conducted. They are not numerous, but they provide qualitative insights into the way the Taliban narratives are constructed. Unlike most Islamist movements, the Taliban have no manifesto elaborating their religious ideology, and this makes the insights gained from the interviews especially valuable. My interviews in Pakistan did not follow a rigid structure but were organized loosely around six analytical themes that I hoped would help elicit their ideas of jihad: a) their definition of jihad; b) their justifications for militant activism; c) what they saw as legitimate conditions for engaging in militant jihad; d) their view on legitimate means in militant jihad, including the legitimacy of suicide bombings; e) their demarcation of legitimate targets and definitions of the enemy; and f) their demarcation of who is a true Muslim.

Most of my conversations and interviews were with leading figures in the movements affiliated with the Taliban. They, therefore, can be seen as complementary to the communication materials. The Pakistani Taliban have an interest in reaching a mainstream Western audience but are selective as to whom they will speak with. This is not different from other marginalized militant movements.[9] My impression was that because of my Muslim and Pakistani background, they saw me as a trustworthy medium for their messages to the West. Collecting these statements myself gave me an opportunity to compare the material aimed at potential Muslim recruits and the interviews. The informants' perception of me as a fellow Muslim meant that their justification of jihad did not always follow the typically superficial pattern of communication with someone they saw as being fundamentally hostile to Islam.

Talking to the militants brought me intellectually closer to the topic I am interested in and gave me a better sense of the context and the issues at stake. Methodologically, it is always important to take an empathetic approach in the interview situation and abandon any preconceived notions about the truth or falsity of the views of the world of either the subject or one's own. This does not mean that the interviewer should approve of destructive or violent action or gullibly accept the subjects' visions of the world. Rather, it means accepting that the business of the interviewer is to understand the world view of the subject and to reserve judgement for later.

I believe that most political scientists and anthropologists who supplement their theoretical work with actual field studies and observations would confirm my impression that getting closer to the subject under scrutiny informs and complicates the researcher's predefined conceptual schemes. Hence conducting the interviews also informed my interpretations of the written statements and videos and thus reduced possibilities of misunderstandings that often exist in a remote sender–receiver relationship. As the anthropologists Antonius Robben and Carolyn Nordstrom have argued, '[t]o be able to discuss violence, one must go to where violence occurs'.[10]

Initially, I also wanted to include interviews given to Western and international media. This turned out to be quite difficult, because the Pakistani Taliban have given strikingly few interviews of this sort: the few that exist have appeared mostly in niche magazines or websites (and interestingly, have been conducted by journalists with Muslim-sounding names). Those that have appeared in more prominent publications tend to have been conducted and reported very superficially. There may be several reasons for such deficiencies, among them media tendencies to focus on events rather than discourses and conceptual differences, the fear of spreading violent ideologies, the militants' mistrust of mainstream Western media, and the priority they give to convincing the local Muslim audience about the justice of their cause.

Whereas many scholars who study terrorism and Islamism dismiss public statements as mere rhetoric that glosses over the 'real' intentions of the actors, I am in fact particularly interested in these kinds of statements because of the political effects they produce.[11] The stories they tell have considerable mobilizing and legitimizing capacity. When I elaborate on my research interest in the narratives of the other side, I am often met with sceptical questions: do they really mean what they say, or are they using words strategically in order to hide their real beliefs and motivations?

Failing to take the words of one's study object seriously reflects a sharp distinction between the subject and the object, especially given the positivist ideals of science, based on the image of the individual who has an inner side that cannot be verified by positivist test methods. Those who work within a positivist paradigm of science discount the 'inside', and statements representing the 'inside' are, therefore, also regarded as invalid because there is no theorized bond between the inside and outside.

In contrast to this view, my understanding of the mind is congruent with those strands of discursive psychology or social psychology that dissolve the mind–body dichotomy.[12] Scholars within these traditions do not see discourse or speech as the product or expression of thoughts or the mind lying behind it; rather, the mind is immanent in discursive practice.[13] This view is an output of the second cognitive revolution that challenged the idea that mental and psychological entities are discrete and self-contained.[14] Instead, it brought forward the idea of *socio-mental practice* and positioned these seemingly psychological entities in 'the social world of action and interaction'.[15] Thus, my interest in the narratives is based on the view that beliefs or emotions cannot be isolated or identified outside the context in which they are expressed, and the mind (a concept encompassing beliefs, emotions, attitudes, and intentions) comes into existence only 'in the performance of actions'.[16] This conception facilitates a dynamic view of the relationship between psychological entities and the social world and implies that the discourses and narratives I have studied are simultaneously reflective of the Taliban mind.

So, to return to the original question, do they really mean what they say, or are they using their words strategically to mask their real beliefs and motivations? To answer this question, it is first important to note that there .can be differences in the messages conveyed through the different means of communication I deal with in this book. Some modes of legitimization are directed towards a Western audience, some towards potential recruits, and some might even be directed towards the individual speakers or writers themselves as a means of self-legitimization. From an individual perspective, political ideology might not fully explain a person's involvement in the Taliban, but it is still a part of their self-understanding. These different audiences are contexts that call for different forms of argumentation and different types of language. Thus, variations in discourse, even from the same source, do not necessarily constitute evidence of ideological inconsistency or strategic dissembling.

The use of religious imagery in the narratives of the Taliban, which I discuss in some depth, can either be dismissed as purely instrumental—on the assumption that these actors do not really believe in the religious ideology they are invoking but are calculating their words as if they had taken a course in strategic communication—or it could be taken seriously, as a frame of understanding that reveals the lenses through which they interpret the events they are part of. My meetings with the Taliban activists made it clear to me that the religious imagery and myths could not be reduced to expressions of strategic communication. Rather the imagery and myths, as I will explain in further detail, appeared to be the frame of understanding through which they interpreted the political events they are part of.

An argument that is sometimes used to dismiss the relevance of narratives and listening to one's study objects is that the interviewees do not realize their own motivations and hence would be unable to explain them. However, a researcher is hardly in a better position to understand the minds of terrorists than the terrorists themselves. For me, the attempt to seek the truth behind their words sounds more like the task of a psychologist than of a social scientist. Moreover, asking questions in an interview situation is not merely a neutral path to obtaining information about what is inside the interviewees' heads or determining the objective reality of a matter. An interview is always a dynamic: both parties are influencing each other and are simultaneously bound together by their linguistic and cultural context.

Another reason for focusing on the narratives of the Taliban is that invoking religion and religious vocabulary can mobilize and rationalize violence. To understand why it has these potential effects requires an investigation into the religious terminology and theological concepts that are employed. However, it also demands an understanding of the social setting of the actors. Mark Juergensmeyer and I have drawn the contours of what we

call a *sociotheological approach* to the study of religious violence—
an approach that encourages social scientists to take stock of
the religious justifications for social action, and for theologians
and scholars of religious studies to be more aware of the social
significance of spiritual ideas and practices. Sociotheology takes
religious thinking and social context seriously, eroding a stone-
wall dichotomy between theology and the social sciences.[17] This
approach, I believe, is crucial to understanding the way in which
the religious and the political are interwoven in the world views
of the Pakistani Taliban.

One of the challenges for social scientists in Western academia is to avoid taking an outsider and West-centric approach
to the ideas and concepts of religious activists in the Muslim
world. Magnus Ranstorp, among others, has noted the Anglo-
Saxon dominance in academic discourses influencing terrorism
research.[18] This bias, and the lack of a self-reflexive stance, is
largely due to the fact that much research in this area has been
event-driven and funded by governments, and has thus accord-
ingly been associated with particular political demands. It can be
mitigated by taking seriously the definitions and concepts of the
activists who are studied, thus attempting to understand them
on their own terms.

I hope and believe that an enhanced understanding of the
'other side', their concepts of violence, and of the nature of
the conflict can contribute to the development of better policy
tools for dealing with the challenges of violence from Taliban-
related groups. A deeper understanding of the mindset of the
Pakistani Taliban can be helpful, especially for those engaged in
resolution and negotiation attempts, since—rather obviously—
knowing them better will make such processes more efficient.
Peacemakers can benefit significantly from basing their efforts on
insights produced by qualitative approaches to the study of violent religious activism rather than on emotional and judgemental
diagnoses of terrorist groups. Anthropologist Cynthia Mahmood
has also argued: 'In a culturally plural world, those whose calling

is translation across cultural divides have a critical role to play.'[19] With my Pakistani roots, my upbringing in the West, and my academic interest in security studies and the study of terrorism, I have felt a particularly compelling obligation to take on this role.

Political Sensitivities

The issues I deal with in this book are highly politicized, which means that they are often approached emotionally and polemically rather than intellectually. This is true even within the academic community, which—as veterans in this field of study have also noted—is often influenced by the security–political nature of the topic and the strong opinions that often accompany fear, despite the existence of strong ideals about the neutrality of research in Western academia. Within the US and Western Europe, terrorism, especially since 9/11, has been a highly sensitive topic to engage with, and even the intellectual definition of terrorism is highly contested. I have chosen to avoid using the terms 'terrorism' and 'terrorists' in reference to my study objects because, due to their controversial and contested meaning and range, these words can be more confusing than illuminating, more stigmatizing than elaborative.

The polemical or fearful reader might go so far as to charge parts of the book with conveying dangerous terrorist messages. I experienced this type of reaction on my return to the US (where I then lived) from my fieldwork in Pakistan. At one point, I was encouraged to produce a series of portraits of Taliban militants for a newspaper. After extensive discussion of the draft of the first article portraying female militants and their world view, the editor had second thoughts, and the article was rejected with the explanation that the paper was uncomfortable presenting the women's perspectives without an explicit critical rejection. Although newspaper portraits typically try to get very close to the ideas of the individuals or movements portrayed, the editor did not want to be seen as publishing unfiltered terrorist perspectives on a conflict in which many Western countries, including my own homeland of Denmark, have a stake.

This is a reaction frequently encountered by researchers dealing with the sensitive issue of terrorism and the world view of our adversaries: attempts to understand are interpreted as attempts to be apologetic or explain away horrific acts. This book might encounter the same type of criticism, since the main idea behind it is to present the 'other point of view' as unfiltered as I have been able to—this insight can be used to condemn, learn, or sharpen our policies, but it is up to the reader.

To take another example, it caused outrage among some segments of American society when the international-relations scholar Richard Falk implied in a general comment, in the wake of the Boston Marathon bombings in 2013, that terrorist attacks should make the US reconsider its foreign policies. The challenge is that the public demand for condemnation often clashes with the intellectual attempt and necessity to understand the motivations and grievances of those who commit acts of terrorism. In response to the frequently invoked argument that writing about the perpetrators of violence romanticizes who they are and what they do, Cynthia Mahmood rightfully contends that 'until it becomes fully normal for scholars to study violence by talking with and being with people who engage in it, the dark myth of [the] evil and irrational will continue to overwhelm more pragmatic attempts to lucidly grapple with the problem of conflict'.[20]

This is why I find it necessary from the very outset to stress that my representations of the Taliban's viewpoint are intended to provide insights into an unexplored and largely underestimated mode of justifying violence. I do not seek to promote violence but rather to enable measures to efficiently deal with it, prevent it, and ultimately combat it—just not in ways that are likely to escalate conflict and lead to further violence. Much of the material I include here presents the defensive dimensions of the Pakistani Taliban's security narratives. I engage with this defensive rhetoric on the discursive level, and my discussion of it should, therefore, not be read as a justification. As already indicated, I do not recognize that the enemy referred to in the security and political narratives of Taliban activists constitutes a real threat in objective terms; nor do I condone their use of violent measures to avert the perceived danger.

I have no sense of loyalty, political or religious, towards religiously and politically extremist groups such as the Taliban—quite the contrary. The statistics on the expansion of Taliban factions and increased numbers of suicide attacks in Pakistan since 2001 show that the existing political measures have proven frustratingly insufficient and counterproductive in combating the violent activities of these movements. It is this failure that is my personal concern, politically, intellectually, and as a religious being. The diplomatic art of conflict containment urgently needs creative thinking to break the spirals of violence triggered even by defensive action. Understanding the phenomena we are dealing with is the first step in that direction.

The Structure of the Book

This book is an attempt to understand the mindset of Taliban activists, and it particularly seeks to present a nuanced and detailed examination of the role of religion in the Taliban narratives on violence. In both intellectual and political debates, the role of religion in violent conflicts is often questioned. These discussions frequently boil down to polarized disputes between those who attribute to religion an overly strong explanatory power and those who argue that religion is not a real or intellectually significant factor compared with social, economic, political, or other motivations. The truth lies somewhere in between. Clearly, religion can lend legitimacy to a violent movement: my study is unusual, however, in seeking to elaborate just how it does so. My research also demonstrates that there is no 'bulletproof' distinction between secular and religious justifications for

embracing violence. Among the Pakistani Taliban, the justification of violence draws on a distinctive combination of religious
and secular rationalizations.

Chapter 1 presents the history and background relevant to
understanding the Pakistani Taliban as a movement and as an
ideology. It describes the main events that led to the creation
of the neo-Taliban movements in Pakistan and identifies the
distinctive features of the Pakistani Taliban. This chapter also
displays the fragmented nature of the movement and the few
ideological and religious characteristics that unite it. Finally, it
places the Pakistani Taliban in the broader context of Pakistani
politics and the battles over the role of religion since Pakistan's
creation in 1947.

The next three chapters portray select Taliban activists, leaders, and sympathizers through descriptions of my meetings and
conversations with them. The selected interviews and themes I
draw forward are illustrative of the recurrent trends I encountered during my field trips to Pakistan. Chapter 2 presents the
narratives of representatives from the main umbrella organization
of the Taliban, the Tehrike Taliban Pakistan (TTP). This chapter
particularly highlights the Taliban claims of defending sharia and
the sovereignty of God. Chapter 3 features my meeting with a
female activist who was once the principal of a religious seminary for girls in Islamabad. The seminary was demolished in an
attack by the Pakistani military in 2007, an event that led to
the establishment of new Taliban-affiliated movements. Several
of the girls who survived are either active supporters of such
movements or militants themselves. This chapter also contains
material from an interview with the principal of the religious
seminary where the original Taliban of the 1990s received training. This principal, Sami ul Haq, was appointed by the TTP to
represent them in their negotiations with the Pakistani government in the beginning of 2014. This chapter highlights the
Taliban claims of defending a more material dimension of Islam,
namely the mosques and religious seminaries, and illuminates

the role this narrative has played in expanding sympathy for the Taliban movement throughout Pakistan. Chapter 4 is based on interviews with two spokesmen of movements that are often related to the Punjabi Taliban. This chapter highlights the Taliban claims of defending the true doctrines and faith. Taken together, these accounts demonstrate both the organizational fragmentation of the Pakistani Taliban and the Taliban arguments that justify violent measures.

Chapter 5 moves on to examine the written, audio, and video communications of the Taliban movement and contains a systematic analysis of the different ways in which religion is represented in the Taliban narratives. It elaborates how religion simultaneously appears as an object to be defended, as a threat, as the purpose of violence, as the source of rules and limitations on violent action, and as the source of motivational imagery and myths.

Chapter 6 contains a conceptual discussion of the implications of my findings. It displays how the Taliban narratives can be both secular and religious at the same time and thus challenge any clear-cut divide between religious and secular motivations for violence. Furthermore, it highlights the way in which the Taliban activists' framings of jihad counterpoint justifications behind conventional warfare expressed in just war discourses.

The concluding chapter returns to the question of policy responses to Taliban violence. It argues that an empathetic approach to the world view of our opponents and a more self-critical stance in relation to the question of what triggers their violence can improve the strategies to deal with the phenomenon. A militaristic strategy until now has not only failed to eradicate the problem but has actually contributed to the further growth of the Taliban movements. This growth, I argue, calls for a new thinking on how to deal with a phenomenon that has seemingly come to stay.

∽

Notes and References

1. During the 1990s, the main critique by Osama bin Laden was directed against the US support of the Saudi Arabian royal family and exploitation of the country's oil resources. Eventually, his critique broadened to condemn the US policy and military activity in the Middle East. His position implied a rejection of all forms of Western political, cultural, and social influence in the region. See Bruce Lawrence (ed.), *Messages to the World: The Statements of Osama bin Laden* (London: Verso, 2005).

2. President Bush invoked this expression in a speech on 16 September 2001: 'This crusade—this war on terrorism—is going to take a while.' See Kenneth R. Bazinet, 'A Fight vs. Evil, Bush and Cabinet Tell U.S.', *New York Daily News*, 17 September 2001, available at www.nydailynews.com/archives/news/fight-evil-bush-cabinet-u-s-article-1.919650 (accessed on 1 April 2008).

3. Jonathan Z. Smith, *Imagining Religion: From Babylon to Jonestown* (Chicago: University of Chicago Press, 1982), p. xii.

4. For the basic texts of the Copenhagen School, see Ole Wæver, 'Securitization and Desecuritization', in Ronnie D. Lipschutz (ed.), *On Security* (New York: Columbia University Press, 1995), pp. 46–86; Barry Buzan, Ole Wæver, and Jaap de Wilde, *Security: A New Framework for Analysis* (Boulder, CO: Lynne Rienner, 1998). See also Barry Buzan and Ole Wæver, 1997, 'Slippery? Contradictory? Sociologically Untenable? The Copenhagen School Replies', *Review of International Studies*, 23(2): 241–50.

5. Although there is disagreement over the exact figures, there is no doubt that the numbers of both civilian and military casualties since 2001 have been very high. See Neta C. Crawford, *War-related Death, Injury, and Displacement in Afghanistan and Pakistan 2001–2014* (Providence: Watson Institute for International and Public Affairs, Brown University, 2015).

6. 'The Taliban's Letter to Yousafzai', *The Daily Beast*, 17 July 2013, available at www.thedailybeast.com/articles/2013/07/17/the-taliban-s-letter-to-malalayousafzai.html (accessed on 1 October 2015).

7. Declan Walsh, 'US had "Frighteningly Simplistic" View of Afghanistan, says McChrystal', *The Guardian*, 7 October 2011, available at www.theguardian.com/world/2011/oct/07/us-frighteningly-simplistic-afghanistan-mcchrystal (accessed on 1 October 2015).

8. See 'Taliban Communication Materials' for an overview of the materials. They can be found in the Taliban Communications Archive hosted by the Danish Institute for International Studies.

9. Cynthia K. Mahmood, *Fighting for Faith and Nation: Dialogues with Sikh Militants* (Philadelphia: University of Pennsylvania Press, 1996).

10. Antonius C.G.M. Robben and Carolyn Nordstrom, 'The Anthropology and Ethnography of Violence and Sociopolitical Conflict', in Carolyn Nordstrom and Antonius C.G.M. Robben (eds), *Fieldwork under Fire: Contemporary Studies of Violence and Survival* (Berkeley: University of California Press, 1995), pp. 1–23.

11. Manni Crone, Ulrik P. Gad, and Mona K. Sheikh, 2008, 'Dusting for Fingerprints: The Aarhus Approach to Islamism', *Distinktion: Scandinavian Journal of Social Theory*, 9(2): 189–203.

12. Derek Edwards and Jonathan Potter, *Discursive Psychology* (London: SAGE, 1992); Horace R. Harré and Grant Gillett, *The Discursive Mind* (London: SAGE, 1994); James Gee, *The Social Mind* (New York: Bergin and Garvey, 1992).

13. Derek Edwards, 2006, 'Discourse, Cognition and Social Practices: The Rich Surface of Language and Social Interaction', *Discourse Studies*, 8(1): 41–9.

14. The first cognitive revolution brought forward the realization that all experience is mediated, that there are cognitive processes behind words and actions. See Harré and Gillett, *The Discursive Mind*, pp. 17–34.

15. Gee, *The Social Mind*, p. xvii.

16. Harré and Gillett, *The Discursive Mind*, p. 22.

17. Mark Juergensmeyer and Mona K. Sheikh, 'A Sociotheological Approach to Understanding Religious Violence', in Michael Jerryson, Mark Juergensmeyer, and Margo Kitts (eds), *The Oxford Handbook of Religion and Violence* (Oxford: Oxford University Press, 2012), pp. 620–43.

18. Magnus Ranstorp, *Mapping Terrorism Research: State of the Art, Gaps and Future Direction* (London: Routledge, 2007).

19. Mahmood, *Fighting for Faith and Nation*, p. 3.

20. Mahmood, *Fighting for Faith and Nation*, p. 272.

1

The Rise of the Pakistani Taliban

This chapter goes through the history and background relevant to understanding the dawn of the Pakistani Taliban as a movement and an ideology. I describe the main events that led to the creation of Taliban movements in Pakistan and identify the distinctive features of the Pakistani Taliban. I also seek to initially point at the fragmented nature of the movement by elaborating on who counts as the Taliban in Pakistan, and describe the few ideological and religious characteristics that unite the movement. Finally, this chapter places the Pakistani Taliban in the broader context of Pakistani politics characterized by historical battles over the role of religion.

To understand the current influence of the Taliban in Pakistan, particularly in the northwest, it is necessary to review the recent history of conflict in the region. The situation in and around the tribal areas in Pakistan has been fragile at least since the end of the 1970s, when Afghanistan was invaded by Soviet forces. The Federally Administered Tribal Areas (FATA) in northwestern Pakistan became increasingly unstable after the US and NATO forces invaded Afghanistan in October 2001, in the wake of the 9/11 attacks in New York and Washington, DC.[1] Thousands of Afghan Taliban activists, Al-Qaeda members, and their foreign affiliates (more or less organized groups of Uzbeks, Chechens, and Tajiks) escaped into Pakistan looking for bases from which to fight against the American and NATO forces. In recent years, the chaotic situation in the tribal areas has been further complicated by the presence of insurgent groups who are working for changes in the neighbouring countries. For example, the area has attracted members of the East Turkestan Islamic Movement (ETIM), representing Uighur Muslims who want an independent Xinjiang. Particularly since 2007, ETIM militants have been waging a war on Chinese interests from hideouts in the Waziristan mountains, where the Taliban allegedly have sheltered them.[2]

When the Afghan Taliban regime fell in 2001, the Taliban and the foreign fighters gradually settled just across the border in FATA and the adjacent provinces of KPP and Baluchistan. They were initially welcomed here, and in many places they were reportedly protected by the local tribes. Some analysts have ascribed this willingness to protect the refugees to the ethical code of the Pashtun population (*pashtunwali*), which emphasizes hospitality and asylum.[3] Other analysts point to the use of threats or exchanges of money and protection between the tribal leaders and the foreign militants.[4] In any case, after 2001, the Taliban ideas of governance, punishment, and public morality became disseminated very efficiently, leading to the 'Talibanization' of all tribal areas' agencies—a total area of 27,220 square kilometres—and also parts of the provincially administered areas of the KPP.

One of the reasons behind the rapid Talibanization was the vacuum left behind after 2003, when the Pakistani army deployed thousands of troops in the tribal areas to drive out warriors associated with the Al-Qaeda. The army operations and the subsequent Taliban control of the areas caused the collapse of local political systems. Until then the tribal areas had been run relatively autonomously by local councils of elders (jirgas) and had not been susceptible to Taliban influence.[5]

The Talibanization increased as a result of other local and international events between 2001 and 2007, culminating in the formal organization of a Pakistani Taliban umbrella movement in 2007. Apart from the invasion of the neighbouring Afghanistan, the most significant events in this context took place in 2002, when the Pakistani army began a campaign (Operation al-Mizan) in Waziristan to eliminate Al-Qaeda militants, sending in 70,000–80,000 soldiers. This was the first time since Pakistan's creation that its army had deployed troops in the region.[6] The campaign caused a backlash: militant groups proliferated, and several groups originally formed to fight in Afghanistan instead became engaged in the fight against the Pakistani security forces. In the tribal areas, the Pakistani army's intrusion was perceived to be a violation of their autonomy. At the same time, President Pervez Musharraf banned different religious–political movements suspected of militant activities.[7] This ban, too, had the unintended effect of increasing the popularity of the Taliban, bringing it new recruits and fostering alliances with other Islamist organizations.

Another army operation that contributed immensely to the proliferation of Taliban movements and sympathizers was the 2007 strike against the Red Mosque in Islamabad. The heavily armed deployment ordered by Musharraf also demolished the adjacent Jamia Hafsa, the largest religious seminary for girls in Pakistan (discussed in more detail in Chapter 3). In April 2009, the Pakistani army also initiated a heavy offensive in Swat after a failed peace deal. This led to a massive humanitarian crisis, with more than two million displaced Pakistanis. These refugees were vulnerable to Taliban recruitment. In the absence of effective aid from the Pakistani government, Islamist charities, including those connected with the Pakistani Taliban, used the refugee crisis to push their anti-US agenda.[8]

Yet another factor that has contributed to the proliferation of Taliban movements in Pakistan is the expansion of US operations from Afghanistan into Pakistan. Since 2004, when the US intensified drone attacks and acts of war in the Pakistani tribal areas in an effort to eliminate Taliban-affiliated activists and Al-Qaeda leaders, Pakistani factions of the Taliban have been further encouraged to organize a unified resistance.[9] For instance, in September 2008, when four American missiles struck in southern Waziristan at a time when people in the villages were breaking their day-long Ramadan fast, a *New York Times* correspondent reported that thousands of Waziris met that evening and swore to raise an army of volunteers to fight against the NATO forces in Afghanistan, if the Americans continued their raids in Pakistan.[10] The drone attacks have been perceived both as an insult to Pakistani sovereignty and as an example of the Pakistani government's neglect of its own people. Critics have insisted that the US attacks on the Pakistani soil would not have been possible without permission from the Pakistani government.

Other factors that have encouraged resistance are the enormous expansion of the US embassy in Islamabad since 2001; the Kerry-Lugar aid bill (formally known as the Enhanced Partnership with Pakistan Act of 2009), which many Pakistanis saw as an affront to Pakistani sovereignty;[11] and rumours about the growing presence of the private US security company Blackwater and its operatives in Pakistan. (The company was renamed Xe Services in 2009 and Academi in 2011.[12])

In 2009, after the announcement by US President Barack Obama that 21,000 more US troops would be sent to Afghanistan, an alliance encouraged by Mullah Omar, the deceased emir of the Afghan Taliban, was formed among three powerful Pakistani Taliban leaders—the late Baitullah Mehsud, the late Mullah Nazir, and Hafiz Gul Bahadur—known as the Council of United Mujahideen (Shura Ittihad-ul Mujahideen).[13] These three leaders had historically disagreed fiercely over issues such as whether foreign fighters should be protected, whether the targeting of Pakistani security forces was legitimate, and whether to negotiate peace deals with the Pakistani government. Although this alliance was always fragile, the fact that the three leaders joined hands at that point illustrates the important and often overlooked effects in Pakistan of the war that was taking place in Afghanistan.

The increase in US troops and the expansion of the war zone into the tribal areas of Pakistan made it easier for the mushrooming Taliban factions in Pakistan to find common ground with the Afghan Taliban.[14] New alliances that cross the conventional ethnic and sectarian demarcations of the Pakistani Taliban have also been formed since 2009: some of the Taliban groups have recognized mutual interests with Punjabi militants, foreign Salafi militants from the Al-Qaeda, and the Islamic Movement of Uzbekistan (IMU), with whom the tribal-based Pakistani Taliban do not share a culture, ethnicity, or religious school of thought.

In 2008–9, the media reported that segments of the Pakistani mainstream were also beginning to show solidarity with the militant activists. A June 2008 poll found that in spite of the increasing terrorist attacks within Pakistan, around 75 per cent of Pakistanis opposed US military action against the Taliban and the Al-Qaeda, and 44 per cent pointed to the US as the greatest threat to their personal safety (India, the historical 'enemy' of Pakistan, was next with 14 per cent). By contrast, only 6 per cent identified the Al-Qaeda, 4 per cent identified the Afghan Taliban, and 8 per cent identified the Pakistani Taliban as the biggest threat.[15] The results of such opinion polls often fluctuate, but they still indicate that in a war-torn territory, violence by either side may be resented, no matter how noble the justifications might be.

News coverage of controversial political issues has also played into the mobilization capabilities of the Taliban. These include international events such as the Cartoon Crisis of 2005–6, which has been invoked by the Taliban as evidence that the West is on an aggressive campaign against Islam. Revelations of the abuse of detainees in the US detention centres of Guantanamo Bay and Abu Ghraib have also been used to justify violent measures by the Taliban. Another incident involved the terrorism suspect Aafia Siddiqui, reported in 2008 to have lost her sanity after the mistreatment she endured during five years in US custody. Even today, Aafia Siddiqui is often regarded as a nationalist symbol and referred to as 'the Daughter of Pakistan' despite the fact that she was charged with facilitating terrorism. In this case, the conduct of the Taliban was immediately posed as a counterexample. On television, Pakistani analysts repeatedly invoked the case of the British journalist Yvonne Ridley, who was captured by the Afghan Taliban in 2001 but, impressed by their behaviour, converted to Islam after her release.

A final factor worth mentioning as a driver of the Talibanization of Pakistan is the occurrence of natural disasters. During the past decade, Pakistan has experienced a series of earthquakes, floods, and other disasters that have been interpreted by Taliban-affiliated groups as either a punishment for un-Islamic behaviour or a wake-up call from above to implement a true Islamic rule of law. After a massive earthquake in the KPP in 2005, Taliban mullahs quickly began to broadcast propaganda on FM radio stations, saying that the earthquake was God's punishment for the people's misdeeds and un-Islamic behaviour, and public sympathy for the Taliban increased. After the initial earthquake, parts of Kashmir, the KPP, and Punjab were severely affected by tremors and aftershocks that continued for months. Reports indicate that more than 82,000 people were killed and more than 3.3 million left injured or homeless.

The year 2010 saw the worst natural disaster in Pakistan's history: devastating floods across the northwest of the country left 1,600 dead, 3 million homeless, and over 20 million people severely affected. The World Bank estimated that crops worth USD 1 billion were wiped out, and damage to irrigation canals increased the risk of short- and long-term food shortages.[16]

Following these disasters, Taliban-affiliated groups initiated relief efforts among the affected and displaced communities. Relief, whether offered by the Taliban or by Western charitable organizations, increases sympathy for the sponsoring organizations among those who benefit. The massive need for aid did not temper the anti-Western rhetoric of Taliban-affiliated groups. Thus in a media interview, a spokesman of the TTP, Azam Tariq, said: 'We condemn American and other foreign aid and believe that it will lead to subjugation. Our jihad against America will continue.' He proposed that the relief work could be led by the TTP instead: 'We will ourselves distribute relief under [the] leadership of our chief Hakimullah Mehsud among the people if the government assures us that none of our members will be arrested.'[17]

After the floods there were also reports that the TTP was planning to kidnap foreign aid workers delivering assistance and that the local population had been warned against accepting foreign aid.[18] Banned Islamist organizations emerged at the forefront of aid efforts, using the emergency to win hearts and minds. For instance, it was noted by US officials that the refugee camp Sukkur Falahe Insaniat in northwest Pakistan is a charity with ties to the LeT, parts of which have become known as the Punjabi Taliban. Both the LeT and its so-called humanitarian or missionary wing Jamaat ud Dawa (JuD) are blacklisted by the Pakistani government and the UN. Generally, crises like these increase people's susceptibility to simplifying extremist viewpoints that appear to offer explanations for the misery they are experiencing. Observers have pointed out that mass migration and mass destruction of property and livelihoods are great traumas, and the frustration that especially youngsters feel in the wake of such experiences accelerates the spread of extremist ideology.[19]

Talibanization has led to, among other things, the enforcement of a harsh system of justice, including public executions of those judged to be criminals according to Taliban readings of divine law. Many of the Taliban campaigns have been aimed at banning music: music stores, video shops, and Internet cafes have been closed. In some places, the Taliban has threatened those indulging in such practices as shaving their beards, attending traditional fairs, and watching cable TV. In areas strongly under Taliban influence, such activities have been explicitly prohibited. Talibanization has frequently also implied the enforcement of a parallel administrative system and a conservative view of gender relations.

To disillusioned young men, the Taliban has offered what is seen as a just cause for fighting. It has also provided a system of quick justice and dispute resolution, and in some areas of the KPP and the tribal areas, the Taliban has functioned as a surrogate government, offering not only judicial but also financial and social services. It has offered financial incentives for support, in the form of funds paid to families of martyrs. As a result, it has gained considerable local support in large parts of northwestern Pakistan. As explained by Joshua White, Talibanization can be seen as a co-option of state authority at the local level: by playing off local discontentment with the judicial system, policing, and other state services, the Taliban have gained a strong foothold throughout the tribal areas.[20]

Who Counts as the Taliban?

Compared to the 1990s' Taliban movement that took over most of Afghanistan, today's Taliban is amorphous.[21] The name covers a conglomeration of groups and actors: some recently formed; some reorganized movements that have redefined their specific agendas to focus on Afghanistan or Pakistan; some consisting of only Afghan members; some consisting of only Pakistani members; and some with a blend of both, united by their common Pashtun identity, religious interpretation, or commitment to resistance. Though this book focuses on the Pakistani Taliban, a rigid distinction between the Afghan and Pakistani Taliban is impossible because of the groups' historical bonds and contemporary cross-boundary activities and alliances.[22]

It is hard to create even a snapshot of the Pakistani Taliban and its affiliated movements because alliances and the leadership change rapidly, and new movements emerge and disappear frequently. The Pakistani Taliban movement has increasingly become a magnet for other Pakistani religious–political movements dissatisfied with the societal and constitutional role of religion in Pakistan. The TTP is the largest umbrella movement, with chapters in most of the tribal areas (FATA) and a few in the settled areas (KPP). Among the most noteworthy organizations that are part of the TTP are the Janude Hafsa, led by Asmatullah Muawiya; the Jaishe Islami, led by Waliur Rahman in Bajaur; the Karwane Niamatullah, led by Maulana Niamatullah in Bajaur; and the Dr Ismael group in Bajaur. Examples of major organizations that have worked closely with the TTP but go by their own names include Ansar al-Aser, led by Adnan Rasheed, and Ansarul Mujahideen, led by Mufti Shafique.

Another cluster of Taliban movements is the so-called Muqami Tehrike Taliban (MTT). In North Waziristan, this is led by Hafiz Gul Bahadur, while the South Waziristan branch is led by Bahawal Khan. Among the most noteworthy organizations that typically collaborate with the MTT are the Amr Bil Maruf Wa Nahi Anil Munkar (enjoin the good and forbid the evil), Lashkare Islam, Tehrike Taliban Islami Pakistan, Ittehade Mujahideen Khurasan, and Ansar ul Islam. Each of these movements has its own leadership structure.

The Pakistani Taliban is hence a highly decentralized phenomenon that is hard to depict using conventional organizational diagrams. As with many other Islamist parties and movements, the adherents of the Pakistani Taliban can be divided between the core members (*arkan*), the affiliates (*mutaffiq*), and the sympathizers (*hamdard*). Although some local leaders and commanders were deeply loyal to the strategic leadership around Mullah Omar, not all Pakistani Taliban supporters acknowledged him to be the supreme authority in religious or strategic matters.

The Pakistani Taliban organization may best be understood as a decentralized network, with local groups organized relatively autonomously around their local leaders or commanders. Such groups emerge at the grass-roots level: the Quetta Shura, the main leadership committee of the Afghan Taliban (headed by Mullah Omar until his death in 2013), does not initiate the opening of new chapters in Pakistan. Local Taliban chapters gain some form of recognition from movements that are higher in the Taliban hierarchy—primarily the TTP leadership and its shura. The individual units mostly conduct their own intelligence collection, operations, and logistics, and their insurgency is also believed to have a highly decentralized character. Their size and the degree to which they cooperate with, or receive aid from, other units vary. Different units do seem to cooperate in training militants in special skills, for instance, by jointly operating camps that give training in suicide attacks.

Before 2001, the Taliban was typically described as a Pashtun movement. This is no longer accurate: non-Pashtun movements have merged with the Pakistani Taliban. Moreover, some elements of the new Taliban movements are in direct conflict with traditional Pashtun culture and norms, and the Taliban have killed tribal elders and attacked jirgas that stand as symbols of Pashtun identity.[23] Pashtun nationalist movements such as the ANP are among the fiercest opponents of the Taliban, and the affiliates of Pashtun nationalist movements often clash, verbally and physically, with Taliban adherents. The organizations that are not part of the TTP have only weak connections, if any, to the Afghan Taliban and the Quetta Shura. Some simply designate themselves as the Taliban; others, like the Punjabi Taliban, have forged such close relationships with the Taliban that the original organization has been dissolved into different factions.

Now I describe some of the major groups within the Pakistani Taliban and the issues that unite and divide them. One of the more recent controversies within the movement is whether to engage in peace talks with the Pakistani government. There are also divisions between the Taliban groups in the tribal areas and the increasing number of groups operating in large cities like Karachi.

Tehrike Taliban Pakistan (TTP)

The TTP is the main constituent organization of the Pakistani Taliban. Its roots go back to FATA in 2004, when the powerful tribal leader Baitullah Mehsud replaced Nek Mohammad as the informal leader of the nascent Taliban movement in Pakistan. Nek Mohammad was an adherent of the Afghan Taliban, who was killed in a US airstrike in South Waziristan.[24] From being a gym instructor in his tribal village, Mehsud became the leader of the TTP in 2007, which united about 27 disparate Taliban factions under one umbrella. Nek Mohammad and Baitullah Mehsud were the first two prominent Taliban leaders in Pakistan. In a biography of Baitullah Mehsud, who died in 2009, the TTP spokesman Azam Tariq describes the dawn of the movement:

> At the fall of the Islamic Emirate of Afghanistan, he [Baitullah Mehsud] busied himself with transporting the Mujahedeen of Al-Qaida to safe havens, and for a long time he remained in their service. When the Mujahedeen of Afghanistan started to regroup and reorganize to retaliate against the American aggression, the martyr, Amir Baitullah Masood (may Allah accept him) established Tanzeem-e-Taliban, Masood Division, with the approval of the leadership of the Islamic Emirate of Afghanistan. . . .
> Since Baitullah (may Allah accept him) was inherently equipped with leadership and marksmanship, a new and bright chapter was added to the Afghan Jihad called 'The Caravan of Baitullah'. In the beginning, he opened an office adjacent to Madrasah Nizaamia for his Jihadi activities. The youth joined the Caravan of Baitullah in abundance, and the numbers of Mujahedeen kept increasing.[25]

The movement that Azam Tariq describes as the 'Caravan of Baitullah' was the beginning of a phenomenon that later became known as the Pakistani Taliban. Mehsud's movement was initially meant to attract mujahedeen to Afghanistan, and it was initiated with the blessings of Mullah Omar, the emir of the Afghan Taliban. Since then, several additional Taliban chapters have been formed, and today there are TTP units in almost all tribal agencies and frontier regions: North and South Waziristan, Orakzai, Kurram, Khyber, Mohmand, Bajaur, and Darra Adam Khel. In the KPP, the Taliban have gained footholds in Swat, Dir, Buner, Bannu, Lakki Marwat, Tank, Peshawar, Dera Ismail Khan, Mardan, Charsadda, and Kohat.

Figure 1 Taliban presence in the tribal agencies and northwest frontier regions of Pakistan

Source: Based on the author's inputs.

In contrast to Nek Mohammad, Baitullah Mehsud not only set up recruitment offices to organize volunteers who wanted to fight in Afghanistan, but he also began a Talibanization campaign in South Waziristan in May 2005 by establishing a force called the Taliban Commandos to enforce the Taliban version of public morality and order. Its first task, according to reports from the area, was to apprehend all kidnappers and thieves, and some of the prisoners were publicly executed. In 2006, Baitullah gave the men of his village three weeks to grow their beards, warning them that no mullah would conduct their marriage or death ceremonies if they did not follow this custom (*sunnah*) of the Prophet.[26] In addition, the Taliban forbade playing music in public places. As a result, businesses like music stores, cosmetics shops, and Internet cafes were more or less forced to shut down. Baitullah Mehsud also seemed to have greater strategic ambitions. This became clear when he was accused of being behind the assassination of the former prime minister Benazir Bhutto in December 2007. He died in August 2009 from a missile strike on his father-in-law's house in South Waziristan. Shortly afterwards, Hakimullah Mehsud—another member of the Mehsud tribe and commander of the central tribal agencies Kurram, Orakzai, and Khyber—was appointed the new leader of the TTP.

Under Hakimullah Mehsud, the TTP strengthened its ties with Islamist militants from other countries, including the IMU, a dissident group that fled persecution in Uzbekistan and settled down in the mountainous region of Waziristan, between Pakistan and Afghanistan, following the fall of the Afghan Taliban regime in 2001. In terms of religious ideology, the Baitullah Mehsud-led TTP was not particularly sectarian, in the sense that it had nothing against cooperation with Ahl Hadith or Salafi movements (see the section on Taliban religious ideology ahead). In July 2008, the Taliban commander of Mohmand Agency of the tribal areas, Abdul Wali (also known as Omar Khalid), started attacking militants affiliated with the Shah Group, a local Ahl Hadith movement originally led by activists from the LeT operating in Kashmir.[27] Baitullah Mehsud was displeased with the fragmentation and internal frictions within the movement, and some observers believe that the Shah Group was a proxy of the Pakistani security agencies seeking to influence the Taliban alliance led by Gul Bahadur and Mullah Nazir against the anti-government network of Baitullah Mehsud.[28] However, when it comes to their attitude towards Shia Muslims, the TTP under Hakimullah Mehsud have proved more sectarian than the rival organizations.

Differences over relationships with foreign fighters and the targeting of Pakistani government members and security forces soon led to lasting splits within the TTP. The fact that an outsider, Mullah Fazlullah from the valley of Swat, was chosen to replace Hakimullah Mehsud when he was killed in a drone strike in 2013, suggests unresolved tribal disputes about naming an appropriate successor to Hakimullah Mehsud.

Mullah Fazlullah is the third leader of the TTP. He led the Swat and Malakand chapters of the TTP until he was ousted by the Pakistani military in 2009. Under his leadership the TTP remained divided, particularly because large parts of the tribal-based Taliban were reluctant to acknowledge him as their leader. Another issue that continues to divide the TTP is the question of entering into negotiations with the Pakistani government. When Asmatullah Muawiya, a Punjab-based Taliban leader, welcomed Prime Minister Nawaz Sharif's offer of dialogue with the Taliban in 2013, a dispute between Hakimullah Mehsud and Muawiya broke out. Mehsud declared that Muawiya had nothing further to do with the TTP. In response, Muawiya hit back by saying that Mehsud had no authority to dismiss him, that he ran his affairs independently and had his own decision-making shura.

Mullah Fazlullah was known from his earlier reign in the Swat valley. He took over the area after the Pakistani government initiated the military operation Silence against the Red Mosque in Islamabad in July 2007.[29] Expressing his support for the imam brothers of the Red Mosque in broadcasts on his FM radio channel, Fazlullah declared war against the Pakistani security forces.[30] After this incident, Fazlullah reportedly joined with other religious leaders in Pakistan to form a new organization, Tehrike Tulaba wa Talibat Barae Nifaze Shariat, to promote the enforcement of sharia.[31] With this movement he formally joined the TTP in December 2007, presumably to strengthen his capabilities against Pakistani government forces. At that time he also got appointed as one of Baitullah Mehsud's deputies.[32]

Before Fazlullah joined the Taliban, he used to be known as 'Mullah Radio' because he preached throughout the KPP through an illegal FM radio channel based in Swat. He established a sharia court that handed down sentences according to his interpretation of Islamic law for offences such as theft and fornication. Like Baitullah Mehsud, Fazlullah also set up an armed police force, the Shaheen Commandos—the Fazlullah version of a public-morality corps and traffic police. According to some reports, abandoned factories and schools were converted into prisons for men and women deemed guilty of violating the morality and gender codes of the Tehrike Nifaze Shariate Muhammadi (TNSM).[33] The Fazlullah-led group in Swat also blew up girls' schools and video and CD shops, and it spectacularly opposed polio-vaccine campaigns in the area in 2008. It also set up a parallel civil bureaucracy to provide judicial, financial, and social services.[34] The tyrannical rule in Swat under Fazlullah is well described through the eyes of a young schoolgirl in the biography of Malala Yousafzai.[35]

Muqami Tehrike Taliban (MTT)

The most prominent rival of the TTP is the MTT, an alliance of 14 groups opposed to conflict with the Pakistani central government. Its leaders are the powerful Taliban commanders Hafiz Gul Bahadur (North Waziristan) and Bahawal Khan (South Waziristan), who replaced Mullah Nazir in January 2013, when he was killed in a drone strike. Beginning in early 2007, Mullah

Nazir fell into dispute with Baitullah Mehsud over the issue of protecting foreign fighters belonging to the Al-Qaeda and the IMU.[36] The friction arose when Mullah Nazir started actively fighting the Uzbek Salafists of the IMU in 2007–8.[37] The MTT has periodically cooperated with the TTP, but the differences over cooperation with foreign fighters and with the Pakistani government have created tension between the two.

The rise of the MTT has its roots in tribal and ideological disputes. Baitullah Mehsud was a member of the Mehsud tribe, which constitutes about 60 per cent of the total population of 700,000 of South Waziristan. Its historical rivals are the Ahmadzai Wazir tribes. Although they constitute only 35 per cent of the population, they are richer, controlling about 70 per cent of local businesses.[38] The Taliban followers from the Ahmadzai Wazir tribe were led by Mullah Nazir until he was killed in 2013.

While the TTP has seemingly been fighting a larger jihad that is also directed against the Pakistani government, the Mullah Nazir group (originally called the Mujahideene Haq) advocated fighting only against foreign troops in Afghanistan. This may be one reason why reports state that the Afghan Taliban leadership became dissatisfied with Baitullah Mehsud and the expansion of his focus from Afghanistan to Pakistan. According to news sources, the Mullah Nazir group—also known as the 'soft' or pro-government Taliban—had allegedly been approached by the Pakistani government or military to fight the 'hard' Taliban, led by the Mehsud tribe.[39]

The Baitullah Mehsud group also had clashes with Hafiz Gul Bahadur, a member of the Tori Khel Waziri tribe of North Waziristan and a former deputy leader of the TTP. Their disagreements emerged when Mehsud, despite objections from Bahadur, carried out an attack on the Pakistani security forces in the North Waziri town of Razmak in the fall of 2007.[40] Since Bahadur had signed a peace deal with the government, he refused to help the Mehsud faction when the Pakistani army carried out a reprisal attack in South Waziristan in the winter of 2007–8.[41] Bahadur now leads a larger faction of Taliban commanders, including Mullah Nazir's followers. Among the Taliban movements that the MTT collaborates with, even though it is not formally part of the MTT, is the movement Amr Bil Maruf Wa Nahi Anil Munkar based in Khyber Agency, one of the tribal areas in FATA.[42] In February 2009, Baitullah Mehsud, Mullah Nazir, and Hafiz Gul Bahadur met to try to resolve their differences, allegedly at the request of Mullah Omar, the leader of the Afghan Taliban. They made an announcement designating Mullah Omar as their supreme leader and formed a new 13-member council, the Shura Ittihad-ul Mujahideen, to direct the new alliance.[43] However, reports about leadership rivalry following the death of Baitullah Mehsud make it clear that this union was fragile. The split between the Afghan-oriented and the Pakistan-oriented Taliban has remained deep since then.

The Urban Taliban

Apart from the TTP and the MTT, the emergence of the Punjabi Taliban represented a new development within the Pakistani Taliban and new patterns of alliances during 2008–10, especially for the TTP. The label designates activists and movements with Punjabi rather than Pashtun origins. However, in practice it is something of a catch-all category: not all Punjabi Taliban activists are ethnically from the Punjab province of Pakistan. Sindhi- and Urdu-speaking militants are part of this group. Sometimes all non-Pashtuns, with the exception of non-Pakistanis like the Uzbek militants, are referred to as the Punjabi Taliban. Movements frequently designated as part of the Punjabi Taliban include the Sipahe Sahaba Pakistan (SSP), Lashkare Jhangvi (LeJ), Jaishe Mohammad (JeM), and the LeT.[44]

Some of these new alliances are more natural than others, particularly those between movements that share a religious ideology. For instance, the LeJ, like the Taliban, follows the Deobandi school of Islamic thought, while the LeT is an Ahl

Hadith movement (see the definition ahead). The ties between the TTP and the anti-Shia groups, mainly the SSP and the LeJ, became stronger after the death of Baitullah Mehsud. Qari Hussain Mehsud, known as Ustadhe Fidayeen (teacher of the fidayeen), who is believed to be the mastermind behind many suicide attacks across Pakistan, was known for his strong anti-Shia sentiments and his close ties with the LeJ.[45] Because of the increased cooperation with parts of the SSP and the LeJ under the leadership of Hakimullah Mehsud, the TTP became more engaged in attacks against Shia Muslims.

The LeJ, which first emerged in Punjab in the 1990s, has recently split into different factions.[46] Its activities are spread countrywide and mainly directed against Shia Muslims, symbols of the Pakistani government and armed forces, and westerners. According to reports, its militants have established hideouts in North Waziristan, the area controlled by the network of the veteran Afghan jihadist Jalaluddin Haqqani. Its so-called North faction operates in all tribal territories, but especially in Kurram and Orakzai, where there is a sizeable Shia population.

The JeM, a Kashmir-oriented movement, is another movement that is often denoted as part of the Punjabi Taliban. It was founded in Pakistan in 2000 to overthrow Indian rule in Kashmir and has grown rapidly since its inception. Among its adherents are not only Pakistanis and Kashmiris but also Afghan and Arab veterans from the conflict in Afghanistan. This is the movement that attracted international media attention for its alleged involvement in the murder of the American journalist Daniel Pearl. It has since been suspected of having close ties to the Al-Qaeda leadership and to other militant movements in northwest Pakistan and across the border in Afghanistan, including the Taliban. The group targets Indian forces, westerners, and non-Muslim Pakistanis.[47]

The LeT (which I return to in Chapter 4) is probably the movement that is most typically referred to as the Punjabi Taliban. Generally, the relations between the TTP and the

Punjabi militants are complicated. The Pakistani journalist Hassan Abbas once explained in an interview with *Foreign Policy* magazine, 'They never merged and the nature of this collaboration remained restricted to distribution of tasks for a limited number of terrorist attacks in Punjab. Of course, they learned from each other, provided useful information and training to each other, but their larger goals remained distinct.'[48]

The reorientation of some LeT activists, or the breakaway factions of the LeT, does not suggest that it is actually merging with the TTP. The classical LeT, backed by the United Jihad Council (UJC), is still focused on the struggle against India in Kashmir. But some factions within the movement are in favour of cooperating with the TTP against the Pakistani government in retaliation for what they see as the betrayal of the cause of Kashmir. The divisions are, however, deep, since the movement embraces both activists who are strongly opposed to attacking targets inside Pakistan and activists who were alienated from the Pakistani army after 2002, when Musharraf banned the LeT, or in 2007, when the government attacked the Red Mosque activists.

The Punjabi Taliban has increasingly embraced ideas of global jihad and has been connected with attacks on symbols of the West, such as the 2009 attack on the UN World Food Programme office in Islamabad, and the planning of terror plots to be carried out in the West.[49] The collaboration between the tribal-based Taliban and the Islamist movements that were previously known for their sectarian or Kashmir-oriented agendas reflects the Pakistani Taliban's evolution from being a support organization for the Afghan Taliban (as was the case under the leadership of Nek Mohammad) to becoming a more autonomous organization that includes the Pakistani government and security forces among its targets. It has played a role in the expansion of the Taliban beyond FATA and the KPP to the heartland of Pakistan.

Since 2009, after the Swati Taliban (led by the present TTP leader Mullah Fazlullah) were ousted from Swat by the Pakistani army, the Taliban have reportedly become active in the port city of Karachi. Located in the Sindh province, Karachi is Pakistan's largest city with a population of more than 15 million, and is considered to be the commercial capital of Pakistan. The Swat operation triggered an exodus of refugees and Taliban militants, and some of them became active in Karachi. In fact, Karachi, historically, has not been a stranger to the Taliban: students of the Jamia Binoria and Jamia Farooqia religious seminaries in the city had close links to the student movement that arose in Peshawar at Darul Uloom Haqqania when the original Taliban movement was born. During the past decade, the city has been ravaged by violent clashes between parties representing different ethnic constituencies (primarily the Mohajirs and the Pashtuns), criminal gangs, and mafia-like groups seeking to seize land. The recent emergence of the Taliban has worsened the security situation in the city and added yet another layer of complexity to the violence. Evidence of growing Taliban influence includes the emergence of informal Taliban courts in suburbs dominated by Pashtun groups, Taliban attacks on the Shia population living in the city, and the arrest of a series of Taliban leaders. At the same time, the Taliban conflict with the Pashtun nationalist movement, the ANP, has expanded from the KPP to Karachi, which is home to several million Pashtuns.[50]

Rivalries among adherents of different TTP factions in Karachi have made it increasingly clear that the movement has an extraordinary capacity to multiply and expand without being ideologically or ethnically coherent. The most powerful faction of the TTP in Karachi is dominated by the Mehsud tribe. It was divided into two groups, one loyal to the TTP's former chief Hakimullah Mehsud and the other to the TTP chief in South Waziristan, Waliur Rehman Mehsud. In 2013, the two factions clashed, and the faction loyal to Waliur Rehman Mehsud killed dozens of Hakimullah Mehsud's adherents. Another Taliban faction active in Karachi largely comprises Swati militants who are loyal to Mullah Fazlullah, the present leader of the TTP umbrella. The Swati and Mehsud militants migrated to Karachi after military operations began in Swat and South Waziristan in 2008 and 2009, respectively. Evidence of a fundraising campaign suggests that the Mohmand chapter of the TTP has also been active in Karachi since 2011.[51]

In June 2014, one of the largest TTP attacks took place at the Jinnah International Airport in Karachi. After a siege that lasted for hours, 36 people were dead, including the assailants. The TTP immediately claimed responsibility and justified the attack with reference to the drone attack that killed Hakimullah Mehsud in North Waziristan in 2013 and the Pakistani army's air strikes in the tribal areas. They also stated that Karachi airport was a target because Karachi handles the US and NATO cargo bound for Afghanistan. Although subsequent evidence pointed to the IMU's involvement in the airport attacks, these developments show the degree to which the Taliban phenomenon has become entrenched in the urban areas of Pakistan.

Taliban Religious Ideology and Discourse

Unlike other Islamist movements that appeared in the twentieth century, the Taliban has never had strong ideological or intellectual roots. While Islamic revivalism in Muslim countries has often been based on a tradition of scholarly debate and writing, the Taliban leaders and followers often were, and are, poorly educated in the corpus of Islamic studies. Indeed, although it employs an active religious vocabulary, the movement is often linked to outright criminal networks, smugglers, and gangs.[52] Thus, ideologically and in practice, the Taliban remains a unique movement with no real precedent in Islamist ideas and movements.

Nevertheless, some core aspects of the Taliban creed and ideology can be identified with and categorized among well-known positions within Islamic or Islamist thought. Most of the Taliban movements identify with the Sunni branch of Islam, which is the most common in both Pakistan and Afghanistan (accounting for approximately 75 per cent of the Pakistani population).[53] Many of the groups that have joined the 'caravan of the Taliban' also have strong anti-Shiite sentiments. Thus these movements have a narrow definition of what it means to be a true Muslim.

Within the Sunni branch of Islam, most Pakistani Taliban factions follow the Hanafi school of jurisprudence,[54] though parts of their jihad discourses, as I show ahead, arguably deviate from classical interpretations of the conduct of jihad. This is the most common tradition in Pakistan and Afghanistan. However, the 'classical' Taliban factions that arose in the tribal areas of Pakistan also adhere to the Deobandi school of thought. The Barelvi (constituting approximately 60 per cent of the Pakistani population), the Ahl Hadith (approximately 4 per cent), and the Deobandi (approximately 15 per cent) schools of thought are the three main Sunni traditions in Pakistan.

Deoband is a city in India with an influential religious seminary (madrassa), the Darul Uloom Deoband. The theological position of the Deobandis is heavily influenced by the views of the eighteenth-century Muslim reformer Shah Wali Allah. He addressed what he saw as the decline of faith, moral degeneration, and an increase in superstition among Indian Muslims by approaching metaphysical issues with a rational interpretation.[55] The religious scholars (*ulama*) from the Deoband seminary in British India called for resistance to the encroachment of Western culture through adherence to authentic Islamic values and rejection of practices that they believed had watered down the true Islam.

A key difference between the Barelvi and Deobandi schools of thought is that the Barelvis believe in intercession between humans and divine grace by means of an ascending chain of holy personages (pirs), reaching ultimately to the Prophet Muhammad, who intercedes with Allah on their behalf. Wali Allah was against this belief and argued that intermediaries create distance between the divine (and the scriptures) and the individual believer.

The Deobandis thus reject many of the traditions related to Sufism (which in Pakistan is often equated with the Barelvi school) and claim that Barelvis are guilty of (harmful) innovation (*bidaat*) and thus deviate from the true path. Nevertheless, the Deobandis do not reject mysticism as such: they believe in the cultivation of God-consciousness (*tassawuf*) through prayer and other rituals. They believe that God can directly guide pious Muslims, for instance, through dreams.

Although the original core of the Taliban was influenced by Deobandi culture, the Taliban in Pakistan are also inspired by Ahl Hadith groups, especially since their collaboration with the Punjabi Taliban. The Mehsud-led Taliban's protection of Al-Qaeda-affiliated activists also points to the fact that the Ahl Hadith followers are not considered to be apostate Muslims like the Shia Muslims. The Ahl Hadith (the people of prophetic narrations) are the Pakistani Salafis, a puritanical movement closely linked with the Wahhabism of the Arabian Peninsula. The principal tenet of Salafism is the view that Islam was perfect and complete during the days of Muhammad and his companions, but that undesirable innovations have been introduced through materialist and cultural influences from the West.

Brought to India in the late nineteenth century, the Ahl Hadith tradition reasserted the Quran and the *Hadith* (narrations about the deeds and sayings of the Prophet Muhammad) as the only supreme authorities and sources of law in Islam. More than the Deobandis, the followers of Ahl Hadith are critical of Sufi practices such as superstitions, festivals, and temple and saint worship, seeing in them polytheistic influences. To Ahl Hadith followers, the Sufi adoption of some Hindu and Buddhist rituals constitutes idolatry (*shirk*). The number of Ahl Hadith adherents in Pakistan has historically been low because of the long-established Sufi traditions in South Asia, but the followers of Ahl Hadith enjoy the support of wealthy Saudi patrons. The Ahl Hadith movement has grown in popularity since the end of the Cold War, mainly because of this patronage and the return to Pakistan of many Pakistani workers from the Gulf region, who have been influenced by Wahhabi doctrines.

Although they share the Salafis' opposition to Western influence and their call for authenticity, the Deobandis are strict believers in adherence to prior legal rulings (*taqlid*). Deobandi groups proliferated in Pakistan, especially under the Zia-ul-Haq regime and during the jihad against the Soviet army in Afghanistan. Many of the religious seminaries established during that period followed the Deobandi school of thought and provided sanctuary to refugees, some of whom joined the Taliban. However, as Joshua White has observed, the era of jihad against the Soviet army led to a new ideological emphasis in madrassa culture. The new, less rigorously trained clerical class, 'the petty ulama', had only loose connections with the intellectual Deobandi establishment. These changes brought along 'new legitimating ideologies of jihad that had previously not held a significant place in Deobandi religious thought, combined with a newly decentralized educational infrastructure'.[56] In White's view, they paved the way for the Taliban ideology and the proliferation of a 'Kalashnikov culture'.[57] Ahmed Rashid also observes that the Taliban fit poorly into the existing and historical Islamist landscape: he describes their ideological base as 'an extreme form of Deobandism'.[58]

Lacking a coherent ideological manifesto or intellectual foundation, the ideological inclinations of the Pakistani Taliban are best defined through their actions and communications. Since their inception in the 1990s, the 'original' Afghan Taliban have embraced a highly conservative interpretation of sharia propagating a view of true Muslim moral behaviour cleansed of what they regard as bad influences, especially from TV and music (which they see as corrupted by cultural influences from the West). Further, they have promoted a conservative view of the rights and conduct of women, enforcing the wearing of the burka in public and often (though not unanimously) opposing women's education and their participation in public and political life. And finally, they have defended or actively created parallel justice systems to enforce the Taliban interpretation of sharia, with harsh summary punishments meted out to offenders. The use of stoning, whipping, and amputation of body parts has been one of the main means of establishing a Taliban social order. Still, their understanding of Islamic thought is blurry and incoherent, and it is unclear how their vision of an ideal punishment system connects to doctrinal interpretations in other areas.

The Taliban started out in the 1990s as an idealist reform movement, intended to stop the ex-mujahedeen and warlords from fighting each other rather than cooperating to establish a stable Afghan society. They introduced the idea of divine law as the guarantor of peace and order and thus promoted a highly legalist and formalist concept of sharia, which they placed at the very heart of Islam. This ideology offered a simple and relatively successful means of uniting a country divided by affiliations to particular tribes, ethnic or linguistic groups, and clans.

The concept of sharia, literally meaning 'path' or 'way', carries a wide range of connotations and has been implemented in widely different ways in different historical periods and geographical contexts.[59] It remains the basis of many battles over private religious practice and the role of religion in public life. One common interpretation of the concept is 'divine law', but another view represents it as an inflexible set of divine laws that can be directly implemented as 'the law of the land' (*qanun*). When the Taliban opted for a larger role for religion in Pakistan, they adopted this latter concept of sharia. In the Taliban interpretation, the sovereignty of sharia (as the law of the land) is equivalent to the sovereignty of God. So when the Taliban represent themselves as the guardians of sharia, they are simultaneously casting themselves as the guardians of God.[60] In Pakistan, the Taliban allies itself with religious–political movements that criticize the state for its failure to implement sharia, which they regard as a constitutional obligation of an Islamic state. As such, the Pakistani Taliban is part of a century-old battle about the role of religion in state and society, as I elaborate in the next section.

Within religious discourse, sharia has been the focus of a struggle between the legalistic approach to religious practice and the ethical and mystical approach advocated most strongly by the Sufis. As Muhammad Masud recounts, the Sufis challenged the literalist and legal interpretation of religious obligation and 'suggested an emphasis on the inner meanings of *shari'a* and personal commitment as the motive for obedience to *shari'a* laws, instead of punishment and coercion'.[61] Nevertheless, the orthodox legalistic view of sharia has always been powerful, and this is also the one embraced by the Taliban. One of the early (fourteenth-century) attempts to categorize the objectives of sharia as law (*maqasid al-sharia*) concluded that the purpose of sharia as law is to protect five basic human interests: life, property, family, faith, and intellect.[62] These purposes arguably have become part of an orthodox jurisprudential discourse, which was codified in different schools of law within both Sunni and Shia Islam.

Today many Muslims still abide by one of these schools of thought; however, managing societal relations demands a reinterpretation of rules and injunctions to fit the changing social contexts.[63] To deal with this question, jurists often make a distinction between universal law and context-dependent law by distinguishing those parts of the Quran that can be taken as containing a universal message and those that should be understood as applicable only in the particular historical context in which they were revealed.[64] The Taliban movements are notable in that they do not recognize the potential for change in the rules that concern societal relations as a positive capacity of religion; instead, they represent it as a threat. Their resistance to change is often accompanied by the tendency to declare those who do not follow the footsteps of the early generations of Muslims closely enough as apostates or unbelievers (*kuffar*).

The jurisprudential arguments that the Taliban use represent a mix between classical sources and the specific Taliban emphasis on a system of punishment for wrongdoing. An example is a video issued by the TTP, which in accordance with orthodox jurisprudential views, defines the purpose of sharia (maqasid al-sharia) as protecting 'religion, intelligence, honor, life, and wealth/property'. However, the video continues by elaborating a specific scheme of punishment that is not derived from classical sources: 'For the protection of wealth, cutting off a thief's hand; for the protection of life, killing the culprit, hanging, or banishment; for the protection of honor, lashing the unmarried or stoning the married; for the protection of intelligence, flogging the drunk; and for the protection of religion [*deen*], liquidating an apostate [*murtad*] and performing jihad against the kuffar.'[65]

Besides sharia, another central concept of Taliban religious vocabulary is jihad. This has often been a catalyst for political change in Muslim societies, for example, during the Taliban takeover in Afghanistan, and today in parts of Pakistan. Contrary to the common public perception in the West, where the term is often mistranslated and oversimplified as 'holy war', jihad is a complex concept that has had many different connotations throughout Islamic history.[66] The word literally means 'striving', and such striving can take many forms. However, as David Cook observes, central to the concept is a struggle that has some sort of spiritual significance.[67] In some Muslim discourses, jihad refers mainly to an inner struggle against the lower soul, whereas other discourses use the term to refer to actual warfare, waged with a religious or spiritual purpose. While early Muslim legal scholarship, which is the source of formalistic interpretations of sharia, was concerned mostly with jihad as warfare, the mystical tradition embraced by the Sufis in the first half of the ninth century stressed a struggle against lust and worldly passion, which were seen as the main obstacles on the path towards God.[68] Following the tradition of the famous Muslim theologian and Sufi Al-Ghazali (d. 1111), this struggle against the lower self is widely known as the greater jihad (al-jihad al-akbar), whereas the militant struggle is known as the lesser jihad (al-jihad al-asghar).

The two main discourses on jihad are often presented as diametrically opposed: jihad is conceived of either as a militant struggle against human enemies or as a moral and spiritual struggle against the Devil and personal sins. In reality, the distinction is less clear-cut. Though many interpreters of the main Islamic legal sources (the Quran and Hadith literature) deal with jihad as a militant doctrine, the concept of jihad as warfare does not exclude the idea of a cosmic struggle against evil or the quest for self-purification. The jihad-as-warfare discourse often also draws on the self-purification discourse, and hence jihad is a multilayered concept with an attraction and effect that can be understood properly, only if these layers and their interplay are identified and disentangled. For instance, militant movements and ideologues often stress the redemptive aspect of jihad: a *mujahid* who has sinned throughout his life will be forgiven if he repents and joins warfare jihad. The Arab term 'fidayee', which has been adopted by the Taliban, draws more directly on the idea of self-sacrifice.[69] The infinitive *fida* means 'redemption' and the noun 'fidayeen' is widely understood to mean those willing to sacrifice themselves for a religious cause. It thus carries an altruistic and spiritually noble connotation.

The conditions, boundaries, and proper conduct of militant jihad were given a relatively coherent expression by Muslim jurists between the years 1,000 and 1,500, when Muslim rulers had expanded their powers through extensive conquests but also faced the Christian crusades and Mongol invasions. Thus they had engaged in both offensive and defensive types of war. These events prompted a debate about questions such as when jihad is legitimate, defining the conditions that justify jihad, deciding when those conditions are fulfilled, and specifying who is authorized to declare it. Related issues included standards for the proper conduct of warfare—the extent and type of damage that can be inflicted on the enemy, who can be killed and where, and how prisoners of war should be treated—and questions such as who should participate in jihad and the moral qualities required of leaders. These debates produced the criteria that have been used for centuries to differentiate jihad from warfare without a noble cause, thus placing the early legal definitions and regulations in the same category as Western just war traditions.

The justifications of jihad as warfare have varied depending on the historical context. They have ranged from expanding Muslim territory to defending religion against infidels, to a more socialist vision of creating justice and equality.[70] In Muslim jurisprudence and legal discussions, jihad as warfare has often been presented as part of the overall Quranic doctrine of 'enjoin the good and forbid the evil' (al-amr bil maruf wa nahi an al-munkar). This doctrine has been encoded in sharia as three sorts of activities (sometimes presented hierarchically, with warfare jihad as the last stage, and at other times presented on equal footing): missionary (dawa) activities, educational (tarbiyyati) activities, and warfare jihad. With the influential Muslim reformers and modernists Muhammad Abduh and Rashid Rida in the early twentieth century, jihad became a central concept in Islamic theology, since it was linked to the concept of shahada, which is the Muslim declaration of faith, literally meaning 'to bear witness'. (The same word's root form denotes a martyr or shaheed.) The ideas of Abduh and Rida have mainly been interpreted as speaking the truth before an unjust ruler and opposing injustice. They have also been interpreted as critiques of earlier Muslim doctrines of total compliance and loyalty to political leaders.[71]

Among militant movements like the Taliban, being a mujahid carries considerable spiritual prestige, as expressed in martyrdom praise and miracle stories. Among some of the stories that flourished during the Soviet occupation of Afghanistan were, for example, that the wounds of mujahedeen heal miraculously quickly, a martyr's body has a sweet smell, light shines from martyrs' graves, mujahedeen are assisted by divine or angelic intervention through dreams and prognostications, and so on.[72] In Islamic historical literature, Islam's first conquests are also often described as miracles confirming the truth of the religion. Similar imagery is evident in Taliban narratives (see Chapter 5).

The Taliban concept of jihad also incorporates an apocalyptic and messianic aspect. What triggers the necessity of jihad, apart from the imperative to spread the faith or to defend it from hostile attack, are signs of the last days, which may include moral decay, political injustice or instability, natural disasters, or the appearance of an Antichrist (in Muslim terminology, the *Dajjal*). The apocalyptic basis of jihad raises the expectation of the appearance of the Messiah (*imam Mahdi*), who will lead the battles of the last days. In this view, jihad is also seen as a path to salvation, since the last days are expected to separate the righteous from the damned. The belief in an approaching apocalypse is especially germane to the Taliban view of jihad, since traditional literature on the apocalypse relates messianic expectations to the geographical area historically known as Khurasan, of which Afghanistan is a part.[73]

Taliban and the Project of Pakistan

> The real objective of Pakistan and the slogan on which it came into being was *la ilaha illallah* [there is no God but God]. We will continue our jihad against the government of Pakistan until the system of la ilaha illallah is established in the country. (Hakimullah Mehsud, the former head of the TTP)

The product of a religious divide since its inception, Pakistan has contained stark contradictions, plural identities, and multiple positions over the role of religion in state and society. The Taliban nationalist discourse appears in the context of a Pakistan that has always disagreed on what role religion should play in state and society. This context is an important backdrop to understanding the narratives of the Taliban that I will go deeper into in the next chapters.

During the years that I have studied the Pakistani Taliban's communications and recruitment materials, I have noticed a transformation in its rhetoric about the raison d'être of the movement. Since 2012, the communications of the TTP have increasingly engaged with the question of why Pakistan was established in the first place. This discourse goes back to the moment when Pakistan was formed following the partition of India in 1947. Put simply, the discourse on Pakistan's religious identity has been shaped by a battle between parties who argued that Pakistan was created as a state for Muslims and those who argued that Pakistan should be defined by a particular interpretation of Islam, and hence be an Islamic state.

This dispute over the religious identity of Pakistan and the role religion should play in state and society are becoming increasingly important questions for the Pakistani Taliban. With the foreign combat forces' withdrawal from Afghanistan in 2014, the original Taliban raison d'être of a war against foreign occupation diminished, and parts of the Pakistani Taliban acquired a permanent voice in national affairs, on par with Islamist movements such as the Jamiat Ulamae Islam (JUI) and the Jamaate Islami (JI), which have long been part of the national political discourse.

The history of Pakistan is—like every other history—only one story about the creation and purpose of Pakistan. Creating one nation out of people who primarily identified with India or with their ethnic background—whether Baluch, Sindhi, Pathan, or Punjabi—was not an easy task.[74] Somewhere during this process, competing stories about what Pakistan's identity should be were suppressed. Violent resistance, whether from Taliban-related groups or ethnic nationalists, can be seen as signs of attempts to write a different history of Pakistan.

The dominant narrative of the birth of Pakistan puts Muhammad Ali Jinnah (1876–1948) at the centre, together with the nationalist poet Muhammad Iqbal (1877–1938). In 1938, when Jinnah advanced the two-nation idea at a Muslim

League conference, he argued that Pakistan was a separate nation by virtue of its religious identity.[75] However, since the founding of Pakistan, there has never been lasting consensus about the implications of the common Islamic legacy in the country. The unsettled relationship between Islam and the Pakistani nation has, on the contrary, created a space for Islamism and religious militancy. A glance through the political history of Pakistan shows that Islam has never been manifest as an unambiguous basis of rule, but has appeared in many different roles under different governments.

Three days before Pakistan was born, Jinnah framed it as a Muslim *homeland* rather than an Islamic state. He elaborated: 'You may belong to any religion or caste or creed—that has nothing to do with the business of the state.... We are starting with this fundamental principle that we are all citizens and citizens of one state.... [I]n the course of time Hindus would cease to be Hindus and Muslims would cease to be Muslims, not in the religious sense, because that is the personal faith of each individual, but in the political sense as citizens of the state.'[76]

Against such an understanding, the JI, now Pakistan's oldest religious–political party, rallied for the creation of an Islamic state, with a rule of law based in religion.[77] Pakistan's first constitution (of 1956) was a compromise between two normative notions of the place of religion in a Muslim country: the nation was simultaneously declared an Islamic republic and a parliamentary democracy.[78] The same constitution stipulated that the head of state should be a Muslim and that no law could contradict Islamic sources of jurisprudence (meaning primarily the Quran and Sunnah).[79] Since then, the practical definition of a common Muslim identity and what it should imply for state institutions have been questions at the core of Pakistani politics, dividing the nation along theological, political, and sectarian lines.[80]

When Mohammad Ayub Khan established the first military regime in Pakistan in 1958, he sought a greater separation of religion and state. In the new constitution, the word 'Islamic' was removed from Pakistan's official name. Nevertheless, he used religion to legitimize selective reforms. His government sponsored educational organizations that would advance what he saw as rational and liberal interpretations of Islamic belief and challenge the powerful interpretations of the clerics (ulama), which were disseminated through the conservative religious seminaries. The successor to the military regime, Zulfikar Ali Bhutto (1971–7), replaced what he saw as a westernized concept of religion with a socialist model, at first retaining the divide between religion and state. Bhutto commonly invoked Islamic principles to explain foreign policy and domestic decisions inspired by socialism. With the civil war in 1971, which led to the secession of Bangladesh, questions about Pakistan's identity as a Muslim homeland re-emerged. Thereafter, religion occupied an increasingly prominent position in the political discourse. The constitution of 1973 restored the word 'Islamic' to the title of the Republic of Pakistan.[81]

For some political actors, however, this name change was hardly sufficient. General Zia-ul-Haq, who succeeded Bhutto, legitimized his military takeover in 1977 in the name of Islam and promised to create a real Islamic system. Under Zia-ul-Haq, particular versions of Islamic law were invoked to postpone free elections, enforce strict media censorship, prohibit political parties, ban alcohol and gambling, reform the penal codes, and introduce economic reforms such as interest-free banking. Divisions between competing religious orientations became highly visible in Pakistani society, leading to serious clashes.[82] For some observers, these events proved the impossibility of developing consensus about the role of religion in Pakistan.[83] Sectarian differences made it difficult to create national and official religious institutions like those established in other Muslim countries, such as Egypt or Saudi Arabia. Conversely, the limited power held by religious institutions at the national level has always given Pakistan's political leaders the latitude to interpret religion in different ways and contexts.

With the democratic elections in 1988, Benazir Bhutto of the Pakistan People's Party (PPP) became the prime minister. Although she made a highly publicized pilgrimage to Mecca after her appointment and made use of Islamic vocabulary and symbolism, she articulated a less powerful role for Islam. She was challenged by the Islamic Democratic Alliance (IDA, a coalition of nine parties). By 1990, the IDA had won the elections, and Nawaz Sharif (of the Muslim League-N) replaced Benazir Bhutto. Under Sharif, Pakistan became engaged in ensuring a political leadership in Afghanistan that adhered to a Sunni interpretation of Islam and respected the border between the two countries.

Pervez Musharraf's military takeover in 1999 led to the suspension of the Pakistani constitution, and once again triggered intense public debate about how to negotiate a harmonious relationship between religion, pluralism, and democracy.[84] Musharraf, somewhat paradoxically, argued for the establishment of a true democracy but also made it clear that the government should follow true Islam.[85] In October 2002, free elections were held again, and the coalition Muttahida Majlise Amal (MMA, or the United Action Front), consisting of six religious–political parties with strong rhetorical connections to Islam, the PPP, and Muslim League-Q (Quaide Azam faction) won a majority.[86] With the general elections, Pakistan officially returned to democracy, but Musharraf remained in power, this time as the president of the country. The MMA was strongly opposed to the anti-terrorism campaign in Afghanistan that had ousted the Taliban from power. Claiming that Musharraf had become a tool of US foreign policy, the group campaigned on promises to enforce sharia and rallied to call for the withdrawal of US forces.[87]

The period under Musharraf's rule saw a significant increase in militant religious–political movements.[88] Many were banned but simply resurfaced under different names. The emergence of Pakistani Taliban organizations after the US-led invasion of Afghanistan was part of this picture. Some of the militants who fought in solidarity with the Afghan Taliban saw their resistance as a repetition of history: a battle against foreign occupation like the battle against the Soviet forces. With the Pakistani army's deployment of troops in the tribal areas during the period between 2002 and 2004, the Taliban loyalists gradually consolidated an independent Pakistani identity. Between 2003 and 2007, the armed rebellion against the army's intrusion into the tribal areas gradually turned into a religious battle. The Taliban declared the Pakistani army to be apostates, thus defining them as legitimate targets of jihad. In 2007, the TTP was established with the dual aims of fighting the invading forces in Afghanistan and the Pakistani army and government. After Musharraf resigned from the presidency in 2008, Asif Ali Zardari of the PPP became the new president after a tumultuous campaign period during which his wife, Benazir Bhutto, was assassinated in a plot allegedly planned by the now-deceased leader of the TTP, Baitullah Mehsud.

This tumultuous political history illustrates the ebb and flow of different religious discourses in Pakistani politics.[89] Religion has been framed both as a somewhat diffuse component of national identity and as a well-defined religious and social order based on sharia. The Taliban factions in Pakistan today represent segments of Pakistani society that want Islam to play a larger role not only in the country's constitution but also in its civil laws. This historical struggle is an important backdrop to the narratives of Taliban leaders, adherents, and sympathizers I introduce in the next three chapters.

༚

Notes and References

1. Since the establishment of the state of Pakistan, FATA has been relatively autonomous. The seven tribal agencies—Bajaur, Mohmand, Orakzai, Khyber, Kurram, North Waziristan, and South Waziristan—are each administered by a political agent (PA) who

is in charge of the agency overall, while the tribal leader (*malik*) mediates between the administration and the tribes. The PAs report to the KPP governor, who is appointed by the Pakistani president. Criminal cases and disputes are traditionally settled by the tribesmen through a council of tribal elders (jirga) that determines the guilt of the accused under customary law—which, among other things, allows collective punishment. The provincially administered tribal areas (PATA; administered by the KPP) include the districts of Swat, upper and lower Dir, Buner, and Shangla.

2. See Mona Kanwal Sheikh and Gareth Price, 'Pakistan: A Stage for Regional Rivalry', in Mona Kanwal Sheikh, Farzana Shaikh, and Gareth Price (eds), *Pakistan: Regional Rivalries, Local Impacts* (Copenhagen: Danish Institute for International Studies and Chatham House, December 2012).

3. Muhammad A. Rana and Rohan Gunaratna, *Al-Qaeda Fights Back: Inside Pakistani Tribal Areas* (Islamabad: Pak Institute for Peace Studies, 2007).

4. Laila Bokhari, *Waziristan: Impact on the Taliban Insurgency and the Stability of Pakistan* (Oslo: Norwegian Defence Research Establishment, 2006).

5. Rana and Gunaratna, *Al-Qaeda Fights Back*, pp. 120–1.

6. The Pakistani security forces initially assisted the US-led Operation Enduring Freedom (2001–2) in Afghanistan by deploying more than 70,000 regular troops in the tribal areas. Thereafter, the army launched Operation al-Mizan (2002–6) and Operation Zalzala (2008), both of which consisted of a series of operations in Waziristan. Then again in 2009, the Pakistani army began Operation Rah-e-Nijat in South Waziristan against the TTP leader Hakimullah Mehsud. In Swat, the army launched Operation Rah-e-Haq in November 2007 and its so-called second phase in July 2008. In April 2009, when Mullah Fazlullah and his militants captured the district headquarters in Mingora and marched into the neighbouring district of Buner, the Pakistani army launched Operation Rah-e-Rast. In Bajaur Agency, the Pakistani security forces launched Operation Sherdil in August 2008. In Khyber Agency, a series of military offensives under the name Operation Sirat-e-Mustaqeem were conducted in 2008. In Kurram Agency, the military launched Operation Koh-e-Sufaid in July 2011. In June 2014, the Pakistani army launched

operation Zarb-e-Azb in North Waziristan. See Daud Khattak, 2011, 'Evaluating Pakistan's Offensives in Swat and FATA', *CTC Sentinel*, 4(10): 9–11; Zahid Ali Khan, 'Military Operations in FATA and PATA: Implications for Pakistan', Institute for Strategic Studies, Islamabad, available at www.issi.org.pk/publication-files/1339999992_58398784.pdf (accessed on 17 June 2014).

7. When Musharraf came to power, he initially banned five organizations under the Anti-Terrorism Act of 1997: Lashkare Tayba (LeT), Jaishe Muhammad (JeM), Sipahe Sahaba Pakistan (SSP), Tehrike Jaferia Pakistan (TJP), and TNSM. All of them, except for the Shia TJP, have either a Deobandi or an Ahl al-Hadith orientation. The Sunni Tehreek, which has a Barelvi orientation, was placed under observation but not banned. Since then, the list of banned organizations has been revised and expanded.

8. Jane Perlez and Pir Zubair Shah, 'In Refugee Aid, Pakistan's War Has New Front', *The New York Times*, 2 February 2009, available at www.nytimes.com/2009/07/02/world/asia/02aid.html (accessed on 1 October 2015).

9. On the US drone strikes in Pakistan between 2004 and 2010, see International Security Program, 'Drone Wars Pakistan: Analysis', available at http://securitydata.newamerica.net/drones/pakistan-analysis.html (accessed on 11 June 2014).

10. Ismael Khan, 'Pakistanis Say 5 are Killed by U.S. Missiles in Tribal Area', *The New York Times*, 17 September 2008, available at www.nytimes.com/2008/09/18/world/asia/18pstan.html?_r=0 (accessed on 1 October 2015).

11. This bill, authorizing support to the Pakistani government of USD 1.5 billion annually over five years, generated a great controversy in Pakistan. The ruling party, led by Prime Minister Yousaf Raza Gilani, praised it as a linchpin for strengthening Pakistani democracy, but opponents criticized it for authorizing greater American interference in Pakistani affairs (for example, by broadening airstrikes, submitting Pakistan's nuclear programme to US oversight, and controlling the appointment of military leaders). The text of the bill is available online at 'S.1707 (111th): Enhanced Partnership with Pakistan Act of 2009', GovTrack.us, www.govtrack.us/congress/bills/111/s1707 (accessed on 20 December 2013).

12. Qandeel Siddique, *Tehrik-e-Taliban Pakistan: An Attempt to Deconstruct the Umbrella Organization and the Reasons for Its Growth in Pakistan's North-West*, DIIS Report, no. 12 (Copenhagen: Danish Institute for International Studies, 2010), p. 21.

13. General David McKiernan, who in May 2009 was replaced by General Stanley McChrystal as the US commander in Afghanistan, asked for 10,000 more soldiers. Adding NATO troops, including those deployed through the August 2009 Afghan elections, boosted the total number of Coalition troops to approximately 100,000 in 2010.

14. The collaboration between the Afghan Taliban and the Pakistani Taliban was intensified to prepare for the deployment of 17,000 new US troops to Afghanistan later that year. See Carlotta Gall, 'Pakistan and Afghan Taliban Close Ranks', *The New York Times*, 26 March 2009, available at http://www.nytimes.com/2009/03/27/world/asia/27taliban.html (accessed on 9 May 2016).

15. The poll results are available at www.terrorfreetomorrow.org/upimagestft/PakistanPollReportJune08.pdf (accessed on 5 January 2011).

16. Saeed Shah and Jonathan S. Landay, 'Pakistan Flood Crisis Raises Fears of Country's Collapse', *McClatchy Newspapers*, 13 August 2010, available at www.mcclatchydc.com/2010/08/13/99180/pakistan-flood-crisis-raises-fears.html (accessed on 24 March 2011).

17. See 'Taliban Urge Government to Reject US Aid', *The Express Tribune* (Pakistan), 11 August 2010, available at http://tribune.com.pk/story/38118/taliban-urge-government-to-reject-us-aid/ (accessed on 29 July 2014).

18. Rob Crilly, 'Pakistan Floods: Taliban Vows to Kidnap Foreign Aid Workers', *The Telegraph*, 26 August 2010, available at www.telegraph.co.uk/news/worldnews/asia/pakistan/7965241/Pakistan-floods-Taliban-vows-to-kidnap-foreign-aid-workers.html (accessed on 1 October 2015).

19. Shah and Landay, 'Pakistan Flood Crisis'.

20. Joshua White, *Pakistan's Islamist Frontier: Islamic Politics and U.S. Policy in Pakistan's North-West Frontier*, Religion & Security Monograph Series 1 (Arlington: Center on Faith & International Affairs, 2008), p. 87.

21. For a comprehensive account of the origins and formation of the original Taliban, see Ahmed Rashid, *Taliban: Militant Islam, Oil and Fundamentalism in Central Asia* (New Haven, CT: Yale University Press, 2000). A more recent analysis of actors and policies is provided by the same author in *Descent into Chaos: The United States and the Failure of Nation Building in Pakistan, Afghanistan and Central Asia* (New York: Viking, 2008).

22. For an overview of the ideology and alliances of various militant Islamist movements in Pakistan and Afghanistan, see Mariam Abou Zahab and Olivier Roy, *Islamist Networks: The Afghan–Pakistan Connection* (London: C. Hurst, 2004).

23. See White, *Pakistan's Islamist Frontier*, p. 87.

24. Rana and Gunaratna, *Al-Qaeda Fights Back*, p. 93.

25. Azam Tariq, 2009, 'Biography of Baitullah Mehsud', *Hitteen*. Translation titled 'The Life of Baitullah Masood', available at https://azelin.files.wordpress.com/2010/10/e2809cthe-life-of-baytullah-mee1b8a5sude2809d-by-ttp-spokesman-azzam-e1b9adariq.pdf (accessed on 1 March 2011).

26. Rana and Gunaratna, *Al-Qaeda Fights Back*.

27. Iqbal Khattak, 'Mohmand Agency Now under Taliban's Control', *Daily Times* (Pakistan), 24 July 2008.

28. See Syed S. Shahzad, 'Plot to Divide the Taliban Foiled', *Asia Times Online*, 23 July 2008, available at http://atimes.com/atimes/South_Asia/JG23Df01.html (accessed on 1 June 2011).

29. Delawar J. Banori, 'Commandos on the Other Side', *The News International* (Pakistan), 21 October 2007.

30. 'Swat Attacks Leave Two Policemen, 4 Others Dead', *Dawn*, 5 July 2007, available at http://archives.dawn.com/2007/07/05/top6.htm (accessed on 24 March 2011).

31. See Banori, 'Commandos on the Other Side'.

32. Tariq, 'Biography of Baitullah Mehsud'.

33. Siddique, *Tehrik-e-Taliban Pakistan*, p. 40.

34. Siddique, *Tehrik-e-Taliban Pakistan*, p. 62.

35. Malala Yousafzai and Christina Lamb, *I Am Malala: The Girl Who Stood Up for Education and Was Shot by the Taliban* (New York: Little, Brown and Company, 2013).

36. Sadia Sulaiman, 2008, 'Empowering "Soft" Taliban over "Hard" Taliban: Pakistan's Counter-Terrorism Strategy', *Terrorism Monitor*,

6(15), available at http://www.jamestown.org/programs/tm/single/? tx_ttnews%5Btt_news%5D=5080&tx_ttnews%5Bback Pid%5D=167&no_cache=1#.VzXUiE3Owdk (accessed on 11 June 2014).

37. Rahimullah Yusufzai, 2008, 'A Who's Who of the Insurgency in Pakistan's North-West Frontier Province, Part One: North and South Waziristan', *Terrorism Monitor*, 6(18), available at http://www.jamestown.org/programs/tm/single/?tx_ttnews%5Btt_news%5D=5169&tx_ttnews%5BbackPid%5D=167&no_cache=1#.VzXVn03Owdk (accessed on 1 October 2015)

38. Aamir Latif, 'Taliban vs. Taliban', *Islamonline.net*, 30 January 2008, available at www.islamonline.net/servlet/Satellite %3Fc %3DArticle_C %26cid %3D1199280033146 %26pagename %3DZone-English-News %252FNWELayout (accessed on 24 March 2011).

39. Latif, 'Taliban vs. Taliban'.

40. Rahimullah Yusufzai, 2008, 'The Impact of Pashtun Tribal Differences on the Pakistani Taliban', *Terrorism Monitor*, 6(3), available at http://www.jamestown.org/single/?no_cache=1&tx_ttnews%5Btt_news%5D=4712#.VzXV7E3Owdk (accessed on 1 October 2015).

41. Yusufzai, 'A Who's Who of the Insurgency, Part One'. See also Rahimullah Yusufzai, 2009, 'A Who's Who of the Insurgency in Pakistan's North-West Frontier Province, Part Two: FATA Excluding North and South Waziristan', *Terrorism Monitor*, 7(4), available at http://www.jamestown.org/single/?tx_ttnews%5Btt_news%5D=34574#.VzXWJk3Owdk (accessed on 1 October 2015).

42. Yusufzai, 'A Who's Who of the Insurgency', Part One and Part Two.

43. Yusuf Ali, 'Taliban Form New Alliance in Waziristan', *The News* (Pakistan), 23 February 2009.

44. Hassan Abbas, 2009, 'A Profile of Tehrik-i-Taliban Pakistan', *CTC Sentinel*, 1(2): 1–4.

45. In October 2010, Qari Hussain Mehsud was reported killed by US drone attacks in North Waziristan. However, the TTP contradicted this report and described it as part of a campaign to demoralize its fighters. See 'TTP's Top Gun Qari Hussain "Killed"', *Dawn*, 16 October 2010, available at http://archives.dawn.com/archives/75228 (accessed on 5 January 2011).

46. On the split-up of the LeJ, see also Zia Khan, 'The Fission of Lashkar-e-Jhangvi', *The Express Tribune* (Pakistan), 17 November 2010, available at http://tribune.com.pk/story/78500/the-fission-of-lashkar-e-jhangvi/ (accessed on 25 July 2014).

47. Mark Burgess, 'Jaish-e-Muhammad', *CDI Terrorism Project*, 8 April 2002, available at www.cdi.org/terrorism/jem.cfm (accessed on 24 March 2008).

48. Hassan Abbas, 'AfPak behind the Lines: Punjab's Growing Militant Problem', *Foreign Policy*, 22 June 2010, available at http://foreign-policy.com/2010/06/22/afpak-behind-the-lines-punjabs-growing-militant-problem/ (accessed on 1 October 2015).

49. One example is the case of Faisal Shehzad, who pleaded guilty to an attempted car bombing in New York's Times Square in May 2010 that was linked to the TTP in Pakistan. The TTP also claimed responsibility for a failed bomb plot in Barcelona in 2008 involving 12 men with Pakistani origins. In 2009, two men were charged for plotting an attack on the Danish newspaper *Jyllands-Posten*, which published the Muhammad cartoons: this case was linked to the Punjabi Taliban (specifically to the LeT). The TTP was allegedly also involved in the 2009 suicide attack carried out against a Central Intelligence Agency (CIA) base in Khost, Afghanistan.

50. 'Karachi: Enter TTP', *Dawn*, 9 March 2014, available at www.dawn.com/news/1091918 (accessed on 1 October 2015).

51. 'TTP Network in Karachi', *Dawn*, 9 March 2014, available at www.dawn.com/news/1091918 (accessed on 1 October 2015).

52. The Afghan Taliban has been linked to the opium trade in the region, and in Pakistan, the TNSM has reportedly been infiltrated by gangs as well as by the local 'timber mafia'. See White, *Pakistan's Islamist Frontier*, p. 86.

53. The Sunni and Shia traditions are normally regarded as the two major branches of Islam. The historical split reflected a disagreement over who was the rightful successor of the Prophet Muhammad, and thus also what should be the criteria for political authority. The historical schism has led to contemporary differences in both rituals and doctrines.

54. In the Sunni Islamic tradition, four schools of jurisprudence (*madhab*) evolved during the ninth century: Hanafi, Maliki, Shafi, and Hanbali. The followers of these four schools follow the same

basic belief system but differ in the practice and execution of rituals and in juristic interpretations of sharia. However, all four are generally considered to be equally valid in the Sunni tradition.

55. Shah Wali Allah also argued for a direct approach to the Quran, since Quranic scholarship had been the exclusive domain of specialists. Breaking with the notion that the Quran may not be translated, Shah Wali Allah translated it into Persian in order to make the revelation accessible to common people in the subcontinent. Wali Allah saw the Sunnah, the traditions about the Prophet Muhammad, as a commentary on the Quran itself rather than something independent of it. The idea of an organic relationship between the Quran and the Sunnah is characteristic of Deobandis, who make very active use of Hadith literature.

56. White, *Pakistan's Islamist Frontier*, p. 31.

57. White, *Pakistan's Islamist Frontier*, pp. 31–2.

58. Rashid, *Taliban*, p. 88.

59. Muhammad K. Masud, *Muslim Jurists' Quest for the Normative Basis of Shari'a* (Leiden: International Institute for the Study of Islam in the Modern World, 2001); Anthony Black, *The History of Islamic Political Thought from the Prophet to the Present* (London: Routledge, 2001).

60. Muslim jurisprudential discourse distinguishes between sharia and *fiqh* (jurisprudence) in an attempt to distinguish between the divine nature and origin of sharia and the interpretations that jurists derive. In political language, references to sharia rather than fiqh thus, in effect, downplay the human interpretive role and emphasize the divinely given nature of the law.

61. Masud, *Muslim Jurists' Quest*, p. 7.

62. Abu Ishaq Al-Shatibi, *Al-Muwafaqat fi usul al-Sharia* (Cairo: Al-Maktaba al-Tijaniyya al-Kubna, 1975).

63. See, for example, Tariq Ramadan, *To Be a European Muslim: A Study of Islamic Sources in the European Context* (Leicester: Islamic Foundation, 1999).

64. Tariq Ramadan, *Radical Reform: Islamic Ethics and Liberation* (Oxford: Oxford University Press, 2009).

65. 'Bloodshed and Revenge', video released by the TTP headquarters, Umar Studio, July 2009, retrieved from www.2shared.com/file/7370960/8370331e/TTPENGDVD.html (accessed on

11 January 2011). Translation released by the producers, available at www.alqimmah.net/showthread.php?t=9318 (accessed on 11 January 2011).

66. For further discussion on the point that religious discourse within Islam fluctuates widely, see, for instance, Ayesha Jalal's analysis of the shifting discourse on jihad in South Asia over three centuries in *Partisans of Allah: Jihad in South East Asia* (Lahore: Sang-e-Meel Publications, 2008).

67. David Cook, *Understanding Jihad* (Berkeley: University of California Press, 2005), p. 2.

68. Cook, *Understanding Jihad*.

69. Some Taliban activists argue that there exists a technical difference between suicide missions and fidayee missions. The latter technique is not the same as using the body as a bomb but rather entails trying to get close to the target with explosives and then attempting to escape alive.

70. This last argument was especially promoted by Hassan al-Banna and Abul ala Mawdudi, the founders of the Egyptian Muslim Brotherhood and the Indian–Pakistani Jamaate Islami (JI), respectively. Interestingly, these influential intellectuals, who are often designated as the chief ideologues behind Islamism, describe jihad as purely defensive in nature and regard offensive strategies as legitimate only if the objective is to liberate or to advance the cause of justice. Sayyid Qutb, another influential ideologue behind contemporary Islamism (and an early Muslim Brotherhood intellectual), is among the few Muslim intellectuals who have argued for the legitimacy of offensive jihad, even dealing with the sensitive issue of whether jihad can be proclaimed against an unjust Muslim ruler—and concluding that it can.

71. Black, *The History of Islamic Political Thought*.

72. Cook, *Understanding Jihad*, pp. 153–4.

73. Cook, *Understanding Jihad*, pp. 160–1.

74. For a comprehensive description of Pakistan's history and the battles over the idea and identity of Pakistan, see Stephen Philip Cohen, *The Idea of Pakistan* (New Delhi: Oxford University Press, 2004).

75. Freeland Abbot, *Islam and Pakistan* (Ithaca, NY: Cornell University Press, 1968).

76. Jinnah cited in Abdus Sattar Ghazali, *Islamic Pakistan: Illusions and Reality* (Islamabad: National Book Club, 1999). See also Ayesha Jalal, *The Sole Spokesman: Jinnah, the Muslim League, and the Demand for Pakistan* (Cambridge: Cambridge University Press, 1985).

77. The JI ('Islamic Congregation' or 'Islamic Party') is among the most influential Islamic revivalist movements in the world. It was founded by Sayyid Abul Ala Mawdudi on 26 August 1941 in British India as a rival to the Muslim League and its vision of an Islamic state. See Mona K. Sheikh, 'Jamaat-e Islami', in Wade C. Roof and Mark Juergensmeyer (eds), *Encyclopedia of Global Religion* (Thousand Oaks, CA: SAGE Publications, 2011).

78. Robert Wuthnow (ed.), *Encyclopedia of Politics and Religion* (Washington, DC: Congressional Quarterly, 1998).

79. It is interesting to note that the constitution did not say that the Quran should govern Pakistan. Instead, no constitutional basis is provided for governing against the Quran. Governing by the Quran requires a much higher degree of consensus on the interpretation of religion and on Islam's political substance. In consideration of the many sectarian differences in Pakistan, reaching such a consensus is troublesome, if not impossible.

80. For the early history, see Jalal, *Sole Spokesman*; Damodar Singhal, *Pakistan* (Englewood Cliffs, NJ: Prentice Hall, 1972).

81. The constitution of Pakistan is available online at www.pakistani.org/pakistan/constitution (accessed on 4 April 2011).

82. During this period a militant version of jihad was cultivated and, as Zahid Hussain describes in his article, the first Pakistani jihadi group emerged in the 1980s, and by 2002, Pakistan was home to 24 militant groups. See Zahid Hussain, 'Battling Militancy', in Maleeha Lodhi (ed.), *Pakistan: Beyond the 'Crisis State'* (New York: Columbia University Press, 2011), pp. 131–48.

83. John L. Esposito, *Islam: The Straight Path* (Oxford: Oxford University Press, 1998), pp. 199–200.

84. This assessment is based on TV debates dealing with the issue of the Pakistani constitution on PTV (Pakistan Television Corporation) between October 1999 and October 2002.

85. In a public address, Musharraf stated: 'Islam teaches tolerance, not hatred, universal brotherhood and not enmity, peace and not violence, progress and not bigotry. I have great respect for the Ulama

THE RISE OF THE PAKISTANI TALIBAN | 65

and expect them to come forth and present Islam in its true light. I urge them to curb elements, which are exploiting religion for vested interests and bringing a bad name to our faith. I would like to reassure our minorities that they enjoy full rights and protection as equal citizens in the letter and spirit of true Islam.' Pervez Musharraf, 'General Pervez Musharraf's Address to the Nation', 17 October 1999, available at www.pakistani.org/pakistan/constitution/post_12oct99/musharraf_address_17oct1999.html (accessed on 24 March 2008).

86. The coalition consisted of JI; Jamiat Ulamae Pakistan (N); the two factions of the pro-Taliban JUI (JUI-F and JUI-S), which represent the Deobandi School; Jamiate Ahle Hadith; and Tehrike Jafria Pakistan, which is also known as Pakistan Islami Tehrik.

87. The partial adoption of sharia law in the tribal areas is a relatively recent development, one that came about during the 1980s. With the Soviet presence in Afghanistan and the Shiite revolution in Iran, the Sunni religious sector in Pakistan was supported heavily by external donors to counter what were seen as ideological threats from Shiites and communists.

88. For a detailed journalistic description of the development of religious militancy in the era of Musharraf and George W. Bush, see Zahid Hussain, *Frontline Pakistan: The Struggle with Militant Islam* (New York: Columbia University Press, 2008).

89. Singhal, *Pakistan*.

འ

2

Jihad to Protect God
and His Laws

In 1998, Osama bin Laden, Ayman al-Zawahiri, and three other leaders of Islamic movements in Egypt, Pakistan, and Bangladesh published a famous statement in *Al-Quds al-Arabi*, an Arab daily newspaper published in London, that seemed to voice a widely shared image of Islam under siege and a world at war.[1] The statement characterized American military operations in Muslim countries as 'a clear declaration of war on God, his messengers, and Muslims', and called on every capable Muslim to 'resist' and 'liberate' by fighting the Americans and their allies in jihad. Analysing such statements and perceptions, researchers have established that rhetoric invoking war and the perception of being under attack are common to various manifestations of violent religious activism.[2]

In this chapter, I look into the concept of defensive jihad as it is constituted in the narratives of two of the Taliban activists I interviewed in Pakistan, Muslim Khan and Matiul Haq. Though religious violence often has a more offensive dimension as well, as it is reflected in related narratives about the restoration of order or justice that also incorporate religious imagery,[3] the dominant tendency in the narratives displayed in this chapter is that they see a hostile enemy that is on a mission to attack Islam. I have chosen to cluster Muslim Khan and Matiul Haq together due to their emphasis on their duty to defend and spread the laws of God, that is, sharia, and because they are both part of the broader TTP umbrella. I examine their perceptions of threat and the conditions under which they consider armed warfare to be an obligation for Muslims.

This chapter and the next two chapters are based on my interviews, whereas Chapter 5 is based on my analysis of Taliban recruitment materials. The chapters that are based on my interviews are like my analysis of the recruitment materials, illustrative of the larger trends I have identified in the Taliban narratives, but at the same time I try to introduce the readers to some of the activists that identify and sympathize with the banner of the Taliban.

Hence, the two interviews ahead (and my description of the interviews in the next two chapters) are not intended to provide a basis for a systematic comparative analysis of different Taliban groups or activists. Rather they provide the basis for enhancing a culturally sensitive understanding of the discourses of religion, defence, and justice that provide legitimacy to the Taliban use of violence.

Without exception, all the activists I interviewed explained their engagement in warfare as defensive. In most cases their definition of jihad also implied a struggle to establish an Islamic system characterized by the enforcement of a particular concept of sharia. The examples given ahead illustrate exactly how this defensive jihad discourse is constituted.

Although religion is placed within the defensive discourse, it also constitutes a parallel discourse that offers religious–ethical justifications for a more offensive stance. At the same time, the invocation of religion places discursive and practical constraints on engagement in warfare through jurisprudential discourses that set limits on the practice of jihad. The various roles of religion are examined in detail in Chapter 5, where I explain how religion serves both as a justification for jihad and a limitation, since it entails rules for discrimination and just war.

Muslim Khan: One of God's Guardians

The valley of Swat in northwestern Pakistan became known to the world when the schoolgirl Malala Yousafzai was shot in the head by Taliban gunmen while riding in a school bus in 2012. Muslim Khan, who was known as the 'Butcher of Swat' at the height of his TTP career, was part of the TTP leadership and the spokesman of the TTP Swat faction before he was arrested in April 2009. I interviewed him on his satellite phone shortly before his arrest and during the period when the TTP had taken control of Swat.

My conversation with Khan demonstrates the centrality of the concept of defence in the Taliban discourse on jihad. When I introduced myself and my interest in his reasons for embracing violence, he claimed: 'We have never attacked anyone unprovoked. They [the US] come and impose war on us.'[4] In their conversations with me, Muslim Khan and other militants frequently invoked the image of Islam being under systematic attack.

When I asked Muslim Khan about how to stop the growing violence, he began by complaining that the Taliban view on this point would never be published, since the global media represents only the viewpoint of the US and European countries. He went on to stress that 'the simple solution to this war is that the European countries and the US forces take their armies out of here and return to the regions of the North Atlantic Ocean. Then I will give the world a hundred per cent guarantee that all these mujahedeen will go to sleep in peace and live peacefully.' Khan's perception of the conflict established a clear link between the military presence of the US and NATO forces on the one hand and the jihad of the Taliban activists on the other. From his responses, I immediately sensed that the reason he had agreed to talk with me—a Muslim with Pakistani roots, born and raised in the West—was his frustration about being misrepresented in the Western media. To Khan and the other militants I talked to, it was clearly very important to stress that their war was justified.

Khan had been part of the TNSM movement's leadership since 1994. The TNSM was banned in 2002 by former president Pervez Musharraf following the US overthrow of the Afghan Taliban regime in November 2001, when between 5,000 and 10,000 TNSM followers including their leader Sufi Muhammad crossed into Afghanistan to fight alongside the Taliban against the US-led Coalition.[5] The TNSM lost most of its cadres during US raids in Afghanistan.

Khan was appointed spokesman of the TTP Swat faction in 2008, when segments of the TNSM joined the TTP. He has often been cited in the Pakistani media as one of the authoritative representatives of the TTP. He was one of the fiercest critics of an anti-polio campaign organized by the World Health Organization (WHO) in 2008. Khan publicly stated that anyone who became crippled or died of polio would become a martyr, honoured for refusing to take a vaccine containing forbidden materials (the vaccine, according to Khan, was derived from pig tissue). In the Pakistani media, he questioned the motives behind the vaccination campaign: 'There are other diseases also—like hepatitis, typhoid, etc. Why is everyone concentrating on polio? See, this is an American conspiracy.'[6] His position was consistent with that of the TNSM leader Fazlullah (the leader of the TTP since 2013), who, in a radio sermon, deemed the immunization campaign a US conspiracy to make Pakistanis impotent and infertile.

The reason Khan originally joined the TNSM movement was, he explained, to implement sharia (nifaze sharia) in Pakistan. According to him, the purpose of the TTP and the TNSM was the same: 'Our aim is to establish the law of God in this country.

That was the reason why this country was established. The law the government has not implemented. We only want the system of Islam.'

'Muslims cannot stay Muslims without an Islamic system,' said Khan and argued that it is, therefore, a religious obligation (*fard*) for Muslims to establish a system like the one established by the Taliban in Afghanistan. Hence 'those who engage in the struggle for an Islamic system' are the only true Muslims according to his viewpoint. Khan put this obligation on an equal footing with the five pillars of Islam: the declaration of faith (*kalma*/shahada), prayers (namaz), pilgrimage (hajj), the fast (*roza*), and giving alms (*zakaat*). Further, he was keen to convince me that:

> To believe in other systems or base any decisions on other systems amounts to idolatry (*tagruth*). This is why Allah is not accepting our [the Pakistani people's] deeds. In my opinion, this is like living as animals, or as the foreigners live, like the Jews live or like the Christians live. We are Muslims, and we only have one system with us, which is Islam.

Specifying what he meant by an Islamic system, he explained that 'our parties want a system which is based on the heavenly revelations. That means the Quran and the Sunnah of the Prophet. Not just for our sake, but there are benefits in it for everyone. The decisions that are based on such [a] system are both taken faster and bring inexpensive justice.' Thus for him, an Islamic system entailed the enforcement of sharia as the basis on which disputes are resolved and criminals punished.

The framing of sharia as a formalized justice and punishment system in turn is a very narrow interpretation of the concept and one of the main characteristics of the religious ideology of the Taliban. In public debates in the West, there is often an erroneous tendency to accept the Taliban's (and other extremist groups') very particular framings of religious concepts as representative of all believers. The interpretation of sharia is a vivid example. From the twelfth century onwards, sharia was conceived by the Sufis as a set of spiritual and ethical guidelines, in reaction to the legalist interpretation of the concept maintained by the more orthodox class of the religious elite (the ulama).[7] Although the Taliban's legalist interpretation is in one sense quite orthodox, their heavy emphasis on sharia as a system of quick and efficient public justice is a reading coloured particularly by the situation in the tribal belt of Pakistan.

According to Khan, the US attacked Afghanistan in response to the Taliban's embrace of sharia. I noticed that he did not mention 9/11 at all. The US, he explained, was on an offensive and aggressive mission to 'prevent every Islamic system from existing in the world'. For Khan, there was a fundamental doctrinal difference between Islam and other political systems. This difference was the real reason for the attacks by the enemies of Islam, whom he also described as the 'crusaders'. Hence Khan, like the other militants I spoke to, was convinced that US military actions in Afghanistan were part of an expansionist religious crusade.

Becoming increasingly eager to convince me about the real nature of the conflict, Khan stated: 'It is in reality a war between religions that Bush has started.' Even though he believed that militant jihad need not be only defensive, he kept stressing that the jihad fought by the Taliban (and other mujahedeen groups) was indeed purely defensive: 'History is witness that Muslims have always fought defensive wars.' Still, he argued, somewhat paradoxically, that the ultimate object of jihad is to 'bring about God's law on earth'.

During my conversation with Muslim Khan, I repeatedly found myself in a kind of verbal game in which I sought to turn him towards elaborating the 'offensive' dimension of his jihad, where the implementation of sharia was seen as mandatory for Muslims, while he tried to move the conversation towards the actions of the West and thus constitute his jihad as a defensive action. However, his specific interpretation of the duty of jihad remained conditioned by the US-led invasion of Afghanistan. Khan individualized the duty of jihad by making it incumbent on every Muslim. When there is no country in the world left with a real Islamic system, he argued, no proper authority exists to declare jihad, as originally prescribed in Islamic jurisprudential literature.[8] Without such an authority, according to his logic, jihad can be undertaken only if it is defensive, and 'in a defensive war every Muslim is obliged to participate, both men and women'.

During my conversation with Khan, he used the term '*jihad bil qital*'. The Arabic term '*qital*' means 'fighting', and this usage implies a distinction from other types of jihad, for example, *jihad bin nafs* (the jihad of the soul) or *jihad bil lisan* (the jihad by word). However, he used the word 'qital' interchangeably with jihad, thus centring the jihad discourse on the militant struggle. By framing jihad as a response to an emergency and as an individual obligation, he distinguished the present struggle of the TTP from the quest to establish an Islamic system—though both, according to him, could in principle be part of jihad bil qital. At one point he argued that 'jihad bil qital is to establish the Islamic system, and fight wars for that cause', which added a new dimension to his position that the current jihad was entirely due to the crisis created by the foreign invasion in Afghanistan. At the same time, he maintained that jihad to create an Islamic system is a collective duty (*fard al-kifaya*), albeit one that is not obligatory for every Muslim so long as a sufficient number of the community (the army) fulfils this duty. While he argued for offensive or system-transforming jihad as one meaning of the term, he also maintained that using force to create an Islamic system was allowed only at the instigation of a just imam. Khan's position contained some inherent inconsistencies, because he wanted to stress that his jihad was defensive while holding on to the premise that with a just imam, offensive jihad was legitimate. It remained unclear whether he considered Mullah Omar to be a just imam.

Despite the fact that the TTP had had several violent clashes with the Pakistani authorities and security forces, Muslim Khan insisted that the main problem was foreign intervention in the internal affairs of Pakistan and Afghanistan. Thus he linked the objectives of defending territorial borders (and thereby 'life and property') and political autonomy with the Islamic system that, according to him, was the main target of the US–NATO invasion. He also argued that the former American president George W. Bush launched the war for ideological reasons, because otherwise it would not make sense that 'the CIA-sponsored mujahedeen of yesterday suddenly are the terrorists of today'. He was referring to the Afghan militants who fought the Soviets with covert US support. From the Taliban's perspective, Muslim Khan stressed, '[t]here is after all no difference. Back then we were chasing out foreign occupation forces, and today we are chasing out foreign occupation forces.'

When we discussed the role of suicide tactics in jihad, he told me that he had 'no doubt' that they were legitimate means not only in a situation of desperation but also in other non-defensive situations, so long as they were accompanied by the right intention (*niyat*): 'to fight along the path of God and pave the way for His system.'

Niyat is a very powerful concept in Islamic theological discourse. It is traditionally regarded as the main premise for validating an action as pious. In the Sahih al-Bukhari volumes, the Prophet Muhammad is quoted in the very first Hadith as saying that 'actions are according to their intentions'.[9] Another often-quoted Hadith (al-Qudsi)[10] in Muslim legal literature from the same compilation begins in this way:

> Allah has written down the good deeds and the bad ones. Then he explained it [by saying that] he who has intended a good deed and has not done it, Allah writes it down with Himself as a full good deed, but if he has intended it and has done it, Allah writes it down with Himself as from ten good deeds to seven hundred times, or many times over.

Many theologians and jurists (*fuqaha*) have elaborated on the concept of intention. Among the most notable is the twelfth-century scholar Al-Ghazali, who stressed the importance of a clear intention accompanying ritual acts of worship. It is a widely accepted practice among Muslims to clarify their intentions, sometimes ritualized by a direct proclamation before prayers or a day-long fast. Generally, it has been interpreted to mean that a religiously wrong action can still be considered a pious act if it was carried out with the right intention. Conversely, right actions are regarded as worthless if they are carried out with the wrong intention (for example, greed or the desire for prestige). Relating to this, another widely cited Hadith from the Sahih Muslim compilation[11] narrates how the first three men in hell will be the mujahedeen who seemingly fought for God but actually fought to be called brave warriors, the *qari* (reciter of the Quran) who seemingly spread the word of God but actually coveted the title of scholar, and the wealthy man who seemingly spent for religious causes but actually coveted the prestige of being called a generous man. Such conduct has also been considered a lesser form of shirk, because the purpose is not to serve God but rather to attract the attention of human beings.

Besides stressing the importance of a sincere niyat as the condition for lawful jihad, Muslim Khan further made a point of distinguishing between suicide, which he regarded as unlawful (haram) according to Islam, and self-sacrifice. Yet, although he argued that voluntary death was permissible in the fight against the enemies of Islam, he gave me no references to religious texts, maintaining only that the divine permission was 'clear' in the Quran and Hadith literature. He justified extraordinary measures such as suicide or self-sacrifice primarily by linking them to the importance of defending the Islamic system. The measures he was discussing (suicide, violence, and so on) were implicitly justified by the importance of the ideals he was defending (religion and the sovereignty of God). This means that Khan invoked both religious and security justifications (that Islam is under deadly attack) for such actions, invoking the latter when his theological arguments or references to religious texts were weak.

Matiul Haq: A Call for an Islamic System

My interview with Muslim Khan from the TTP shows how the security arguments, that is, the notion of being under attack and, therefore, justifying a violent response, are very strong. However, the idea that the Taliban need to protect God and his laws also had a more offensive dimension, which stressed to a higher degree the importance of implementing sharia. This dimension became clear to me when I interviewed Matiul Haq, the son of Sufi Muhammad, the original leader of the TNSM, based in the Swat valley. Though the TNSM existed in Pakistan even before 2001, a faction of it took up arms in Pakistan and joined the TTP under the leadership of Fazlullah, the son-in-law of Sufi Muhammad and a leader of the TTP umbrella. Matiul Haq was among the TNSM followers who joined the TTP under the leadership of Fazlullah, who at that point was leading the Swat chapter of the TTP.

Sufi Muhammad was convicted by the Pakistani government for fighting in Afghanistan after 2001. After his release in April 2008, he returned to Swat, advocating an end to militancy in the region, and openly criticized Fazlullah. However, Muhammad was arrested again in 2009, and by the end of 2010, four of his sons were also arrested and charged by an anti-terrorism court for various offences, including treason.[12] Among them was Matiul Haq, who also used to be the spokesperson of the TNSM.

My conversation with Matiul Haq was one of my most uncomfortable interviews. My use of the term 'khudkash hamlay' (suicide attacks) instead of fidayee attacks immediately put him into a defensive mode. Judging from his increasingly loud and aggressive tone of voice, I felt that he had stamped me as an outsider, a non-Muslim westerner. Some of his responses to my questions were outright scornful. When I asked him about what defines a Muslim, he exclaimed, 'Don't you know? Oh Lord!' followed by a guffaw that sounded as if he found my ignorance both tragic and ridiculous.

Although his father had criticized the violent means of Fazlullah and his followers, Matiul Haq did not reject the legitimacy of suicide attacks when I spoke with him. However, he corrected my use of the word 'suicide' (khudkash) to 'self-sacrifice' (fidayee) in order to stress that suicide is forbidden in Islam. His distinction was based on a differentiation between the possible intentions behind a suicidal act: if the intention is to fight the enemies of God, then the act is considered legal, whereas taking one's own life for selfish motives is unlawful. In his words:

> Fidayee attacks against the *kafir* [infidel] are completely legal, not only legal in Islam but also dominant [as an idea] in Islam. But when Muslims use this method against other Muslims, then it is haram. I am saying that in a confrontation with a kafir, you cannot call these suicide attacks. When Muslims attach bombs to their bodies and go to the kuffar, then we call it fidayee in our language. This is completely justified in the Quran and the Hadith, from the *sahaba karam* [early 'honourable' followers of the Prophet Muhammad], and from the fuqaha.

Haq's argument for the legitimacy of extraordinary means such as fidayee attacks depends not only on the intention but also on the target. Thus the justification is based more on the nature and scale of the threat than on the nature of what is being defended.

According to Haq, the original aim of the TNSM was to establish 'God's system' on Pakistani soil. He invoked the idea that Islam has six different sectors, encompassing 'a system of law, a system of politics, a system of economy, private life, society, and education': according to Haq, it constitutes a holistic and comprehensive ideology for conducting not only private but also public and political–legal matters. He declined my requests to be more specific, and I believe that he judged that I, as an outsider, would not understand anyway.

When I asked him about how the conversion to an Islamic system would happen, he said that it should be done by proselytizing jihad (*dawa*). At the same time, he stated that there are three conditions for the successful establishment of an Islamic system: first, Muslims unite against their enemies; second, they boycott foreign systems; and third, they initiate jihad against those who are trying to prevent it. In his view, the present Pakistani government is an accomplice of the enemies of Islam because it has embraced a foreign system, namely democracy. He argued that 'the present government came with democracy, and whatever it then does is non-Islamic and against sharia'. This legitimizes a violent course of action against government representatives and security forces, which is especially embraced by the followers of Fazlullah. Thus militant jihad is framed as a necessary step towards establishing a true Islamic system.

During the interview Haq suddenly changed his rhetorical tone and voiced a call to all Muslims to abandon 'the Western democratic way' and 'hold on to the Islamic way'. I sensed that at that moment he had come to regard me as a potential ally, a channel for broadcasting his views to fellow Muslims. The shift made it very clear that it was hard for him to conceive of any middle ground between being a hostile outsider and a loyal follower. Although this made me uncomfortable, I didn't protest but continued listening.

The Islamic way, he explained, was demonstrated during the five years of Taliban rule in Afghanistan, which he described with words such as 'peace' and 'order'. In contrast, the proponents of other 'worldly and secular systems', most notably the US, were associated with images of 'war and destruction', and described as idolaters (*mushrikeen*). Contrasting the Taliban regime with Afghanistan's long history of conflict, Haq argued that 'in the five years when the Emarate Islamiyya [the Islamic Emirate] was established, the country was peaceful. Then the US came. They have removed all peace and order. This is a clear example in front of you.' 'The secular governments came and removed all peace and order,' he said.

In his defence of 'God's system', Haq quotes a Hadith in which the Prophet Muhammad is reported to have said: 'Do jihad against the idolaters through your money, body, and tongue. Spend money in the cause of God, use your body in the service of religion, and use your tongue to speak against false systems.' In his justifications of the actions and ideology of the TNSM movement, he frequently invoked such sayings of the Prophet, along with references to Hanafi jurists who have interpreted the sources of jurisprudence (notably Hadith literature and the Quran) as a formalized set of rules. The same is true of his explanations of the TNSM's embrace of militant jihad (jihad bil qital).

Matiul Haq's call for jihad bil qital does not immediately appear to be part of the same narrative as his vision of establishing an Islamic system, though they are linked. He casts militant jihad in mainly defensive terms, presenting a snapshot of 'history' as evidence: 'History can witness that we are fighting for our defence. In Afghanistan we were attacked by the US; here in Pakistan they come and call us terrorists in different areas. But here, too, we are fighting in defence, because the army is attacking us. They attack innocents. When people fight back, it is nothing else but defence.' This reasoning helps to explain Haq's sharp reaction to the common designation of the TNSM as a terrorist movement: 'If terrorism means that a Muslim is fighting for his rights to establish the system of God, and sacrifice whatever he can in this endeavour, then ok, we are indeed terrorists. If terrorism means to kill and attack innocents, then we are not that kind of terrorists. We are only asking for our rights. This should not be called terrorism.'

Thus Haq's narrative on the necessity of jihad bil qital was based on the defence of two elements: first, the sovereignty (of Afghanistan); and second, the 'right to establish the system of God', which amounts to the defence of religious–political autonomy. However, the defence of sovereignty was also linked to the defence of religion and an Islamic system. For instance, throughout our conversation Haq referred to Afghanistan as the Emarate Islamiyya and stated that the only true Islamic system in modern history has been 'under the Taliban in Afghanistan'.

By implication, the offensive, system-transforming mode of jihad and defensive jihad are not as distinct as he initially asserted.

Haq also invoked religion to explain the motives of the threats to 'Islamic sovereignty and autonomy'. As in my other conversations with Taliban adherents, he believed the enemy to be acting with ideological and religious motives, driven by 'their struggle ... to wipe out Islam from the world'. These enemies of Islam are identified as an unholy alliance of the unbelievers, the Jews, and the Christians (kuffar, *jahood*, and *ansar*).

By this point in our conversation I had apparently managed to signal that I was not a stranger to Islamic vocabulary or religious traditions, and Haq increasingly referred to the conflict in religious and mythical terms. He explained the invasion of Afghanistan in apocalyptic terms, citing what he called a prophecy of Muhammad that the unbelievers, the Jews, and the Christians would try to demolish Islam: 'It is their misperception that this will ever happen. The Prophet has told us that there will come a time when the Jews and the Christians will become the slaves of Islam. It is their misperception that Islam will be demolished.' He invoked similar reasoning and analogies to explain the actions and decisions of the TNSM (that is, the rationale for engaging in jihad bil qital). His religious discourse was parallel rather than complementary to the security discourse, in which violent action was framed as a necessary response to assaults on sovereignty and on religious–political autonomy. However, these two discourses at times seemed to merge when he equated the defence of sovereignty and autonomy with the defence of God's system.

The main aspect of 'God's system' that militants like Haq seek to implement is the enforcement of sharia. The Swat district of the Malakand Division in the KPP has been a battleground for sharia, and as mentioned earlier, it was for a long time a stronghold of the TNSM, which was created in the early 1990s in the name of implementing sharia. The TNSM was inspired by Ahl Hadith influences and also by the JI's call to implement sharia.

The movement arose in response to Prime Minister Benazir Bhutto's imposition of a new, controversial system of tribal law in the area. Although its leadership was not intellectual like the JI's, the TNSM called for sharia as the proper replacement for the tribal law system.[13] After a series of violent clashes, it succeeded in its goal: a sharia ordinance, also known as the Nizam-e-Adl Regulation, was implemented in Malakand in 2009.[14] This was the result of a peace deal signed on 21 May 2008 between Mullah Fazlullah and the Pakistani government. Fazlullah promised to cease attacks on Pakistani security forces and other government installations in the area, to deny shelter to foreign militants in the Swat region, and to dismantle his militia. The Pakistani government in turn agreed to release Swat militants from jail, to implement sharia in the entire region, to establish an Islamic university in Iman Dehri, and to withdraw troops from Swat.[15]

However, none of the parties upheld their agreement, and the Pakistani government launched a new military operation in Khyber Agency and arrested leading TTP militants in the KPP on 28 June 2008.[16] That summer, the Swat militants increased their attacks on government installations and girls' schools: they destroyed more than 125 girls' schools in 2008.[17] The situation in Swat escalated further after an attempted takeover of Buner, a district near the capital of Pakistan. The fighting between government forces and the Swati Taliban created over two million internally displaced refugees. The Pakistani army claimed that close to 1,600 militants and 90 soldiers had been killed since the fighting began.[18] After this incident, Fazlullah escaped to Afghanistan, where he launched his war against the Pakistani military. He returned to Pakistan in November 2013 in order to take over the leadership of the TTP. Fazlullah is part of the Yousufzai tribe from Swat and the first non-Mehsud leader of the Pakistani Taliban. Since his takeover, he has struggled to impose his authority on the powerful tribe that dominates large parts of the tribal areas.

Notes and References

1. Osama bin Laden, Ayman al-Zawahiri, Abu-Yasir R.A. Taha, Mir Hamzah, and Fazlul Rahman, 'World Islamic Front for Jihad against Jews and Crusaders', *Al-Quds al-Arabi*, 23 February 1998.
2. Martin E. Marty and R. Scott Appleby (eds), *The Fundamentalism Project: Fundamentalisms Comprehended*, Vol. 5 (Chicago: University of Chicago Press, 1995).
3. See, for example, Mark Juergensmeyer, *Global Rebellion: Religious Challenges to the Secular State, from Christian Militias to Al Qaeda* (Berkeley: University of California Press, 2008).
4. All quotations from activists in this and the following sections are my own translations.
5. Muhammad A. Rana and Rohan Gunaratna, *Al-Qaeda Fights Back: Inside Pakistani Tribal Areas* (Islamabad: Pak Institute for Peace Studies, 2007), p. 123. See also Ahmed Rashid, 'A Dangerous Void in Pakistan', *Yale Global Online*, 4 March 2009, available at http://yaleglobal.yale.edu/content/dangerous-void-pakistan (accessed on 1 June 2011).
6. Cited in Ayesha Akram-Nasir, 'Polio-Free Pakistan: Only a Dream?', *Daily Times* (Pakistan), 14 September 2008, available at www.dailytimes.com.pk/default.asp?page=2008\09\14\story_14-9-2008_pg13_7 (accessed on 1 October 2015).
7. Sufism is a broad category that covers many different orders and movements in the world, historically and today, but overall the term denotes the mystical–ascetic aspect of Islam. It is often highlighted as an alternative to the legalist approach to Islamic teachings, and one of its main tenets is that the practitioners of Sufism strive to obtain direct experience of God by making use of intuitive and emotional faculties.
8. The primary sources for the rulings on jihad (*ahkam al-jihad*) have traditionally been the Quran and reports of the practice of Prophet Muhammad. Early jurists like Imam Malik (d. 795), Abu Yusuf (d. 795), and al-Shaybani (d. 804) wrote longer works on the concept of jihad. Al-Shafi (d. 820) and al-Tabari (d. 923) rendered opinions on the conduct of war and of statecraft. They established precedents that were developed in turn by scholars like al-Sarakhsi (d. 1096), al-Mawardi (d. 1058), Ibn Taymiyya (d. 1328), and a

host of others. Some of the most authoritative statements about the demand for a just imam (*imam al-adil*) are made by Imam Ridha and Shaykh Tusi.

9. The Sahih al-Bukhari is one of the six canonical Hadith compilations in Sunni Islam. They were collected by Muhammad ibn Ismail al-Bukhari after being transmitted orally for generations. A translation by M. Muhsin Khan is available at http://www.usc.edu/org/cmje/religious-texts/hadith/bukhari/ (accessed on 25 July 2014).

10. *Hadith al-Qudsi* is a category of Hadith literature containing the sayings of the Prophet Muhammad. In orthodox tradition these are regarded as coming directly from God.

11. The Sahih Muslim is another of the six canonical Hadith compilations within Sunni Islam. The Hadith were collected by Muslim ibn al-Hajjaj. Abdul Hamid Siddiqui has translated the entire compilation into English. The translation is available at http://www.usc.edu/org/cmje/religious-texts/hadith/muslim/ (accessed on 25 July 2014).

12. 'TNSM Chief's Four Sons Sent on 5-Day Remand Friday', *Daily Times* (Pakistan), 21 January 2011, available at www.dailytimes.com.pk/default.asp?page=2011\01\21\story_21-1-2011_pg7_9 (accessed on 1 October 2015).

13. Joshua White, *Pakistan's Islamist Frontier: Islamic Politics and U.S. Policy in Pakistan's North-West Frontier*, Religion & Security Monograph Series 1 (Arlington: Center on Faith & International Affairs, 2008), p. 35.

14. The full text of the Nizam-e-Adl Regulation can be accessed from the online archives of the *Daily Times* (Pakistan). 'Text of the Nizam-e-Adl Regulation 2009', *Daily Times* (Pakistan), 15 April 2009, available at http://archives.dailytimes.com.pk/national/15-Apr-2009/text-of-the-nizam-e-adl-regulation-2009 (accessed on 22 July 2014).

15. I received a copy of the original peace deal (21 May 2008) in Urdu by fax. See also Delawar J. Banori, 'Peace Deal Inked with Militants', *The News International* (Pakistan), 22 May 2008.

16. Faris Ali, 'Pakistan Launches Anti-Taliban Crackdown Near Peshawar', *Reuters*, 28 June 2008, available at www.reuters.com/article/2008/06/28/idUSISL176577 (accessed on 1 June 2011).

17. Zahid Hussain, 'Taleban Threaten to Blow up Girls' Schools if They Refuse to Close', *Timesonline* (Pakistan), 26 December 2008, available at http://www.timesonline.co.uk/tol/news/world/asia/article5397901.ece (accessed on 1 October 2015).

18. 'Pakistan Army Chief Says Tide Turned in Swat', Reuters (Islamabad), 5 June 2009, available at http://www.hindustantimes.com/world/pakistan-army-chief-says-tide-turned-in-swat/story-K2opHb0JGV0wxHoYltIvOP.html (accessed on 17 March 2016).

☙

3

The Demolition of
Islam's Forts

The previous chapter unfolded how sharia and the law of God are central elements of both the defensive and offensive justifications of violence given by the TTP. It also showed how the defence of territory and borders melts together with the defence of the law of God. This chapter illuminates how the defence of more material or physical dimensions of religion are also part of the overall justification of violence. The Taliban battle in Pakistan is also one about defending mosques and religious seminaries, what they typically refer to as 'Islam's forts': the place where the soldiers of God are located guarding the sacred grounds. The defence of mosques and seminaries is a recurrent justification of violence that is particularly embraced by Taliban adherents and sympathizers due to the unfolding of dramatic events in Pakistan in 2007, the year when the TTP was also established.

One of the most polarizing incidents in the Pakistani government's campaigns against Islamist militants was Operation Silence, the 2007 Pakistani army operation against the Red Mosque in Islamabad. The heavily armed deployment, ordered by former president Pervez Musharraf, damaged the mosque and completely demolished the adjacent Jamia Hafsa, the largest religious seminary for girls in Pakistan. After the military operation that killed hundreds of people—including young girls who refused to surrender—the seminary building was flattened with a bulldozer that left behind nothing but the dusty ground. The incident, which provoked public outrage and denunciations and promises of vengeance from Taliban commanders, was a trigger for the escalating violence since 2007. The Red Mosque siege was quickly followed by the deployment of troops in the tribal regions as well as in Swat.

The attacks provoked widespread indignation when the uncensored part of Pakistan's news media showed images of crying mothers who had lost their young daughters and the bulldozed ground where traces of children's clothes and shoes stuck out of the earth. Some attributed the government's action to the West's 'War on Terrorism'. At least one new branch of the TTP was created to avenge the military operation, and several Taliban-affiliated groups still refer to the Red Mosque incident to mobilize support.[1] The Ghazi Force, named after the head cleric who was killed during the raid, has become part of the TTP and has conducted attacks on Pakistani security forces and symbols of the Pakistani government in Islamabad and Rawalpindi.[2] Other groups, such as the Taliban-affiliated Janude Hafsa (referring to the 'revival' of Jamia Hafsa), were also formed in direct response to the event.

One significant consequence of the operation against the Red Mosque is the vehement response it has provoked in young women between the ages of 16 and 30. It is unclear whether any of the girls are actually involved in systematic training for militant activities.[3] On several occasions, however, women have stated their intention to engage in militant jihad and to sacrifice their lives if necessary. Since the military operation against the mosque, young women activists have participated in rallies and demonstrations with shouts of '*Sharia ya shahadat*' (sharia or martyrdom) and 'Tariquna, tariquna: al-jihad, al-jihad' (our path, our path: jihad, jihad).[4] Umm Hasaan, the wife of the Red Mosque imam Mohammed Abdul Aziz, still has considerable authority over the female students, many of whom stayed on in Islamabad. In 2011, the capital administration allotted Jamia Hafsa a new plot of land where the school has been rebuilt. Umm Hasaan still travels throughout Pakistan giving speeches to large rallies of women and girls. After the speeches, many in the audience want to touch her in order to absorb some of her blessed aura. Under the slogan 'You can kill the body, but you can't kill the passion', the Red Mosque and Jamia Hafsa have spent the last several years rebuilding their organizations.[5]

The prelude to Operation Silence was a series of activist incidents in which the girls and young women of Jamia Hafsa were involved. First, they occupied a public library in protest against the Musharraf government's city modernization plan, which entailed the demolition of 81 mosques in the capital.[6] In a rally following the destruction of the historical Amir Hamza mosque, 18-year-old Hamna Abdullah addressed a crowd of thousands of female activists, speaking of the mosque as shaheed (martyred). She declared: 'Our bodies will fall, but mosques will stand. Rivers of blood will flow, but [we] will not let them harm the greatness of Islam.'[7] Throughout her speech, Hamna Abdullah portrayed mosques and seminaries as the 'forts of Islam', thus equating the defence of these structures with the defence of religion.

The young women of Jamia Hafsa have drawn attention for their activism on several occasions. In one instance they took the law into their own hands and kidnapped a brothel-keeper. They had initially reported her illegal activities, but when the police took no action, the girls argued that it was their religious duty to act.[8] A couple of days in captivity later the brothel-keeper was released, after vowing before God that she would close her business.

A few months after their first kidnapping, the girls kidnapped nine employees of a massage clinic, again claiming that they were carrying out un-Islamic acts. This event led to the involvement of the Pakistani security forces. A few days after the hostages were released, Operation Silence was initiated against the Red Mosque and the adjacent Jamia Hafsa and Jamia Faridiya (the affiliated seminary for boys). Only the building of Jamia Hafsa, however, was completely demolished.

The Red Mosque and Jamia Hafsa first came into the international media's spotlight when one of the suicide bombers of the 7/7 attacks in London in 2005, Shehzad Tanweer, was suspected of being linked to the mosque (no formal link has ever been proved). The Red Mosque was subsequently raided by the police as part of a crackdown on religious seminaries. In the early part of 2007, the Red Mosque and its affiliated seminaries gained increasing notoriety for their unlawful activities, including the kidnapping of alleged prostitutes and the public burning of videos and DVDs that the Red Mosque activists considered to be un-Islamic. Some of these actions were carried out by young women from Jamia Hafsa. In the years following the Red Mosque incident in 2007, the number of suicide attacks aimed at the Pakistani army or government representatives also increased significantly, both in the KPP and in large Pakistani cities such as Lahore, Islamabad, and Karachi. These included attacks on the Manawan Police Training School in Lahore and on the Sri Lankan cricket team in March 2009. The most striking example was the September 2008 bombing of the Marriott Hotel in Islamabad.[9] The assassination of Benazir Bhutto of the PPP created a highly tense and polarized political environment.

Jamia Hafsa had more than 6,000 registered students. The Red Mosque was built in 1965 and has thousands of regular visitors every week. The first imam of the mosque, Muhammad Abdullah, was well known for his fierce speeches on jihad against the Soviet army and later for his friendly relations with Osama bin Laden and the leadership of the Taliban during the Soviet operations in Afghanistan. The Jamia Hafsa/Red Mosque movement is not formally linked to the Taliban, but its adherents and leadership (though not all users of the mosque) are sympathetic to their jihad and the system that prevailed under the Taliban rule in Afghanistan.

Because the mosque is situated close to the headquarters of the Pakistani military intelligence service, the Inter-Services Intelligence (ISI), their employees used to be some of its regular visitors. In 2007, however, the imam brothers who were then jointly in charge of the mosque issued a fatwa against the Pakistani security forces who were fighting the Taliban activists in the KPP, stating that they did not deserve Islamic funeral prayers and that soldiers killed fighting the Taliban should not be buried in Muslim graves.[10]

Umm Hasaan: Women and Jihad

I met Umm Hasaan in her home in Islamabad. Passing the front room of the house, where a meeting was going on among a handful of men and the imam of the mosque Abdul Aziz, I was shown into the second room, where Umm Hasaan was waiting with some of the Jamia Hafsa students. There was a very intense and energetic atmosphere in the house: during my conversations with Hasaan, she constantly had to get up to answer the phone, and several women and girls came to visit her. Noticing that we were conducting an interview, they sat down quietly around the bed on which we were sitting. She initially did not allow me to record our conversations, as I believe she did not fully trust my intentions, but after a while, probably in part because I joined her in prayer, she allowed me to use a recorder.

When I finally had Umm Hasaan's attention, I asked her what jihad meant to her. She was a very calm lady in her mid-forties who spoke in a remarkably soft voice. It was hard to imagine that she could embrace the idea of justifiable violence. Her response touched first on the missionary and educational forms of jihad: the first and most important step, she said, is to invite non-Muslims to Islam (dawa), then to educate Muslims and non-Muslims about Islam (*tarbiyat/tabligh*). She acknowledged that offensive jihad—'to take up the sword in defence of oneself or to convince others'—is one of the stages of jihad but stressed that the flourishing of militant jihadi culture in Pakistan is due to the attacks on Islam.

Hence, like other militants I spoke with, she highlighted the defensive character of contemporary jihad: 'In Pakistan, the situation is that Islam has been criticized and ridiculed for many years; its beard, its *bakra* [headwear resembling a turban], its burka, its each and every rule is made fun of. Series and films are produced to do this. For instance, on the topic of jihad.' Drawing on examples from around the globe, she pointed out, 'Muslims are killed wherever you look. Just look at Kashmir, Iraq, Bosnia, or Burma. What options are left for the Muslims? Only one. Kill the one who is coming to kill you. It is tit for tat. The more heavy-handed the government is in trying to crush Islam, the more heavy-handed the reaction should be.'

Hasaan explained the ongoing jihad as being based on the principle of reciprocity against the actions of the enemy, the US. With respect to Taliban clashes with the Pakistani government, she argued that 'during the approximately 60 years that the country has existed, the tribal people have never been disloyal towards the Pakistani government'. She held instead that the Pakistani army has provoked the tribal peoples with their raids in Waziristan: 'They handed the mujahedeen over with bags on their heads to the unbelievers [kuffar], though their fighting had only been confined to Afghanistan. So what do they, then, expect in turn?'

As Umm Hasaan grew more comfortable talking to me, the notion of defensive jihad receded, and dimensions of the imperative to establish sharia by force began to surface. Hasaan held that, ideally, speaking justice (*kalmae haq*) to an unjust ruler is the finest form of jihad, though she maintained that this might not always be enough. Her 18-year-old daughter Hamna Abdullah, who was very loyal to the interpretations of her mother, elaborated on this view when she came to join us in our conversation:

Jihad is mandatory when a Muslim country is attacked by foreign powers. It is mandatory for the people living there, and if the people around them can see that they cannot manage by themselves, they are also obliged to fight. We mean that if there is a need for jihad you should go, but if you can manage with dawa and tabligh [missionary activities], then do. Take a doctor; sometimes he can manage by using medicine, but sometimes an operation is needed. Today if you look at the injustices and violations by America, jihad [as qital] is mandatory for Muslims.

This statement is illustrative of the mathematical logic that is intertwined with religious reasoning, since sufficiency is constituted as a legitimate criterion for deciding the means of jihad. The criterion of sufficiency opens up for the use of measures sufficient to defeat the enemy and to face the threat. Whereas sufficiency can also be applied in a restrictive sense to mark the outer limits of legitimate means, the use here is more enabling of the employment of force. In Hamna's depiction of jihad and the appropriate means to carry it out, the principle of reciprocity for an enemy's actions is similarly constituted: 'The greater the injustice committed against you, the greater the injustice you should return. If they are demolishing a house of yours, you should demolish one of their houses. If they are killing yours, you should kill theirs.' In this context, she continued to argue that Osama bin Laden did the right thing, if he was indeed behind the attacks on the Twin Towers and the Pentagon in 2001 (which she ultimately doubted): according to Hamna, he was simply reciprocating the injustices committed against Muslims by the US.

Jihad is justified not only as a defence against external enemies but also by reference to the sorry state of Pakistani society, a central concern among the Jamia Hafsa affiliates. . Even though the imam brothers in charge of the mosque frequently issued condemnations of what they saw as un-Islamic practices, these statements were accompanied by a defence of the Pakistani underclass. The mosque leadership is known for frequent and loud criticism of corruption among Pakistan's political, economic, and military elite and of the deep social divisions in Pakistani society. This is one of the reasons why the Red Mosque has loyal sympathizers among the poorer segments of Pakistani society. Most of the students of Jamia Hafsa came from the KPP and the tribal areas, along the unmarked border with Afghanistan. Like the thousands of other religious seminaries in Pakistan, it provided free lodging and food for its students. For a poor family from the tribal areas, this kind of support matters more than a westerner can imagine.

Hasaan invoked this condemnation of social and economic inequality in her defence of sharia and thus as part of her jihad discourse. She stated, for example: 'In a situation where there is no peace, no justice, massive unemployment, and criminality, and where Islam and *sharia mutahera* [pure sharia] are being ridiculed, it is natural to take up arms.' Thus her views encompass two parallel discourses: one views militant jihad as a necessary defence against Western attacks on Islam, and the second views it as essential to the quest for justice, equality, and peace in Pakistan. These ideals are also represented as the purpose of 'Islamic politics': Hasaan argued that 'Islamic politics is a politics about doing good; it is about peace and justice and it brings equality between the people and the ruler. The people have the right to hold their rulers accountable without being thrown into jail. It is clean politics, and it is about the betterment of society.' She added that a real Islamic government is tolerant of pluralism (and that differences among Muslims should be regarded as a blessing); however, everyone, regardless of what rules of fiqh they follow, should comply with any rules proclaimed by an Islamic government. In a real Islamic system, she argued, the 'fatwa is over the king'. By this she meant that the jurisprudential rulings of religion and the laws of God have priority over secular rule.

Hasaan was clearly anxious to stress that socioeconomic justice is one of her primary motivations for justifying militant jihad. Justice, of course, is a very fluid concept. In Hasaan's view, it is related to the enforcement of sharia (nifaze sharia) and particularly to the system of punishment for offences. The increasing crime rate in Pakistani society is a recurrent theme in the narratives of female activists, but Hasaan also fiercely criticized the lack of justice infrastructure in Pakistan and the fact that people are kept in jail for years without trial. She also criticized the penal system, describing long prison sentences as inhuman because they effectively take away people's lives and separate them from their families. She argued that sharia, by contrast, prescribes efficient and just punishments, such as cutting off the hands of a thief, which both deter others from engaging in similar acts (because they are carried out as public spectacles) and at the same time give criminals the opportunity to restart their lives immediately. The punishment 'might seem temporarily harsh' but in the long run 'is more human', she argued. In continuation, she invoked an example from Afghanistan: 'For six years there was no theft when the Taliban chopped off the hands of [a] few thieves.... Those who visited Afghanistan were thrilled.... In six years there were only two murders in Afghanistan, because the murderers were efficiently and publicly punished. In Pakistan, a murder takes place every fourth minute!' These kinds of mythical statistics were recurrent elements in my interviews with Taliban sympathizers and affiliates.

Reflecting on the militant actions by the students of Jamia Hafsa and the concept of freedom, Hasaan compared the function of religion with that of the police in enforcing law and order. Defending the young women's activism, she argued that 'freedom always has its limitations, otherwise there would be chaos', and maintained that the state has constructed its institutions based on the exact same realization. Because the police did not act against the brothel-keeper in the kidnapping case, she argues, the girls had to step in. 'Religion has the same function [as the police]. It adds discipline to society so that order can be maintained.' In line with this view, she later argued that when the rulers of the country are not doing their job, the responsibility of the religious scholars (ulama) increases. Thus religion (deen) and politics (siyasat) play the same social role. This logic enables her argument that religion is above politics, and that the Red Mosque affiliates represent the force and voice of religion.

Even though the female activists believe in strongly central- ized leadership and look on the Taliban rule in Afghanistan as an ideal government, the state of emergency that they see themselves living in necessitates the conception of militant jihad as an individual duty (fard al-ayn). 'Under normal conditions,' explained one of the anonymous female activists, whom I refer to as Mubeen, 'it is a Muslim ruler who has to declare jihad. But today there is no such ruler.' The girls noted that some people are exempted from the obligation of jihad bil qital according to the jurisprudential rulings (ahkam al-jihad). Rather unconven- tionally, however, their list of exemptions included the sick, old people, and children—but not women.

In explaining the urgency of jihad, Asia, another anonymous former student at Jamia Hafsa, who was shot in the stomach during Operation Silence, told me that in the beginning she and the other activists only wanted to defend the mosques, the forts of Islam. But today—facing what she described as 'anti-Islamic forces'—they see a need for stronger action: 'We need sharia, and jihad has become mandatory when nobody is listening to us [Muslims], and the religious leaders have failed to show leader- ship.' Asia was among the students who called for young girls to join the ranks of jihad.

The female activists from Jamia Hafsa are all convinced that Islam is under systematic attack. According to their narratives, the first stage of their jihad is about saving Islam from attacks by the 'Pakistani government', the kuffar, and the 'Jews'. Hamna Abdullah was convinced that the aim of Islam's enemies is 'to wipe out Muslims by removing jihad from our minds'. Umm Hasaan was confident that the girls were ready to take up the battle: 'When governments try to demolish Islam, God gives his adherents an inner strength that makes them stand up against injustices.'

The young women's belief in the necessity of jihad affirmed their definition of a real Muslim as someone who both declares the faith (*kalma*) and also implements belief in daily life. Living their beliefs, they claimed, was a central tenet of the madrassa culture of Jamia Hafsa. Their jihad discourse was also coloured by this interpretation. As Hamna argued, 'Muslims are today confined to namaz, roza, hajj, *zakat* [four of the five pillars of Islam]. And what is the result? They [the enemies of Islam] are attacking Islam all the time. What was the case in early history? Muslims stood up, did jihad, answered, so the kuffar remained confined to their own borders.' This statement asserts that ritual acts of worship are considered insufficient when Islam is under attack. Deviance from orthodox behaviour or the expansion of the concept of religious obligations is justified with reference to the extraordinary circumstances and existential threat facing the religion.[11]

The more I talked with the female activists, the more their narratives invoked idealized accounts of either early Islamic history or the Taliban rule in Afghanistan. They also shared a firm belief in a broad conspiracy to 'crush Islam', exemplified by anecdotes. Umm Hasaan referred to early Islamic history as a time of peace and harmony: 'As long as Muslims stayed rulers, there was peace. When the sahaba karam visited new areas, people themselves opened their doors, because they were tired of their own rulers. They could see the advantages of the Islamic system of peace.' The girls used similar language in their heroic narratives about socioeconomic justice and the low crime rate during the Taliban rule in Afghanistan. For instance, Asia told me that under the Taliban, the shops could stay wide open while shopkeepers attended Friday prayers because no one would even think of stealing from them. Hamna told the story of a man who deliberately left his gold watch in a busy bazaar. When he returned the next morning, the watch was still there, and people had protected it from damage by putting small stones around it.

The young women's fear of the enemies of Islam was informed by various types of superstition. Mubeen related to me a religious scholar's explanation of why Waziristan is a particular target for the enemies of Islam:

> It is because they know that the day the number of people who join both the *fajr* prayer [the daily dawn prayer] and the *jummah* prayer [the Friday prayer that is normally better attended] is the same, the unbelievers [kuffar] and Jews will die. In Waziristan this was the case. The unbelievers are creating destruction there, because these places were the only places where the number of people attending fajr and jummah prayers was equal. They know that if the number continued to grow, they would be done.

The women's call for jihad was based on these kinds of mythic stories but also on heroic narratives. Shortly before I met with Umm Hasaan and the girls at her house, they gathered for a rally on the streets of Islamabad. From the loudspeaker, a girl prayed to be sent the courage of the 17-year-old Syrian general Muhammad bin Qasim, who in the eighth century conquered the Pakistani provinces of Sindh and Punjab. He is well known for having brought Islam to South Asia, and during my meetings with the Taliban adherents, his name was mentioned several times as a model of skill and courage. Ending the rally, the female activists turned to God and prayed to be granted sufficient power to defeat the enemies of Islam.[12]

Sami ul Haq: The Taliban's Pakistani Father

Jamia Hafsa is not the only religious seminary that has been associated with terrorism in the Western media. Darul Uloom Haqqania near Peshawar is the largest and most popular seminary in Pakistan and Afghanistan. It is where most of the Afghan Taliban leadership, including Mullah Omar, was educated in Quranic and Hadith studies. Its current leader Sami ul Haq is also the head of a faction of the political party JUI.[13]

Many of the original Taliban members were recruited from Darul Uloom Haqqania during the crisis of authority and chaos in Afghanistan after the Soviet army withdrew in 1989.

Many of them never completed their studies and were generally poorly educated in traditional religious disciplines. Like the two seminaries affiliated with the Red Mosque, Darul Uloom Haqqania identifies with the Deoband school of thought and its political background. The renewed emphasis on the relationship between purified Islam and jihad against foreign occupation forces has revived the spirit of political activism in some of these seminaries.[14]

Despite this seminary's nickname of 'Jihad University', few Islamic educational institutions have consistent positions about engaging in war (Jamia Hafsa is an exception, probably because of the military action taken against it). Though seminaries may demonstrate ideological or political bias through their choice of teachers, curricula, and guest speakers, the idea that particular seminaries are systematically producing jihad warriors disregards the capacity of more decentralized, politically engaged student movements.

Having served as a member of the senate of Pakistan, Sami ul Haq is well known as one of the fiercest proponents of the implementation of sharia in the judicial system. In 1985, he presented the so-called sharia bill in the senate, which contributed to the polarization of the political debate on this issue. He has also openly declared that he and his father had friendly relations with both Osama bin Laden and Mullah Omar. Although he was placed under house arrest in 2001 for calling for a national revolt and leading thousands of people to march through cities across Pakistan, when Washington first threatened war against the Taliban, he is still one of the most outspoken proponents of the lawfulness of militant jihad in Afghanistan and Pakistan. As he told me when I met him in Akora Khattak in the KPP, jihad is justified today for defensive purposes, because 'Islam gives people a right to ensure their security'. Although he is not personally affiliated with the Taliban, he personifies the ideological struggle for sharia that the Taliban movement has embraced.

Sami ul Haq, a joyful older man, treated me in a hospitable and friendly manner from the beginning of our meeting. He seemed straightforward and confident in his replies, perhaps because he was very experienced at giving interviews. His friendly and relaxed attitude was a great relief after my long wait outside his house on a plastic chair in the burning sun (together with a queue of men also awaiting their turn to meet him). After the interview, he allowed me to take a tour behind the gates of the seminary. It looked like the thousands of other religious seminaries all over Pakistan: a school with few modern facilities and kids sitting on the classroom floors learning the Quran by heart. Outside was a huge, empty, dusty playground. I left quickly, feeling conspicuous as the only woman in the male madrassa. Some of the boys in the playground lined up to stare at me. I felt bad observing them as if they were animals in a zoo, and I hated experiencing and sensing the huge social-class difference between us. It is hard to explain, but it felt a bit like guilt—a feeling that admittedly decreased with the miles I put between us on my way home. I was happy, however, that Haq seemed to trust me. He said he had stopped allowing westerners to enter the seminary because of his bad experiences with Western journalists who were intentionally misrepresenting Islam and his seminary.

When I first arrived, one of his adherents had driven me to another house, where I was dressed 'properly' (I was made to put on an extra headscarf). Several young girls and someone who looked like a grandmother stared at me while a woman 'fixed' my attire without a word being said. Then I was taken to Sami ul Haq's house and asked to wait until he was ready. When I was finally taken to meet him, I felt relieved that he seemed to treat me like an insider, albeit one who was expected to go back to the West and correct the media misrepresentations of him.

Sami ul Haq interpreted the situation in Pakistan and Afghanistan as one calling for militant jihad, although non-violent forms of jihad ('demonstrations, education, invitation, and reconciliation') were also part of his discourse. He attributed the militant uprising to US hostility towards Islam, which he characterized as 'a wish to bring chaos and destruction to the Muslims'. He went on:

> One should look at history. America's attitude towards the Muslim world has always been ignorant due to their imperialist policies. Look at their position in Kashmir, in Palestine, Kosovo, and Bosnia. It all started then, not with 9/11. One hundred years of their history is about crushing Muslims. Nobody has yet proved who was behind 9/11. I believe they did it themselves in order to crush Islam.... They want to change the map of the world. And if this was not the case, if Muslims did it, then the perpetrators had a hundred years of history to justify what was done. They were tired of it.... If Muslims did it, it was in defence. To make the US stop.

Sami ul Haq saw American aggression as having ideological and doctrinal roots. And like many of the other activists I met, he backed up his point of view by referring to George Bush's use of the term 'crusade' to describe the 'War on Terror'. He also drew on more ancient history to explain the invasion: 'Since the Prophet [Muhammad] came, the Jews and the helpers [ansar, referring to Christians] have been, from the beginning, part of the struggle to prevent the true religion from spreading.... They have from the very beginning not been able to digest Islam.'

In his view, the contemporary 'enemies of Islam' are the Americans, who have turned against Muslims with the intention of retaining their position as a superpower and imposing their 'world view' on the Muslim world. In Sami ul Haq's interpretation, this means that the US has acted against the word of God. He quoted the Quran, which, according to his reading, states that 'Christianity as a religion is close to Islam'. It is the great threat that Islam represents to the US that has led it to manipulate the Jews, the Christians, the Buddhists, and the Hindus to form an alliance against Islam: 'The EU has accepted slavery, the Far East with their Buddhas has accepted the slavery, Japan has. Now they [the Americans] fear that the Muslim countries won't accept slavery. That is why they started all this propaganda.' The enemy is thus characterized as being motivated by both an ideological fear of Islam's superiority and by the more aggressive agenda of a religious crusade to change the map of the world.

Sami ul Haq sees the defence of the madrassa as central to this conflict. In our discussion about Jamia Hafsa, he stated that:

[the] seminaries are one of their [the Americans'] main targets, because it is here that Islam flourishes. They are the symbols of Islam, the cradle of Islam, and the only keepers of Islam. Today they [secular officials] have removed Islam from the universities and colleges. These [the seminaries] are the powerhouses and forts of Islam. That is why they are coming after the seminaries now.

He equated militant jihad with fighting for the cause of justice and resisting acts of aggression by foreign powers:

Jihad's most important meaning is to stop the hand of those who do injustice, to help the oppressed. To save people from the hands of terrorists.... When the Prophet [Muhammad] came, people were also squeezed between the two powers of Qaiser [Caesar] and Qisra [Khosrau of Persia], like the US and Russia today.[15] He came to save people from terrorism. Jihad's meaning is precisely that: to save people from terrorism. To secure rights, honour, and sovereignty— that is jihad.

Even though Sami ul Haq did not argue that the Taliban system is the only legitimate Islamic system of governance, he supported the Taliban defence of the religious–political autonomy of Muslims. For him, it was a matter of self-determination, and his sympathy towards those engaged in jihad was due to their struggle for the 'sovereignty', 'honour', and 'rights' that the US is violating. According to his view, the two Islamic principles of governance are a bar on dictatorship and an embrace of *ashura* (consultation or deliberation). This could, in principle, take the form of parliamentary democracy. Even so, he idealized the Taliban system, praising the law-abiding and modest society that allegedly existed under Taliban rule in Afghanistan: 'A woman could walk all the way to Herat [a city in western Afghanistan], and nobody would even dare to look. You could have a briefcase full of dollars, and no one would try to rob you.' He claims that this regime was the envy of Western culture: 'The Americans were astonished because they never managed to bring such peace to the streets of Washington.'

When I asked Sami ul Haq what constituted legitimate means in jihad, he answered in terms of the just war principles of sufficiency (using the means sufficient to face the threat) and reciprocity (the expectation that people will respond to each other in similar ways). Invoking stories of innocent people whose lives were ruined by American aggression, he argued that violent resistance by the Taliban and Muslims is driven by desperation and the quest for security rather than by religion or ideology (the motives he in turn ascribed to the US and its allies).

He would not define suicide bombings as unlawful according to Islamic principles. Instead he referred to 'the many rules and conditions' required to justify militant jihad. He stated, for example, that it is not lawful 'to cut off the hands or feet of the enemies, or to mistreat their eyes or faces; it is unlawful to harm their elders, their religious leaders and popes, their women, their patients, or innocent people'. According to him:

> A suicide bombing requires a really desperate situation.... I don't want to give a fatwa against suicide bombings. It depends on each case and the situation of the individual. They won't follow my fatwa anyway. If they are convinced they can reach their real target, then I believe suicide tactics are legitimate. If innocents are at risk of being killed, then it is wrong. But this is war, right? And in war anything can happen.

This response reveals the tension between the religious and worldly explanations he gives for militant action. For Sami ul Haq, as for the militants, the view of the current situation as a crisis of security and sovereignty seems to weigh more strongly than the jurisprudential considerations that might restrict the conduct of jihad. Thus, according to his narrative, Muslims have been pushed to use extreme means to defend themselves. He drew on many religious references, but, paradoxically, he invoked the security discourse (defending Islam) more than the religious discourse (expanding the reign of Islam) to justify the use of extraordinary means in jihad.

Also paradoxical is the fact that although Sami ul Haq is a strong advocate of the implementation of sharia, he does not see militant jihad as a tool for directly advancing this goal. For him the way to sharia is through politics. He observed: 'The politics of the children of Israel [*bani Israel*] was run by the prophets. At that time religion and politics became one. We are struggling for the same.' Nevertheless, defensive jihad is necessary to preserve the security of the Islamic state so that sharia can be implemented through the political system. Thus it is enemy aggression, motivated by fear and envy of sharia, that has necessitated jihad rather than the sharia aspirations of those engaged in jihad.

His views lay bare the conceptual gap between how we, as westerners, perceive ourselves and how we are perceived in another part of the world. Almost all the militants I met with represented the West as an aggressor driven by religious doctrines, whereas we view Islamist militants as driven by expansionist doctrines while identifying ourselves with peaceful secular principles.

ౚ

Notes and References

1. Qandeel Siddique, *The Red Mosque Operation and Its Impact on the Growth of the Pakistani Taliban*, FFI Research Report 2008/01915 (Oslo: Norwegian Defence Research Establishment, 2008).

2. Qandeel Siddique, *Tehrik-e-Taliban Pakistan: An Attempt to Deconstruct the Umbrella Organization and the Reasons for Its Growth in Pakistan's North-west*, DIIS Report 2010, no. 12 (Copenhagen: Danish Institute for International Studies, 2010), pp. 29–30.

3. The present imam of the mosque, Abdul Aziz, is quoted as saying that the women of Jamia Hafsa have been given training at a secret location in the use of automatic rifles and chemical weapons. 'Interview with Abdul Aziz', *Al-Sharq al-Awsat*, 8 July 2007.

4. One of their rallies can be watched on YouTube. Here the slogans are shouted out during the speeches and are also visible on the banners and posters held by the crowd. See www.youtube.com/watch?v=tc5Tg8eVIcU (accessed on 24 March 2011).

5. The slogan was on the Red Mosque website, www.lalmasjid.com (accessed on 12 July 2008), until it was closed down by the Pakistani government after the summer of 2008.

6. Most of the mosques that were categorized as illegal constructions by the Pakistani government are built on the main road connecting the airport with the rest of Islamabad. Many Pakistani critics have noted that the plan reflected Musharraf's need to signal the country's modernity as an ally in the 'War on Terrorism' by demolishing mosques and, at the same time, to secure the route against hostile attacks in case foreign diplomats and politicians visited Pakistan. The Pakistani central administration took action after intelligence agencies reported that certain mosques situated along routes used for VIP movement could be used to carry out terrorist attacks. This information was retrieved in June 2008 when I interviewed Safdar Hussain, a journalist covering the Red Mosque for the *Daily Times* (Pakistan).

7. My translation. A video of the speech and rally was available online at www.jamiahafsa.multiply.com/video/item/62/Jamia_Hafsa_Protest_Taqreer_ (accessed on 24 March 2011).

8. Prostitution is illegal according to Pakistani law. Some journalists covering the case tried to reveal the fact that the reason the police did not react to the complaint against the brothel was that many high-ranking politicians and bureaucrats were frequent customers. Interview with Safdar Hussain, June 2008.

9. Statistics on the frequency of suicide attacks show that violence in Pakistan generally peaked in 2008. Thirty-two of the 59 suicide

attacks in 2008 occurred in the KPP. Information retrieved from South Asia Terrorism Portal, 'Pakistan Assessment 2009', available at www.satp.org/satporgtp/countries/pakistan/# (accessed on 5 January 2011).

10. Stephen Brown, 'Red Mosque Meltdown', *FrontPage Magazine*, 13 July 2007, available at http://archive.frontpagemag.com/read-Article.aspx?ARTID=27394 (accessed on 19 December 2013).

11. Martin E. Marty and R. Scott Appleby (eds), *The Fundamentalism Project: Fundamentalisms Comprehended*, Vol. 5 (Chicago: University of Chicago Press, 1995).

12. See the prayer of Umm Hasaan in Urdu at the end of the speech at www.youtube.com/watch?v=tc5Tg8eVIcU (accessed on 24 March 2011).

13. According to Sami ul Haq, he was appointed the leader of one of the JUI factions because some of the members said that they had received 'signs from Medina', that is, prophetic signs that he should assume the leadership. The disagreement between him and the competing JUI faction was allegedly over the attitude towards the PPP. According to Haq, the JUI-F faction (led by Fazlur Rehman) did not recognize the legitimacy of a female president or the secular agenda of the country and thus opposed collaboration.

14. There are five types of organized religious seminaries in Pakistan: Wafaq ul Madaris al Arabia (Deobandi, affiliated with the JUI), Tanzeem ul Madaris (Barelvi), Wafaq ul Madaris al Salfia (Ahl Hadith/Salafi), Wafaq ul Madaris Shia (Shia), and Rabita ul Madaris al Islamia (JI). The Deoband and Salafi seminaries are most frequently mentioned in the discussions on the relationship between madrassas and jihad. In addition to the seminaries affiliated with the Red Mosque and Darul Uloom Haqqania, the Deoband Binori madrassa in Karachi is often mentioned as being linked to jihadi groups such as the Harkat ul Mujahideen, JeM, and Harkat ul Jihade Islami, and, at some point, having provided shelter to Osama bin Laden.

15. These are references to the Roman Caesars and to Khosrau II, the 22nd Sassanid king of Persia, who reigned from 590 to 628.

4

Anti-Shia and
Punjab-based Resistance

Not all militant action by Taliban affiliates in Pakistan is directed solely against the West or non-Muslims. Since Hakimullah Mehsud replaced Baitullah Mehsud as the leader of the TTP in 2009, there has been increased collaboration between anti-Shia movements and the Taliban, to the point where it has become hard for observers to differentiate between the movements. In addition, activists who were previously fighting their jihad against India on the issue of Kashmir have affiliated themselves with the Taliban. During 2003 and 2004, following the heavy military raids initiated by the Pakistani army in Waziristan, some of the activists affiliated to the Pakistani jihad organizations left their base camps in Kashmir to assist the Taliban.[1] Some of the activists, especially those who joined the Taliban in Swat, and the TTP umbrella, went as far as denouncing the years-old territorial struggle in Kashmir, because, in their view, it was supported by their new enemy, the Pakistani intelligence services, and was not aimed at the implementation of sharia.

This chapter describes my interviews with leaders of two of these movements, the SSP and the LeT—movements that are sometimes referred to as the Punjabi Taliban. The SSP is a sectarian anti-Shia movement while the LeT has traditionally been linked to the battle with India over Kashmir.

Apart from introducing selected perspectives of the Punjabi Taliban, this chapter also brings forward how the defence of the 'true' doctrines of Islam against its false representatives is also part of the Taliban justifications for violence. This is especially visible from my interview with the SSP leader. In this case, the US intentions are interpreted as being on par with those of the Shia Muslims, namely to water down and eliminate the true faith. In the case of the LeT, it appears that it is a doctrinal campaign, a crusade led by the US that is seen as the main driver of the conflict.

Taken together this illuminates that the Pakistani Taliban is far from a uniform movement, and that its narratives that justify violence consist of the defence of different dimensions of Islam, that is, the legal (sharia), the material (mosques and religious seminaries), and the doctrinal (the 'true' faith). The agendas of the different movements that have embraced the Taliban umbrella, however, overlap in the overall perception that Islam is under attack and, therefore, it must be defended with the means necessary to avert the threat.

Sectarian movements such as the SSP and the LeJ have been active in the tribal areas and the KPP since the late 1990s. Since 2008, parts of these movements have developed close ties and collaborations with the TTP. A government campaign against the SSP and the LeJ made them shift their bases to the Taliban-led Afghanistan. After 2001, these groups returned to Pakistan and settled in the tribal areas.[2] Thus some of the militants who were originally based mainly in Punjab gravitated towards the tribal areas considering them safer to live, train, and operate in.

The SSP was established in the early 1980s.[3] At times it has operated as a legitimate political party and participated in democratic elections. In recent years, however, it has been involved in several violent clashes with its rival Shia organization, the TJP. The SSP operates throughout Pakistan and targets both Shia Muslims and other sectarian groups that it regards as non-Muslim. According to Ahmed Rashid, hundreds of SSP militants have passed through the Khost training camp in eastern Afghanistan, which was run by the Taliban and Osama bin Laden until 1998, and thousands of their members have since fought alongside the Taliban.[4]

The LeT has not been driven by the sectarian agenda, but has traditionally been oriented towards the dispute with India over water and territory in Kashmir. The movement has been accused of multiple attacks inside India, including the November 2008 assaults in Mumbai that killed nearly 200 people and injured more than 300.[5] Since its establishment in 1993, it has operated in the Indian side of Kashmir and more recently in Afghanistan. This particular movement is often depicted as a proxy of the Pakistani government, and media allegations of the group's links to Pakistani intelligence agencies are common. It has been well established that the Pakistani army had close relations with the LeT movement in the 1990s,[6] and that LeT activists were trained alongside Pakistani troops. This relationship was, however, formally severed in 2002, when President Musharraf banned the LeT, though it is clear from later events that parts of it still operate in Kashmir as well as the rest of India, and its senior ideologues continue to proclaim their version of jihad in Lahore and Islamabad without interference from authorities.

The relationship between the Pakistani army and the LeT since 2002 can be characterized as a hands-off relationship, rather than an attempt to eliminate the LeT. One very significant reason for this approach has arguably been the fear of fostering more enemies within Pakistan, which has nevertheless been only partially prevented. Still parts of the LeT movement were alienated by the army raids in the tribal areas, Musharraf's formal denunciation of the movement, and the president's alliance with the US.

In 2012, Syed Salahuddin, the head of the UJC, an umbrella organization of which the LeT is a part, said: 'We are fighting Pakistan's war in Kashmir, and if it withdraws its support, the war would be fought inside Pakistan.'[7] My own meetings with representatives of the UJC and the LeT gave me the impression that the Kashmir-oriented movements still have a separate agenda and mentality from the Taliban. Some of the new alliances between the Punjabi Taliban and the TTP are, therefore, more natural than others. Some are likely to be short-lived, since they will only exist as long as there is an overlap in political objectives. As my interview with a member of the LeT will demonstrate ahead, there seem to be considerable differences between the outlook of the Taliban and the LeT with respect to establishing an Islamic state. A complete merging of the TTP and movements like the LeT is, therefore, not a likely scenario, since the ideological differences can have a great impact on how the movements will continue to be organized.

Khalifa Qayum: A Shield against *Sahaba Dushmani*

In order to provide an insight into the narratives of activists who are often identified as the Punjabi Taliban, and display the difficulties associated with treating the Pakistani Taliban as a monolithic entity, I sought to get in touch with both a representative of the anti-Shia movements and a representative of a movement that during the 1990s was solely concerned with the battle over Kashmir, namely the LeT. When I interviewed Khalifa Qayum, he was a senior leader of the anti-Shia SSP and a member of the provincial assembly of the KPP. Some months after my interview with him, he became the target of a bomb attack in Dera Ismail Khan in Peshawar. He survived, but six others were killed.[8] Shia militants were allegedly responsible for the attack. Qayum formerly participated in democratic elections and was elected to the KPP provincial assembly as an independent candidate in 2008. However, he was not allowed to run for election in 2013: instead he was sentenced to three years' imprisonment for seeking to contest the general elections while claiming to hold a university degree that was alleged to be fake.[9]

According to Qayum, the SSP was established in the background of the Khomeinian revolution in Iran to counter 'enmity against the Companions of the Prophet and the enmity against religion' (*sahaba dushmani aur deen dushmani*)'. When I asked him directly about the movement's involvement in unlawful activities, he denied the charge on grounds of principle: 'Yes, we have sacrificed lives, but we are leading our organization according to the law.' There are frequent reports in the Pakistani media about sectarian clashes between adherents of the SSP and the TJP, who in turn see themselves as the defenders of the Prophet Muhammad's family (*ahl al-bayt*, meaning 'followers of the house').

The clashes between Shia and Sunni militants are nourished by references to a historical dispute that arose among the followers of the Prophet Muhammad when he died over who should be appointed as his legitimate successor and the criteria by which political leadership should be decided. The SSP refers to itself as the shield against sahaba dushmani, since it holds the view that one of the companions of the Prophet was his legitimate successor, while the Shia Muslims argue that the true successor should be a descendant of the Prophet and his family. The reasons why this difference sometimes turns into violent clashes are challenging to understand. However, the notion of Pakistan as an arena in which Shia Iran and Sunni Saudi Arabia can fight proxy wars against each other was commonplace throughout the 1990s. Saudi money has been flowing into Pakistan since the 1980s, when the state and private donors funded the proliferation of religious seminaries. Saudi Arabia was a major backer of the military regime of General Zia-ul-Haq, who seized power in 1977 and imposed a particular version of Islamic law in Pakistan. The bulk of Saudi support in Pakistan has been aimed at the

Ahl Hadith movements also known as the Pakistani Salafis, whose doctrines resemble the Saudi Arabian version of Salafi Islam. The formation of militant sectarian organizations such as the SSP and the Sipahe Mohammad are often drawn out as examples of the consequences of foreign Saudi influence. This influence is especially felt in Punjab and Sindh, which have become recruiting grounds for sectarian violence inside Pakistan. The SSP phenomenon emerged in the city of Jhang in Punjab, partly as a reaction to the Iranian Revolution and partly as a reaction to the socio-economic repression of the Sunni populace by Shia feudal lords.

The sectarian conflicts in Pakistan are not limited to Punjab alone. In Baluchistan, for instance, Sunni sectarian extremists have killed hundreds of Shia Hazaras in the past decade. These extremists are allegedly supported by movements linked to (private donors in) Saudi Arabia. The Hazaras are Baluchistan's third major ethnicity, with a Mongolian origin from the central highlands of Afghanistan, and Iranian donors have most likely supported the prosperity of the Hazara community.[10] Similar concerns affect the situation in Gilgit-Baltistan, which is Pakistan's only Shia majority region. Conflicts between Sunnis and Shias have erupted in Gilgit-Baltistan over the years, but the rise of Sunni extremism in general in Pakistan has led to increasing tensions, frequently fuelled by rumours suggesting that the Ismaili Shia community in Gilgit-Baltistan plans to secede from Pakistan.

Today the Saudi ideological influence is reflected in the emergence of hybrid forms of sectarian ideology: for example, the classical Deoband and Hanafi orientation of the Taliban has been considerably influenced by Salafi sources and Wahhabi literature. This development has taken place in tandem with the Pakistani Taliban delinking from its original identity of being a Pashtun movement and becoming integrated with Punjabi militant outfits such as the SSP.

Ideologically, there is also a large degree of resonance between the SSP and the Taliban vision of an Islamic system, which explains why the SSP followers can identify and sympathize with the Taliban movement. Khalifa Qayum told me that 'a few years ago we had a complete Islamic system in the neighbouring Afghanistan'. It was, he said, based on the same model that the SSP wants for Pakistan: the model under the historical leaderships of the first four caliphs (*khulafa ar-rashideen*), considered to be 'rightly guided', who succeeded the Prophet Muhammad when he died (Abu Bakr Siddiq, Umar al Faruq, Uthman ibn Affan, and Ali ibn Abi Talib). Like the others I interviewed, Qayum referred to the ideal state of Afghan society under Taliban rule, equating pure Islamic rule with a state of peace and justice. He told me a now-familiar story about Afghanistan:

> From north to south, from east to west, if an old woman went with a bucketful of gold on her head, no one would scowl at her. No one would even think of stealing from her or robbing her. That was the blessing of the system. When this [Islamic] system is established in practice, peace just comes automatically, because a criminal is punished immediately according to sharia, and the effect of the punishment is that one punishment scares others from doing the same. It was a complete Islamic system.

My meeting with Qayum had a very formal character. I drove to the SSP's offices in Islamabad together with the journalist who had helped me set up the interview. We entered a big, sparingly furnished room, with a handful of Qayum's closest adherents in attendance. He was very polite, but I had the feeling that he was keeping me at arm's length by providing only very formal answers to my questions. Whereas my interview with Sami ul Haq was conversational, the atmosphere in this case was far more tense. Maybe it was because I was the only woman in the room with several men. Maybe it was due to his charisma, which together with his very soft and low tone of voice gave him a mystical authority. I was asked to sit on a stool in front of him, while he sat cross-legged on a charpoy, a traditional woven bed with a wooden frame, wearing a bakra on his head.

Qayum started speaking about jihad in defensive terms, arguing that jihad is mandatory when the enemy is trying to take
away Muslims' right to live or preventing Muslims from observing their own rules. In addition to the defence of life, property,
and religion, he asserted that jihad was justified 'when Muslims
are in danger of losing their faith [*iman*].... The Muslim must
always fight to save his faith'. Qayum told me that he sees the
SSP as the only movement in Pakistan that is truly attempting to
ensure the enforcement (*nifaz*) of Islam and described the SSP
as the 'backbone' of peace in the country.

Compared to the other activists I interviewed, Qayum
seemed to consider true faith as the threatened object, justifying
defensive jihad. According to Qayum, faith should be protected
against the *fitna* that was spread with the Iranian revolution. For
him, the Iranian revolution was an attempt to spread a wrong
and deviant form of Islam, because it was led by Shia Muslims.
As already described, the historical schism between Sunni and
Shia Muslims has led to contemporary differences in both rituals and doctrines, and a movement like the SSP considers these
differences to be a source of harm to religion.

Fitna is often translated as either 'disbelief' or 'upheaval': it
denotes the spread of ideas that lead to harmful disputes among
Muslims. The term is often used to describe the historical disagreements and divisions among Muslims that arose after the assassination of the third caliph, Uthman ibn Affan. Fitna is also a recurrent
theme in Islamic apocalyptic writings, denoting the troubles
attending the last days. In Qayum's narrative, the threats from the
'Iranian fitna' and the 'US fitna' are unified by their common motivation: 'enmity towards Islam' (*Islam dushmani*). Qayum asserted:

> In Afghanistan, there was a pure Islamic government, a *khalifa
> rashida* [rightly guided caliph].... It is only, just only, because of
> Islam enmity that they attacked Afghanistan; it has nothing to do
> with their territory.... The same is true in the case of Pakistan. Those
> who are attacking Pakistan are only doing it because of their enmity
> to Islam ... to crush the Muslims and establish their own power.

This enmity is driven by 'the knowledge that Islam offers a superior system'. To establish this argument, Qayum made an analogy to the business world: 'In business, the one who establishes a bigger business than you is whom you would fear.'

Qayum created an additional link between the defence of faith and the Islamic system of Afghanistan by recognizing Mullah Omar as *Amir ul Momineen* (the leader of the faithful) and by asserting that both Mullah Omar and Osama bin Laden were divinely protected (this interview predates the death of both):[11]

> Their [the US's] 50–60 years of past history is about demolishing Islam in the world and closing the paths of the spread and development of Islam. They are intoxicated by the idea that they want to crush Islam. But no one can ever crush the one that Allah keeps alive. They have yet not been able to touch even a single hair on the head of Osama bin Laden or the Amir ul Momineen.

Qayum, like the other militants I spoke with, vehemently asserted that the Al-Qaeda was not behind the 9/11 attacks, which he regarded instead as a plot by an alliance of Jews and Christians (*jahud wa ansar*). Quite contrary to common opinion, he described the Al-Qaeda as a small organization working to protect 'Islam and Islamic countries'.

When asked about justifications for violence, he responded that it is legitimate only as an emergency measure but claimed that the present situation qualifies as an emergency: 'If a robber comes to your house, you will grab whatever you have to hit the robber.' While Qayum initially denied any link between suicide attacks and Islam, he added, 'But yes, if there is someone who is very powerful and won't let me live, and nobody is protecting me in this situation, there is room. But there is otherwise no place for suicide [fidayee hamlay][12] or qital [the jihad of fighting].'

Throughout the interview, Qayum was thoughtful and attentive to his phrasing, talking slowly with breaks between important words or sentences. The number of people in the room gave the interview a performative quality: sometimes he appeared to be addressing his adherents, and sometimes he seemed to be demonstrating to them how to respond to sensitive questions. Thus while he continuously rejected suicide as unlawful according to Islam, he simultaneously maintained: 'If you know that your life is over anyway, you might as well take the enemy with you.... If one is cornered like a desperate cat, this would not be categorized as suicide.' Therefore, he ended up justifying extraordinary means through a last-resort discourse. At the same time, Qayum rejected calling the situation in Afghanistan a war between two equal parties: 'It's never acceptable for someone to enter your house and destroy your honour,' he said.

To re-establish a true Islamic system, Qayum argued, 'We need a revolution'—not a revolution led by the sword, he added, but a 'moral revolution'. Thus his discourse on the establishment of a true Islamic system was completely independent of his discourse on jihad and suicide, which was shaped by the idea of self-defence. He also expressed hope for a moral revolution throughout Asia. 'If we implement Islam in our lives and show high morals, people will be impressed. The implementation of Islam is the only way to peace in the country,' he ended, looking quite satisfied with his management of the interview.

I thanked him for his time and left the room, feeling perplexed about his arguments. I concluded that he had a strong sense of loyalty and sympathy towards the Taliban, and he seemed to share their vision though most of his followers were from Punjab. Because of his appraisal of Mullah Omar and of Afghanistan under the reign of the Taliban, I could understand why the movement was often designated as the *Punjabi Taliban*.

Muhammad Yahya Mujahid: Averting the Crusade

Through my meeting with a representative of another movement that is also linked to the Punjabi Taliban, namely the LeT, I learnt that the alliances between the Taliban and the pre-existing movements with their own agendas are based on varying degrees of overlapping interest. Adding to this, Punjabi Taliban organizations do not necessarily have anything in common except adherents in Punjab. The SSP and the LeT, for instance, are two very different movements though both are linked to the Punjabi Taliban.

A year after I met Muhammad Yahya Mujahid, a central figure in the LeT movement, he was named in a US treasury department press release as having provided direct support to the Al-Qaeda and having facilitated terrorist attacks, including the July 2006 train bombing in Mumbai.[13] Besides being the head of the LeT's so-called media department, he has also served as their spokesman since mid-2001. In that capacity, Mujahid has issued statements to the press on numerous occasions, including after the November 2008 attacks in Mumbai, which the LeT was accused of having orchestrated.

When I met Mujahid, it was in his capacity as spokesperson for the JuD, an organization that ostensibly provides education, healthcare, and other social and welfare services. Mujahid tried to convince me that the link between the LeT and the JuD was only ideological. However, in 2009, the UN Security Council listed the JuD as an alias of the LeT, and it has been an open secret in Pakistan that the JuD became the public cover name of the LeT when Musharraf banned the latter in 2002. That there is indeed a connection became obvious when Mujahid handed me his business card after the interview: he had crossed out the name LeT with a blue pen and written JuD just beneath it.

This was the only one of my interviews for which I chose the meeting place. We met at approximately 1 a.m. at a private residence the night before I left Pakistan. To accommodate my wish to meet before I left, he drove around 140 kilometres from Muzaffarabad to Islamabad. To me this indicated the degree to which activists of these movements wanted to communicate their message, and that they were looking for understanding. I was very tense when I first opened the door and he stepped in.

I didn't know what to expect and had been close to calling the meeting off several times during the evening. When the doorbell rang, I was afraid that he would be armed. But he wasn't; he was simply a very big man with a bushy black beard and trousers short enough to reveal his ankles, as is common among adherents of Ahl Hadith movements. By the time the interview ended, I was no longer afraid, and he turned out to be a man with a great sense of humour.

Mujahid also appeared nervous at the beginning of the interview, as if he was trying to figure out my agenda. He gave very abstract and imprecise answers to my questions and looked around distractedly, as if he wanted to make sure that the room hid no unpleasant surprises. As the interview progressed, he loosened up and became more cheerful. I noticed a turning point when he told me that there is no difference between the mujahedeen of yesterday and the mujahedeen of today. 'Back then,' he assured me, 'they smelled awfully of sweat, and today,' he paused, 'they still smell awfully of sweat!' The uncontrolled laugh that his own comment triggered seemingly changed his mood. He was a funny man. While we spoke, I found it difficult to believe that he was known as a dangerous terrorist.

Mujahid was not as great an admirer of the Taliban system as Khalifa Qayum was. The LeT and the classical Taliban that arose in the tribal areas hold very different views on how to create an Islamic society. As he stated: 'The Taliban was not an ideal Islamic government, but they tried to govern by Islam. Nowhere do Muslims have power or *sulta* [sovereignty]. That is why they are oppressed everywhere in the world.' Mujahid asserted that before a real Islamic power can be established, civil society must be strengthened through missionary work and education. Thus Mujahid's vision differs from the Taliban's approach of instituting an Islamic society by means of top-down authority.

Even so, in Mujahid's view, the Taliban deserved support for its efforts to defend religious autonomy and self-determination. This followed from his view that 'it matters that it [the US] is

Christian and wants supremacy in the world…. In Afghanistan the agenda was to destroy a Muslim government.' He, too, referred to the 'War on Terror' speech by George Bush, where 'it came out of his mouth that "I am fighting a crusade war"'. Thus according to Mujahid's narrative, too, it is ideology that drives the enemy.

Mujahid saw the main motivation of the enemy, the US, as a combination of superpower aspirations and the urge for doctrinal and religious expansion. The actions of the enemy are hence explained in terms of a crusade-like campaign that aims at expanding the religious doctrines of the West. The interpretation of the conflict as a religious war is interesting to note, since this way of understanding the conflict is recurrent in the Taliban narratives. It is the religion of the enemy, not Islam that is seen as the offensive and expansionist driver of the conflict. According to Mujahid, the doctrinal threat should be averted and Islam must be empowered so that the religion becomes resilient towards the threat.

Remarkably, he did not mention India, the old arch-enemy of the LeT movement, when he talked about 'the enemy'. This points to the fact that the LeT movement has adopted the central concerns of the Pakistani Taliban. To his description of the enemy, he added: 'If the Americans are saying they are fighting a defensive war in Iraq, then it is the same as saying that though the time right now is 12.38 a.m., it is actually 12.38 p.m. That is a complete lie!' At the same time he was careful to note that there was no proof that the Al-Qaeda was behind the 9/11 attacks, indicating that this could not be the real motivation behind the US engagement in Afghanistan.

By his reasoning, the jihad undertaken by the Taliban is solely defensive and, therefore, demands the support of other Muslims:

The religion Islam does not allow terrorism in any way. The first thing to remember is that everywhere Muslims are fighting defensive wars. The ideal jihad, where a caliph sends his army to another place [to conquer], is not going on anywhere. In such a situation, when Muslims are fighting a defensive war, it makes no sense to distinguish between *fard al-ayn* [individual duty required of every Muslim] and *fard al-kifaya* [collective duty that the individual is not required to perform as long as a sufficient number of community members fulfil it]. If a thief comes into this house, we will not start to dispute about whether it is fard al-ayn or fard al-kifaya to defend ourselves. We will take whatever we have in our hands and hit him to defend ourselves.

With this observation he rejected the Islamic jurisprudential concerns of just war as irrelevant in the extraordinary situation contemporary Muslims are facing.

In Mujahid's conceptual attempt to separate jihad from terrorism and in his evaluation of legitimate means, however, religious jurisprudence played a larger role. First he mentioned that it was haram to fight non-combatants and civilians, regardless of their religion. He gave the example of a recent kidnapping of 30 Christians in Peshawar, which he categorized as haram. 'Jihad is a part of our religion. Neither in the defensive nor in the offensive jihad is it allowed to kill civilians, to destroy fields, harm women, children, or elders. Jihad is a very noble practice.' To illustrate examples of offensive jihad, by which he meant the practice of a Muslim ruler occupying non-Muslim territory, Mujahid pointed to historical figures such as Tariq bin Ziyad, who, according to legend, initiated offensive military action to protect a rural girl from being oppressed. Known in Spanish history and legend as Taric el Tuerto (Tariq the One-eyed), Tariq bin Ziyad was a Berber Muslim and Umayyad general who led the conquest of Visigoth Hispania in 711. His name is frequently invoked by modern-day militants.

In evaluating the legitimacy of suicide attacks in defensive jihad, Mujahid held that it depends on where the blast takes place: 'If a person blows himself up in a military installation, as in Iraq or Afghanistan, the case is different from a person who blows himself up among civilians. Blasts in Muslim countries are also haram when targeting other Muslims. And they are also haram in the US or other non-Muslim countries among civilians, among those who are not fighting at all.' This argument was different from the justifications I heard from other interviewees, where there was more room for harming the enemy due to the importance of the object being defended (that is, religion, the rule and sovereignty of God, and so on) and the scale of the threat.

Mujahid's discourse on jihad was also different from the others I heard in that it was not aimed at establishing an Islamic system of rule. Rather, he stressed that civil society must be strengthened before the establishment of an Islamic polity could be envisioned. Thus his narrative framed educational and welfare activities like those carried out by the JuD as central to the progress of Muslims. This remains an important distinction between the ideological agendas of the TTP and the LeT.

To this end, Mujahid stressed the humanitarian functions of the religious seminaries: they were, he told me, 'big NGOs where hundreds of thousands of children get education and food—children that otherwise would be losers in Pakistani society'. Reflecting on the demolition of Jamia Hafsa, he claimed that 'only a few of the European terrorists [that is, the perpetrators of the London and Madrid bombings] had any link to any madrassa'. He saw the secular call for counterterrorism reforms in the religious seminary system as yet another ideological, 'secularizing' scheme of the enemy. He told me, 'We don't oppose having a secular education too. But why at the expense of religious knowledge?'

In Mujahid's view, the demolition of Jamia Hafsa was part of this international 'secularizing' campaign, though Musharraf tried to describe the incident as 'his war' in subsequent statements to the press. Mujahid also claimed that the reason Pakistan was suffering from shortages of water and electricity was that the Pakistani nation passively watched while Musharraf issued an order to turn off the electricity and water supplies to the Red Mosque building in the days preceding the military operation.

Thus Mujahid was suggesting that God punished the entire Pakistani nation for the Jamia Hafsa incident. His narrative ended where it had started when we met, with the assertion that modern Muslims are weak. According to Mujahid, for Muslims to gain power, they must build up civil society.

The difference in focusing on building a strong Muslim civil society or a strong Islamic state suggests that the Taliban is more a powerful slogan than a well-coordinated movement. Though Taliban adherents and sympathizers have been motivated by the particular idea that armed jihad is presently incumbent upon Muslims, their agendas, strategies, and perception of *where the right battlefield is* have varied.

The Pakistani army had close relations with the LeT movement in the 1990s. Musharraf's policies in 2002 were a clear attempt to disassociate the military from the use of the LeT as a proxy, and even though there is disagreement over the degree to which the ISI continued to cultivate relations with the LeT, the formal and public denouncement of the LeT alienated some parts of the movement, which later joined the TTP. They embraced the view that the Pakistani army had betrayed Muslim brotherhood bonds by supporting the US invasion of Afghanistan, and carrying through the subsequent raids in the tribal areas of Pakistan.

The damage caused to the relationship between the Pakistani army and the LeT in the period between 2001 and 2004 (considering the raids in the tribal areas, the ban on the LeT, and the alliance with the US) should not be underestimated. The Red Mosque raids in 2007 represent an important crossroads in this regard—an event that created huge polarization within the country and affected old alliances with proxy movements.

Musharraf also sacked influential army staff who felt loyal towards the proxy model and the Taliban loyalists; for instance, he dismissed two senior generals (the head of the ISI General Mahmood Ahmed and his deputy chief of army staff Muzaffar Hussain Usmani) in an attempt to suppress a growing revolt within the army against his pro-American policies. Both were regarded as hard-line Islamists. Also, ordinary soldiers who refused to carry out orders under the raids during 2002–4 were dismissed.

My impression from my conversations with the Pakistani army personnel is that the discourse on the Taliban has changed considerably since the 1990s, and the narrative of brotherhood between the army and the Taliban activists and loyalists has been replaced with increasing animosity. This is only natural to expect since the communication materials issued by the Pakistani Taliban portray the Pakistani army personnel as apostate Muslims. Facing each other's bullets on the battlefield, it is further hard to imagine that feelings of brotherhood can remain intact.

☙

Notes and References

1. Muhammad A. Rana and Rohan Gunaratna, *Al-Qaeda Fights Back: Inside Pakistani Tribal Areas* (Islamabad: Pak Institute for Peace Studies, 2007), p. 49.
2. Qandeel Siddique, *Tehrik-e-Taliban Pakistan: An Attempt to Deconstruct the Umbrella Organization and the Reasons for Its Growth in Pakistan's North-west*, DIIS Report, no. 12 (Copenhagen: Danish Institute for International Studies, 2010), p. 26.
3. For a detailed description of the SSP, see South Asia Terrorism Portal, available at www.satp.org/satporgtp/countries/pakistan/terroristoutfits/Ssp.htm (accessed on 5 January 2011).
4. Ahmed Rashid, *Taliban: Militant Islam, Oil and Fundamentalism in Central Asia* (New Haven, CT: Yale University Press, 2000), p. 92.
5. One of the gunmen behind the attacks, Ajmal Kasab, was captured, and admitted to having ties with the LeT. The Mumbai attacks were striking events since the perpetrators attacked nine locations during the siege. See Ahmed Rashid, *Pakistan on the Brink: The Future of Pakistan, Afghanistan, and the West* (London: Allen Lane, 2012).

6. Stephen Tankel, *Storming the World Stage: The Story of Lashkar-e-Taiba* (New York: Columbia University Press, 2011).

7. 'Hizb Chief Syed Salahuddin Warns Pakistan against Withdrawing Support on Kashmir', *The Times of India*, 8 June 2012, available at http://timesofindia.indiatimes.com/world/pakistan/Hizb-chief-Syed-Salahuddin-warns-Pakistan-against-withdrawing-support-on-Kashmir/articleshow/13932562.cms (accessed on 1 October 2015).

8. 'Six Dead as Bomb Blast Rocks DI Khan', *Awaz Today*, 27 January 2009, available at http://awaztoday.com/newsdetails.asp?pageId=684 (accessed on 24 March 2011).

9. Qayum was released in December 2013. See Zulfiqar Ali, 'Sentence Served: Former MPA Released in Fake Degree Case', *The Express Tribune* (Pakistan), 2 December 2013, available at http://tribune.com.pk/story/639861/sentence-served-former-mpa-released-in-fake-degree-case/ (accessed on 17 December 2013).

10. Anatol Lieven, *Pakistan: A Hard Country* (London: Allen Lane, 2011), p. 347.

11. This interview took place in June 2008, before bin Laden was killed in a US-led attack on his compound in Pakistan.

12. The word the militants often use for suicide attacks is 'fidayee hamlay', which implies self-sacrifice for a higher cause or for the sake of God.

13. The US Department of the Treasury named him pursuant to US Executive Order 13224 (20 December 2001), and to the UN Security Council Resolution 1267 (15 October 1999). In order to see the implications of this, the order can be retrieved from http://www.treasury.gov/resource-center/sanctions/programs/documents/terror.pdf (accessed on 25 July 2014). The UN resolution can be retrieved from www.un.org/Docs/sc/committees/1267/1267ResEng.htm (accessed on 24 March 2011).

თ

5

Religion in the Taliban Narratives

This chapter explores how the Pakistani Taliban groups invoke religion in their public communications as a justification and motivation for violent acts. It provides an in-depth understanding of the many *different* ways in which religion is invoked in the narratives of the Taliban. The schematic understanding I introduce here might be helpful for analysing and understanding other instances of religious violence also. At the same time, my analysis here also extends the findings of other studies that have tried to deduce the logic of religious violence and it can thus be seen as a contribution to the larger debate on the relationship between religion and violence.[1]

The chapter is organized according to the various ways in which religion appears to play a role in the Taliban narratives justifying violence, namely as (a) an object to be defended; (b) a threat; (c) the purpose of armed struggle; (d) a limit on war; and, finally, as (e) imagery and myth. The analysis in this chapter is mainly based on different genres of public communications issued by the Pakistani Taliban, which complement the material from my interviews. There are moments of overlap between the ideas that become visible ahead and the ideas treated in the three preceding chapters. However, taken together they illustrate what the strong trends in the Taliban narratives are, and can, therefore, contribute to a comprehensive understanding of the religious mind of the Taliban.

The Taliban communications include recruitment videos and recorded speeches, leaflets and pamphlets (shabnamen), jihadi anthems (taranay), and press releases to the local media that take responsibility for violent attacks and explain the reasons behind them. The data was collected between 2007 and 2011, and draws on religious references, concepts, myths, and imagery in a way that makes it evident that they address 'the insider' in order to convince co-religionists about the legitimacy of the Taliban jihad and sharia aspirations, and to convey a clear understanding to the adherents and supporters of the Pakistani Taliban of what they are defending, who the enemy is, and how it should be combated. Religious justifications for violence, therefore, stand out especially clearly in this sort of material. Together with the interviews, these materials have helped me understand the various roles religion plays in the Taliban narratives as well as the limitations of religious discourse. As will be clear, the Taliban are drawing on both secular and religious discourses, attempting to strike a balance between the preservation of religion and tradition on the one hand, and self-defence and security arguments on the other.[2]

The public communications of the Pakistani Taliban are primarily aimed at a local audience. Some, however, are aimed at a larger, transnational Muslim audience and others at adherents of the Taliban and affiliated movements. In the last category, I, for instance, examine a speech delivered by the Red Mosque activist Hamna Abdullah to her fellow students, arguing that the time for militant jihad has come, and a speech delivered by the TTP leader Mullah Fazlullah to a dozen young suicide bombers (fidayeen) just before they left to carry out their missions.

The audio and video recordings I have examined are largely intended as recruitment tools.[3] Some are available on the Internet, but most of the material is distributed locally in the KPP and the tribal areas. The videos include statements made by prospective martyrs before carrying out suicide operations.[4] They also include statements elaborating on the aims and enemies of the various Taliban factions (often accompanied by pictures of beheadings of spies or war scenes). For instance, one video shows the former TTP leader Hakimullah Mehsud explaining why the TTP is fighting against the Pakistani military.

The videos also contain jihadi anthems; most of the anthems I cite in this book are taken from the videos. The anthems are emotional, martial, and nationalistic songs, often glorifying battle and the fighters. They are meant to be emotionally moving and to provide legitimacy for a violent course of action. As described in a report from the International Crisis Group, this sort of material contains 'emotive chanting, archival footage from the fight against Soviet forces and the Soviet-backed regime, images from Iraq and clips from Western documentaries, as well as videos of insurgent training, attacks on government and international forces, and equipment seized or destroyed'.[5]

Taliban-affiliated groups also distribute flyers, pamphlets, and handouts, including the so-called shabnamen or night letters. The shabnamen are a traditional means of communication in the tribal areas: they are unsigned letters distributed clandestinely overnight, often containing handwritten warnings or messages to a particular population. According to the Pakistani analyst Muhammad Amir Rana, these have become the core channel of communication in the KPP and the tribal areas.[6] Shorter messages from Taliban leaders are aimed at the populations of the areas where they operate, whereas the more elaborate statements issued by Taliban leaders and commanders are intended for a larger audience. The leaflets with short messages, which are disseminated by hand, convey concrete imperatives from the Taliban for either security reasons or religious ones. They also generally warn that those who violate the imperatives will be discovered and punished.

Though the Taliban communication material provides religious evidence for their cause in the form of references to the Quran or jurisprudential literature, much of the material seems to be based on the implicit premise that the Taliban interpretation of God's laws represents authentic Islam and is indisputable. Especially in the shabnamen distributed to the local population in the KPP, their interpretation of sharia is presented as religious imperatives, and no argumentation to support their conclusions is considered necessary. An illustrative example is the statement below, which is addressed to the residents of Kurram Agency.

- It is mandatory to keep a beard according to Islamic Sunnah. Cutting and shaving it is a big sin.
- Women should be veiled. They are banned from going into the mountains and fields.
- Lavishness in wedding ceremonies is prohibited, and music is forbidden for everyone.
- Wearing a *tobi* (headwear resembling a calotte or skullcap) is compulsory for every man.
- Prayers in the mosque should be strictly attended, and people should go to the mosque for prayers. The mosque of every village should have an imam and his pay should be at least Rs 5,000.
- Intoxicating materials, hashish, alcohol, and other narcotics and the like are strictly banned.
- Charging interest [on monetary loans] is haram. Those who have charged interest earlier should explain themselves.
- People dealing with NGOs should be arrested. Those having connections with the NGOs should also step forward and explain themselves.
- For women it is haram to attend burials. This means that men should advise their families that women should not attend burials (of non-relatives).
- Tailors should sew clothes according to the Sunnah and not according to the English style.
- Dish antennas should be removed from houses.

- Taking bribes and *halaat* (taking money from a poor party or presenting weak evidence behind a charge) is prohibited in the jirgas.
- Thieves will be given the punishment prescribed in sharia.
- The agreement with the Shia is only about the road.[7] Having friendships or any dealings with them is haram.
- The *haq mehr* (dower) for women at the time of the wedding ceremony is to be fixed at Rs 70,000 and 2 *tolas* [25 grams] of gold. Other traditions are banned. This means the dower should be given at the time of the wedding. In the event of a divorce, women have the right to the valuables and the gold.
- Setting fires in the mountains is banned; anyone who is caught will be punished.
- Those who have relatives in Peshawar or foreign countries should tell them that it is important to grow a beard, and their lame excuses will not be accepted.[8]

In addition to the aforementioned sources, I have examined some special documents, such as the will of Abdul Rashid Ghazi (the imam of the Red Mosque who was killed during Operation Silence) and a biography of the former TTP leader Baitullah Mehsud, written by Azam Tariq, a TTP spokesman. These sources are notable for their use of religious imagery and ideas about divine intervention.

In studying materials of this kind, it is important to understand how they are produced and distributed in order to evaluate how official and authoritative they are, to what degree are they sanctioned by the leadership of the Taliban movements, and who the intended audiences are. Although there have been comprehensive reviews of the Al-Qaeda communications, very little has been published on Taliban communications in Pakistan.[9] It has been observed in some of the few available accounts that the leadership of the TTP is using a media-production entity, the Al-Sahab Media Foundation, and a distribution and translation network, the Global Islamic Media Front—both formerly connected mainly with the Al-Qaeda.[10] In addition to implying collaboration between the TTP and the Al-Qaeda, this connection suggests that the TTP is also addressing a broader, transnational audience.

The TTP also has its own official media organ, Umar Studio. Another outlet, Ummat Studio, seems to have produced far less material, though it can be traced to the TTP.[11] Another lesser-known production entity is the Fateh Studio, which is connected to the Taliban in Swat.[12] I have also examined the Pakistani Taliban material published by independent production entities that are sympathetic to them, such as Studio Intiqam (related to a small Taliban-sympathizing movement, Ittehade Mujahideen Khurasan, which allegedly has formed an alliance with a local Taliban faction), and *Hitteen* (an Urdu magazine addressing a larger, transnational audience). These materials are of interest not only because of the messages they convey but also due to the means by which their productions are distributed. These include popular online jihadi forums, notably Alqimmah.net, and the forums administrated by the Al-Qaeda-sympathizing movement Ansar al-Mujahideen (the Helpers of the Mujahedeen).[13]

Establishing the authenticity of these materials, particularly the leaflets and shabnamen, is sometimes difficult because of the highly decentralized and informal character of such communication. It is conceivable that fake materials that are not issued by the Taliban are also distributed, since the government of Pakistan might have an interest in engaging in the propaganda war. Only a few of the leaflets carry any form of logo or letterhead, most are undated, and many are written by hand and generally reflect a very informal way of communicating. However, they are often signed by the issuing leader or commander (*amir*), and structural and thematic elements in the documents aid in comparison and in establishing their origin.[14] Because of the uncertain provenance of this kind of material, I have treated it cautiously, citing only content and arguments that appear frequently enough to form an identifiable pattern.

بانی تحریک امام المجاہدین
ملا بیت اللہ محسود
(شہید) رحمہ اللہ

امیر تحریک طالبان پاکستان

امیر المومنین
ملا محمد عمر
مجاہد حفظہ اللہ تعالیٰ

بسم اللہ الرحمن الرحیم

تاریخ ـــــــــــــــ   نمبر ـــــــــــــــ

تمام تعریفیں اللہ اس ذات کیلئے ہیں جس کی عزت و کبریائی کے سامنے دنیا کی تمام فرعونی و دجالی طاقتیں پچ و بے تو قیر ہیں لاکھوں درود
وسلام ہوں اس ذات بابرکت پر جو تکوار کے ساتھ مبعوث کیلئے گئے۔

عید الفطر کے اس بابرکت موقع پر ظلم و جبر کی چکی پس رہی والی امت مسلمہ کی مظلوم عوام کو عید کی خوشیاں مبارک ہوں۔ اس موقع پر میں اللہ
رب العزۃ کی رحمت سے امید رکھتے ہوئے امت مسلمہ کو شہاء خلافت ثانیہ اور احیائے خلافت کی تازہ بہاروں کی خوش خبری دیتا ہوں۔
انشاء اللہ شام، یمن، عراق اور صومالیہ سے لیکر پاکستان، افغانستان اور چیچان تک جاری عالمگیر اسلامی تحریکوں ساتھ فتح و نصرت کی واضح
بشارتیں امت کے گہرے زخموں کا بہترین مرہم ہو گئے۔

میں اس موقع پر پاکستان کے مخلص مسلمان عوام کو یہ بتانا چاہتا ہوں کہ ہماری یہ پیاری دھرتی
جو اسلام کے نام پر حاصل کی گئی تھی اسی آج غلام ہاتھوں میں جا چکی ہے اور پاکستانی قوم کو نظریاتی غلام بنایا جا رہا ہے غیور ادار خود دار قوم کسی کے
قوم کسی کے غلام نہیں بن سکتے۔ اس لیئے اس سیکولر اور کفری نظام کا خاتمہ ہم سب پر فرض ہے۔ ہمیں متحد ہو کر ان ظالم و جابر حکمرانوں کا
مقابلہ کرنا ہے۔ علماء کرام سے گزارش ہے کہ وہ اس طاغوتی نظام سے مقابلے کیلئے ان کی صحیح رہنمائی کریں اور نو جوانان اسلام اپنے اکابر
صحابہ کرام کی تاریخ کو دہراتے ہوئے قربانی کیلئے خود کو پیش کر دیں۔
میں اس سیکولر کفری نظام کے خلاف لڑنے والے مجاہدین کو تسلی دینا چاہتا ہوں کہ فتح ہمیشہ حق کی ہوتی ہے۔ جب تک ہم حق پر قائم رہیں گے
اللہ کی نصرت ہمارے شامل حال رہے گی۔
لہٰذا آپ شریعت مطہرہ کی رہنمائی میں اپنی کاروائیاں جاری رکھیں اور اس کفری نظام کی مظلوط کام کرنے والے ہر کار کن کو نشانہ
بنائیں اور اللہ رب العزت کی ذات پر یقین رکھیں وہ مظلوموں کا مدد گار ہے۔
انشاء اللہ نہ صرف پاکستان میں بلکہ پوری دنیا میں خلافت کا سورج ہو گا اور اسلام غالب ہو کر رہے گا۔

حکیم اللہ مسعود
امیر تحریک طالبان پاکستان

دستخط امیر تحریک طالبان پاکستان

Figure 2   Message from the former TTP head Hakimullah Mehsud, distributed on the occasion of Eid ul Fitr on 18 August 2012

Note: The leaflet was collected from Miranshah in North Waziristan in 2012, in which Mehsud argues that it is mandatory for Muslims to overthrow the secular system in Pakistan. He urges Muslims to unite and face the 'tyrannical rulers', and reassures the mujahedeen that God and victory will be with those who are fighting for truth and justice. Mehsud also urges the mujahedeen to continue their activities against the 'infidel' system and to target groups that are strengthening such a system. He tells them to keep up the faith that God helps the oppressed. If God is willing, he says, the Islamic system [*khilafat*] will prevail not only in Pakistan but eventually in the whole world.

Despite the informality of these materials, it would be an error to assume that the local population does not take them seriously. It is likely that public executions of those who have flouted these warnings have instilled fear in the local population and led them to pay greater attention to the messages, regardless of their sources.

The sections ahead are based on an analysis of these sorts of communication materials and bring forward the different ways in which religion appears as a justification for the Taliban embracement of violence.

Religion as an Object to be Defended

One of the most striking features of the Taliban calls to jihad is the repeated claim of exceptionalism and urgency. Militant jihad is deemed urgent because religion—specifically, sharia or religious institutions such as seminaries and mosques—is under dire threat. The defence of these institutions is always equated with the defence of the central religious doctrine of *tawhid*—the oneness and unity of God.[15] Jihad thereby becomes a matter of defending the very foundations of Islam.

Tawhid is the central faith doctrine in Islamic tradition and also the first part of the Muslim declaration of faith: 'There is no God but God' (la ilaha illallah). Any threat to tawhid makes jihad a matter of the life or death of religion. This argument was less prominent in my interviews: tawhid was not frequently mentioned as an object to be defended.

Since the Red Mosque incident in 2007, religious seminaries and mosques have taken on a special significance as physical symbols of Islam under threat. In the speech delivered by Hamna Abdullah in front of thousands of female activists after the demolition of the historical Amir Hamza mosque, she claimed that '[o]ur bodies will fall, but mosques will stand. Rivers of our blood will flow, but [we] will not let the greatness of Islam be harmed.'[16] She equated mosques with 'the greatness of Islam'.

As already noted in Chapter 3, she also referred to the mosques and seminaries as 'Islam's forts' and 'God's house', thus equating the defence of these structures with the defence of Islam.[17] Such claims imply that without the protection of its human guardians, Islam could die out.

Recruitment materials of the TTP also often describe 'martyred' mosques or seminaries, as in a video issued by the Darra Adam Khel faction of the Taliban: 'Look at this madrassa. This is the madrassa of Sherakai. It was attacked in the holy month of Ramadan by the apostate [murtad] and impure [napak] army on a Friday. In this attack, scores of innocent people were killed and many sustained injuries.'[18] Such an image functions to justify violent actions against the Pakistani army. In the public communications, the defence of political sovereignty is also discursively connected to religion and the defence of divine authority. This equivalence was also evident in my conversations with the Taliban activists, who repeatedly depicted Afghanistan as the only place on earth where the rule or system of God was implemented. Thus national borders must be defended because they are simultaneously constituted as Islamic borders. This points to an odd paradox in the Taliban narratives: on the one hand, God is established as sovereign and almighty, yet on the other hand, jihad is justified by the claim that His authority on earth is threatened and in need of human defence.

It is worth highlighting that what, in turn, are related to tawhid and divine political authority are abstract ideas of 'peace' and 'order' attained through the implementation of sharia (depicted as unmediated Godly reign), and with it a particular notion of a more 'efficient' punishment system that, according to the Taliban narrative, can eliminate crimes and immoral acts (according to their narrative, it also presents a more 'human' alternative to the existing Pakistani justice infrastructure). The Pakistani Taliban thereby depict themselves as defending the interests of the Pakistani people.

A video issued by the TTP in the frontier area of Darra Adam Khel claims that Talibanization eliminated crimes in the area:

Darra Adam Khel was earlier home to thieves, dacoits, alcoholics, powder [heroin], hashish, and other criminal acts. Praise be to Allah, through the emergence of the Taliban, the power of the violence-makers was finished. Charg [a name meaning 'chicken' in Pashto] was the leader of the offenders and had heavily tortured the locals. Praise be to Allah, he was killed by the hands of the Taliban and people were freed from him. Hashish, heroin, and alcohol were wiped out from the region.[19]

The virtues of justice as practised under sharia are also expressed in an address by Hakimullah Mehsud recorded in a video: 'In an Islamic government, there is salvation from things such as the police of the English system, complicated court systems, law courts, and offices—what is otherwise interpreted as "law and order" today.'[20]

The same kind of portrayal of the Taliban as the well-wishers of the Pakistani people is often seen in the jihadi anthems. In an address to young men about to depart on suicide missions, Mullah Fazlullah explains the purpose of the Taliban in terms of the common good: 'Brothers, it is our faith that Allah is with us.... Allah is our well-wisher, Islam is the religion of peace, we are the well-wishers of the people, whether they are Hindus, Sikhs, or Christians, or whether it is the kafir army or *mushrik* [idolater] army.'[21]

One of the anthems played in a recruitment video includes the following lines:

We are the well-wishers and admirers of the masses and the country,
We are fighters hailing from every house and family,
O Allah, be our guardian, we are travellers in the black mountains.[22]

The Taliban imperatives in the shabnamen are framed in the same altruistic terms, with the goals of protecting the people and their lands against chaos and establishing peace.[23] These narratives always present sharia and the re-establishment of the glory of Islam as the prerequisites for a stable society. In a statement by Azam Tariq, the spokesman of the TTP, removing the 'secular' leaders is considered to be in the interest of the Pakistani people: 'We can give the Pakistani nation the well-meaning advice that if the Pakistani people want peace in the country, they should take on the responsibility of removing the present establishment of secular rulers and ending the army's American war.'[24]

Despite this avowed altruism, many of these communications are intolerant of religious or moral failings. The call for jihad is based on the premise that true believers never compromise with respect to their religion, and the framing of both religion and the definition of the true believer is, therefore, inflexible. The anonymous editor of the jihadi outlet *Hitteen*, where the Taliban leaders publish their views, describes 'the leadership of truth' (meaning the Taliban) as those who are 'never ready to negotiate with sin, disobedience [towards God], or *kufr* [unbelief] and shirk, and are always ready even to give their lives for the establishment of the sovereignty of Allah'.[25] This uncompromising stance is evident in the shabnamen that describe the ongoing jihad as unending as long as enemy attacks continue and at the same time undertake to 'ensure' that jihad will be continued to the last breath.[26]

Religion as Threat

The defence aspects of the narratives on jihad are clear in the recruitment and communication materials. The militants are defending religion (particular dimensions of it) against elimination attempts by the enemy. This discourse implies that the Pakistani Taliban represent their own actions as *reactions* and devote considerable space in their communication and recruitment materials to displaying the bad intentions and actions of their enemies. Whereas religion clearly appears as something to be defended, it also appears as something to be protected against, namely when it comes to the religion of the enemy. Thus religion is part of the threat image in a particular way, as I describe ahead.

Generally, a common ambivalence can be traced in the material in the way the religiosity of the enemy is constituted. On the one hand, the religiosity of the enemy is constituted as wrong religiosity (driven by 'wrong' faith doctrines, for example, Christianity, Judaism, Hinduism) and on the other hand, the religiosity of the enemy—somewhat paradoxically—consists of adherence to non-religion, disbelief. Thus while references to a crusade war initiated by the 'Jews and Christians' are recurrent, equally present is the tendency to frame the West as devoid of any religion.

The main enemy, the US, is seen as driven by both religious expansionism and the intention to eliminate Islam. In his speech to aspiring suicide bombers, Mullah Fazlullah interpreted George Bush's reference to a crusade in literal terms: 'O Muslims and warriors of Allah's religion, you know that a crusade war is going on. The crusade has been raised, and nearly the whole world is united under it to eliminate Islam and erase the mujahedeen and jihad.'[27] The enemy forces are also frequently described as 'the forces of kufr', while those supporting the US and NATO forces are described as 'crusader slaves'. In TTP materials, this expression is frequently applied to the Pakistani government and security forces.[28]

The enemy, whether ascribed religiously expansionist intentions or the intention to eliminate Islam, is also depicted as an adherent of shirk (idolatry or polytheism). Through a series of metaphoric associations, this phrase often refers to the support of democracy. Through analogies with Quranic depictions of the pharaohs of ancient Egypt, shirk is equated with tyranny, injustice, and oppression.

The pharaohs were seen by their people as the personifications of one of the many Gods that were worshipped in ancient Egypt, and thus they held the status of both kings and gods at the same time. In the Quran, a core element of the story of Prophet Moses is his confrontation with the then pharaoh in Egypt: Moses conveying the message of tawhid and the pharaoh rejecting it, instead asking people to worship him. Thus in

Islamic mythic history, the pharaoh is the ultimate symbol of human arrogance. Furthermore, several verses of the Quran refer to the injustice and crimes the pharaoh committed against his people, making him a symbol of oppression and tyranny.

Besides the kafir (in this case denoting the one who rejects the doctrine of tawhid and sovereignty of Allah) and the mushrik who embraces democracy, others who invite God's anger and are thus designated enemies of the Taliban are the *munafiq* (hypocrite) and the murtad. These latter terms are often applied to the Pakistani government, again because of its embrace of democracy. Democracy is, in turn, equated with kufr and contrasted with sharia. Azam Tariq, for example, continuously describes the conflict that the Taliban is part of as a battle between 'Kufr and Islam'.[29]

The TTP and its member organizations in the tribal areas and the KPP consider the democratic system itself to be a threat. Mullah Fazlullah entreats his video audience:

> My dear friends, save yourselves from sins like democracy. Democracy is a pagan [kufr] system, and it is the opposite of sharia. If there is democracy, then the sharia system cannot be implemented. The Western democracy is the enemy of the sharia of Muhammad [*shariate muhammadi*]. And whoever is in the system of democracy is eliminated from the religion Islam. In democracy, the power is with the people. This is against the Islamic system, where the power rests with Allah Almighty.[30]

Democracy is simultaneously equated with the 'system of the Christians',[31] shirk, and fitna.[32] As stated by Hakimullah Mehsud in his criticism of the Pakistani government: 'This governmental system is democratic, which is shirk in its entirety.' He goes on to characterize democracy as an unjust, despotic, unethical, and tyrannical system: 'We are not the enemies of Pakistan or the Pakistani nation. Instead we are the enemies of this current kufr democratic system that has been forced on us. This system is unjust and despotic. This unethical and tyrannical setup is a kufr system irrelevant to sharia.'[33] Hakimullah Mehsud and Wali al-Rahman Mehsud denounce the government as follows: 'After they have adopted kufr laws, how can they be Muslims? They are most loyal in their friendship with the kuffar, and they are the perpetrators of murder of thousands of Muslims. Therefore, we cannot call them Muslims.'[34]

The Pakistani government and security forces are also depicted as the enemy because of their alliance with the main enemy force, the US. According to the Taliban frame of understanding, this alliance and its adherence to democracy qualifies it to be categorized as murtad or munafiq—an alliance that earns the wrath of God (and thus also the wrath of the Taliban).

Other members of these threat categories include India, the former Afghan president Hamid Karzai, and Shia Muslims. India is constituted as the enemy due to Pakistan's dispute over Kashmir and is framed as being both a kafir and a mushrik country with Hinduism depicted as the driving force behind the actions of India in Kashmir. On par with the former Pakistani president Asif Zardari, the former Afghan president Hamid Karzai was framed as a murtad—an apostate who, due to his friendly relations with the US, has left Islam.[35]

The Shia Muslims are framed as kafir due to their faith doctrines, which, in the Taliban perception, are disrespectful towards the companions of the Prophet and amount to kufr because of the fragmentation they cause among Muslims.[36] With this, India is made equivalent to a mushrik, Karzai and the Pakistani government and its security forces are likened to murtads, and the Shia Muslims to kafirs (disbelievers/'wrong-believers'). In sum, the enemies are not only seen as driven by religion or anti-religious doctrines, but they are also signified through the use of religious terminology.

Religion as the Purpose of Armed Struggle

While the defence of the different dimensions of religion is a constantly present way to explain the purpose of jihad, this is accompanied by parallel references to militant jihad as a faith imperative under the given 'extraordinary circumstances', where Islam is seen as being under attack. Thus another ambiguity can be traced in the role religion plays: whereas religion as an object requiring defence is inscribed in a clear defensive security discourse, more offensive or proactive justification claims related to religion can also be traced in the jihad narrative. These play a double role. On the one hand, the purpose and justification behind the militant engagement in jihad is explained by religion, thus facilitating violence, and on the other hand, religion instructs the legitimate means and behaviour of jihad, thus also constituting its boundaries (the latter aspect will be discussed in the subsequent section).

The more offensive aspects of the role of religion are clear in those parts of the Taliban narratives that explain what the legitimate purposes behind jihad are. As a storyline, this offensive story runs parallel to the defensive story where a foundational religious referent object is being threatened by the 'wrong-believing' or disbelieving enemy. First, the offensive claims of justification are constituted through the active engagement of sources of religious authority (particular religio-textual references, religious jurisprudence, particular exegeses) and religious injunctions depicted as mandatory upon Muslims. My analysis shows that this plays out concretely through the use of references to particular chapters and verses of the Quran that— according to the Taliban depiction—deal with the themes of hypocrisy, Islamic doctrinal exceptionalism, monotheism, idolatry, the forming of alliances with Jews and Christians, sharia, the existence of a vanguard of believers that 'enjoins the good and forbids the evil' (the Taliban) and, not the least, jihad. These verses are interpreted ahistorically and applied as evidence when it comes to demarcating enemies and legitimizing uncompromising measures taken against them.

Given ahead are examples of the Quranic chapters referred to and how they are used:

Surah An-Nisa: Several verses (4:61, 4:63, 4:64, 4:88, 4:138, 4:140, 4:142, and 4:145) of this chapter deal with munafiqs, who are defined as those insincere in their faith, pretending to be good Muslims but in truth driven by other interests. These verses also state that the munafiq earns God's anger. This chapter is especially used to justify jihad against the Pakistani government.

Surah Adh-Dhariyat and *Surah Al-Baqarah*: Some verses of these two chapters establish the doctrine of tawhid in opposition to shirk. They also mention that those who equate other things with God earn His anger and punishment (for instance, verses 51:54, 51:55, 51:56, 51:57, and 51:58 of *Surah Adh-Dhariyat* and verses 2:163, 2:164, 2:165, 2:166, 2:167, and 2:168 of *Surah Al-Baqarah*). These verses are used as evidence that God is with the militants who are fighting shirk.

Surah Al-Maidah: Some of the verses in this chapter are about the distortion of the divine messages spread by Moses and Jesus. This chapter also describes Jewish and Christian scepticism towards the Prophet Muhammad when he claimed to receive revelations from their God. Verses 5:50, 5:51, and 5:52, in particular, are interpreted as a divine warning against making alliances with Jews and Christians, and as a religious justification for the Taliban fight against the Pakistani army because Pakistan has formed an alliance with 'the Jews and Christians'.

Apart from direct references to the Quran, there are also references to classical Sunni Muslim exegesis in, for example, passages defining those who betray the Muslims as kafirs (such as Tafsir Al-Tabari, which is a classical Sunni exegesis from the ninth century, and Tafsir Al-Qurtubi, a classical seventh-century exegesis with the specific objective of deducing juristic injunctions and rulings from the Quran). However, there seems to be no rigid ideological commitment to any particular trend within the various Sunni Islamic interpretational traditions. Despite the original Deobandi background of the Taliban, there are evident influences from major Salafi ideologues, classical as well as modern. These include the medieval theologian Ibn Taymiyya known, amongst other things, for ranking jihad above traditional means of worship (for example, his compilation of jurisprudential rulings in *Majmoo al-Fatawa*),[37] and also Ibn Abd Al-Wahhab (d. 1792), for example, for his work *Kitab al-Tawhid*.[38] The latter is especially used to justify violent measures being taken against those who are constituted as mushrik and those who assist the mushrik.[39]

Besides references to religio-textual evidence, a second way militant jihad is justified more proactively by religion is by representing jihad as a pillar of Islam on par with the its five orthodox pillars: the faith declaration (shahada), prayers (namaz/*salaat*), pilgrimage (hajj), fasting (roza/*sawm*), and paying alms (zakaat); jurisprudentially, all belonging to the sphere of worship (*ibadaat*).[40] Warfare jihad is constituted as the required way of worship under the present extraordinary circumstances and gains priority above the orthodox pillars of Islam. However, it is again the extraordinary context (that Islam is existentially threatened) that is decisive for why there is more emphasis on militant action than on orthodox measures of pious behaviour (praying, fasting, and so on). In the words of Mullah Fazlullah: 'Religion is not just about praying or fasting or missionary activities or [obtaining] traditional Islamic knowledge, but acting out that Allah is Almighty.'[41] Very illustratively, he continues:

> If there are no pillars, then it is not possible to construct the building; similarly, pillars have no importance if they have no roof. Nowadays the situation of Islam is very awful. The pillars of 'prayer' and 'fasting' are standing, but the roof over them is made by Christians and the unbelievers. So, my dear friends, we should take care of this issue.[42]

A third offensive dimension of jihad is based on the religious duty to implement sharia. The following two examples from recruitment materials are clearly illustrative of this sort of trend, where the implementation of sharia seems to be the main justification for jihad.

> A Muslim nation is bound to be regulated by an Islamic system: we [the TTP] struggle for the system not because we beseech it, but because it is our fundamental right. The Tehrike Taliban Pakistan aims to create this Islamic system by engaging in the operation of jihad.[43]
>
> Our aim is to create Allah's rule on Allah's land under the skies of Allah on Allah's people. We will give every type of sacrifice for its establishment; we want nothing short of it.[44]

This argument sometimes forms part of the defensive discourse, whereby the threat from democracy and the crusading intentions of the enemy necessitate the implementation of a just and godly system, but it is also sometimes presented as an obligation to be undertaken proactively in order to realize the glory of Islam. It can be argued that the struggle for sharia inside Pakistan has become increasingly militarized in parallel with the resistance against external forces in Afghanistan, and thus there is no clear-cut distinction between the defensive constitution of jihad and the more aggressive constitution of jihad as the fulfilment of the Muslim duty to establish sharia and the glory of Islam.

A fourth way in which religion plays a more offensive role in providing justification for entering into militant jihad is through ideas of divine intervention. The significance of dreams is clear in the biography of the former TTP leader Baitullah Mehsud written by Azam Tariq and published in the *Hitteen*, disseminated among the adherents and supporters of the Taliban. It is, for example, described that the father of Baitullah Mehsud was initially against his son's engagement with jihad, but then he saw the Prophet Muhammad in a dream telling him to devote his son to the cause of jihad and not create barriers for him. This made him change his mind and after the dream not only did he support his son but also actively engaged in jihad himself.[45]

In another example, Baitullah Mehsud supposedly had a dream before he died (in a missile attack on his father-in-law's house), in which the Prophet told him, 'That is enough, Baitullah, now you should come!' This made him realize, according to Tariq, that 'the time for his martyrdom was near'.[46]

Another interesting and illustrative example of divine intervention and its significance is a speech by Hamna Abdullah, delivered in front of thousands of female followers, in which she explains the background for the Jamia Hafsa's decision to enter jihad, citing divine communication:

> The Lord of Medina was troubled. The Lord of Medina was disheartened and was saying: 'Oh, mujahed daughters, your country [Pakistan] was established for Islam, but 58 years have passed, and Islam is being persecuted here. Mosque after mosque has been martyred, the sacredness of the Quran has begun to be razed; yet I do not see anyone rising up. Clouds of sadness prevail everywhere. Spiritual daughters of Maulana Abdullah Shaheed [the first imam of the Red Mosque], information has reached me that the police attacked you twice. You fought with much bravery and courage; you drove back the police. One hundred of your female students were wounded, but you still stood your ground.'... The Lord of Medina is saying: 'My great daughters, daughters bathed in the longing for martyrdom, daughters waiting for martyrdom: I do not see anyone rising up. No one is seen rising up for the dignity of mosques and the Quran. Thus you [must] stand up for jihad.' O Prophet of Allah, we are weak. We are the weaker sex, we do not have the strength—how do we wage jihad? Then suddenly you [the Prophet Muhammad], peace be upon you, visit a girl in her dream and offer one girl a shining sword, and say: 'Daughters, rise, wage jihad. Allah will help you.'[47]

The power of ideas about divine intervention and support is significant in the Taliban movements led by charismatic and powerful leaders. Their legitimacy is often found in the Hadith narrations that bind the guidance through dreams to the expectation of an approaching apocalypse. In one Hadith, the Prophet Muhammad is recorded to have said that 'when the Day of

Resurrection approaches, the dreams of a believer will hardly fail to come true, and a dream of a believer is one of the forty-six parts of prophecy, and whatever belongs to prophecy can never be false' (Sahih al-Bukhari). In another Hadith, the Prophet is recorded to have said, 'Whoever sees me in a dream, surely he has seen me, for Satan cannot impersonate me' (Sahih al-Bukhari). The belief in true dreams is also based on the example of the Prophet Muhammad, who is reported to have dreamt parts of the Quran. According to observers, the visionary dream has broadly continued to hold an exalted status among Muslims.[48] It appears to be a common trait among activists engaged in militant jihad and the 'worship of fighting' that dreams are seen as guidance: taken as warnings or glad tidings.

Typically, descriptions of dreams and experiences of divine intervention are kept within the circle of followers. Mullah Omar, who is recognized as the supreme leader by both the Afghan and the Pakistani Taliban, allegedly had a dream in which the Prophet Muhammad appeared to him and instructed him to bring peace to Afghanistan. Later he removed a cloak said to belong to the Prophet from its Kandahar shrine and put it on. For his followers, this was a sign of Mullah Omar's divinely conferred authority, because only a true leader of the faithful would be able to remove the cloak. Mullah Omar's authority as the commander of the faithful (Amir ul Momineen) was reportedly based on 'true night dreams' (*ruya*) received by himself or his closest followers.[49]

Religion as a Limit on War

It is remarkable that religion does not appear strong in those parts of the jihad narratives that relate to the rules and means of jihad. Arguably, this is because religious discourses on rules and legitimate means in jihad potentially limit and put restrictive conditions on the practice of jihad. However, rather than restricting the practice of jihad, most of the directions for action given in the jihad narratives establish the basis for action that, according to criteria in classical Islamic jurisprudential literature, would be regarded as unlawful. This is because necessity and urgency arguments take a more prominent role than references to orthodox religion in those parts of the Taliban narratives that prescribe the legitimate rules and means of jihad.

In the materials I have analysed, there are, nevertheless, references to Quranic chapters addressing the topic of appropriate behaviour in jihad (for example, the chapters Al-Anfal, Al-Imran, and Al-Hujurat). Comparatively, however, concrete references to the Islamic sources of law are far more frequent in the discourses on the legitimate purpose of jihad treated in the section above. In some of the material, religion is completely sidelined when it comes to this issue, and necessity and urgency arguments appear to be more prominent in deciding what is seen as appropriate means. For example, a TTP video carries a statement accompanying the beheading of a kidnapped Polish engineer, in which expediency (the 'requirement of the day') takes priority over religious doctrine:

> It is the requirement of the day that all the unbelievers should have the same fate, but we still, on account of our religion, tried very hard not to kill Peter [the Polish engineer]. If Allah wills, this will be the fate of all the foreign hostages that we take, whether they are from China, Britain, or other countries. We will not leave anyone in our grip alive.[50]

This does not mean that the normative rules and principles of jihad are not given any importance. Competing discourses are also to be traced in the communication and recruitment materials putting some kinds of limitations on jihad. Mullah Fazlullah's speech to the suicide bombers includes the observation: 'If we commit cruelties, Allah will give someone else power over us, and they will beat us. May Allah save the Taliban from un-Islamic acts, and may Allah bless us with that jihad which the Prophet Muhammad, peace be upon him, performed.' He continues:

I am ordering the Taliban, rather requesting them, not to break the rules of jihad. Jihad is a holy practice, but also a dangerous one. Remember, if you break the rules of jihad, then even if you kill thousands of enemy personnel, you will not benefit in the life hereafter. Do not include yourselves among those people about whom the Prophet Muhammad, peace be upon him, said, 'Lots of people participated in jihad but would get nothing for it in the life hereafter.'[51]

However, the most central and recurrently mentioned condition deciding the legitimacy of using war as a means is having the right intention or niyat. Interestingly, this requirement establishes the conditions of the possibility of considering unorthodox measures, such as suicide attacks and the killing of spies, as legitimate. For instance, Mullah Fazlullah explains: 'If two, three, or four pious people stand up, they will beat the satanic government, because it is the promise of Allah, but listen: these people should be pious, patient, have strong faith and determination. Their aim should be only to make Allah happy.'[52]

Thus even though limiting civilian deaths is encouraged, they are not considered unlawful as long as the perpetrators had the intention to defend the sovereignty of God, make Him happy, and to fight for Islam. Thus paradoxically, religious conditions of war are represented and interpreted in a way that expands jihad's room for manoeuvre. In a night letter, for instance, it is stated that the kidnapping of people other than spies is against Islamic directives. Kidnapping is, however, considered lawful if it is done in the name of the higher purpose of jihad, whereas kidnapping for ransom is condemned and calls for punishment.[53]

Added to this, there is a very blurred concept of who the legitimate target is. A principle of discrimination is based on representing the enemy (and thus the legitimate target) under the broad category of disbelievers and apostates. Due to the content put into these labels, this means that not only those involved in active combat activities are seen as legitimate targets but also those who facilitate the enemy. Those who are constituted as disbelievers and apostates are encompassed in this flexible category of enemies that ultimately does not put up very strict principles of discrimination. For example, Abdullah Mehsud, a powerful Taliban commander who died in 2007, wrote:

> The people who fight together with the unbelievers against the mujahedeen [the Al Qaeda and the Taliban] and help to get them caught, spy on them, and provide evidence to prove that the activities of the army are right, are all, including the army's unbelievers, apostates. To kill them is mandatory for every Muslim.[54]

It is, however, worth noting that the ideal of keeping collateral damage to the minimum is simultaneously upheld in keeping with traditional Islamic jurisprudence governing the conduct of jihad.[55] In comparison to the means applied by the enemy (drone attacks being one example put forward), the fidayee attack targeting selected buildings, vehicles, and tanks of the enemy is, for instance, highlighted as being more precise, since it leads to less collateral damage. In addition to this, in the Taliban discourse on jihad, civilian deaths can be forgiven as long as they are not intentional. Mullah Fazlullah, for instance, told the suicide bombers:

> We always tell the fidayeen to target two types of people: the Pakistan army and their supporters. And the leaders and members of the Awami National Party [the secular Pashtun nationalist party, driving the main resistance against the Taliban in the KPP]. You people should also act on this principle. Try to target them with minimum damage to the masses, but if there is any collateral damage, then we will not be held responsible for it in the court of Allah.[56]

Another related principle that restricts the practice of jihad, as evident from the material, is sufficiency: to use the required means, but not to exaggerate the use of power. Fazlullah advises: 'Consider yourselves the slaves of the masses; don't get proud when you have power because jihad is about modesty.'[57] The principle of sufficiency is, however, also open to interpretations that can ultimately intensify the use of force, and thus can be an argument for embracing harsher means to match the enemy.

The stress on the importance of following just rules in war is, however, most vocal in the context of evaluating the acts of the enemy. Many of the Taliban videos 'reveal' the brutality of the enemy and its inhuman way of fighting the war. For instance, the dead bodies and faces of massacred children and babies are shown, in some cases paving the way for proportionality arguments when deciding the legitimacy of means (the argument that acts of cruelty should be met with similarly cruel acts) and, in other instances, constituting a contrasting identity for the Taliban self. The treatment of prisoners is also a recurrent theme, as Fazlullah's speech demonstrates:

> People have seen the so-called peace of those who claim peace. Taking prisoners from their cells and throwing them out of helicopters.... Treating innocent and powerless people this way was their peace. Prisoners have rights, even unbelieving prisoners.... In Pakistan, there is no sharia law imposed, no humanitarian or Islamic rights are given to the people. This could be cured by jihad only.[58]

Thus, somewhat paradoxically (considering their initial critique of the means applied by the enemy), this in some instances paves the way for a stronger discourse of proportionality, allowing the Taliban to take harsher measures due to the character and nature of the threat. The abusive treatment of Aafia Siddiqui in US custody and the case of the CIA contractor Raymond Davis, who fired 10 bullets at two Pakistani youngsters in a crowded market in Lahore in early 2011, are used as examples of enemy brutality and immorality that justify proportional acts of retribution.[59] In the shabnamen, the Pakistani government's violation of peace deals is also presented as a violation of the rules of just war.[60] This also means that religious conditions for legitimate war behaviour are evoked mostly to evaluate the conduct of the enemy rather than to regulate and restrict the Taliban use of force.

Religion as Imagery and Myth

The communication materials and militants' speeches are rich in allusions to Islamic history, particularly references to famous battles. These are used to inspire recruits, but they also function to validate contemporary actions as part of the enduring struggle to defend Islam. For example, after the demolition of the Amir Hamza mosque under the leadership of Musharraf, the women's action committee of the Jamia Hafsa seminary adopted the name '313', the number of the Prophet Muhammad's followers who took part in the Battle of Badr against the Quraysh tribe. In addition, contemporary events are often interpreted according to Islamic principles and precepts and as evidence of divine will. In this section, I describe some of the mythic events and religious concepts that hold particular significance for the Pakistani Taliban.

The widespread use of religious imagery and myth adds a transcendental layer to the explanation of jihad and thus ascribes a special spiritual significance to jihad. The conflict is then decontextualized, made ahistorical and cosmic. First, among the identified themes in the constitution of jihad is the willingness to sacrifice oneself for religion, which is framed as a specific pious trait that enhances one's religious standing in the eyes of God. The willingness to sacrifice oneself for religion, with the particular meaning of undertaking a suicide mission, is framed as a sign of devotedness to God.

Theologically, sacrifices are often interpreted as a means of enhancing one's religious standing, though they also have other connotations that have nothing to do with human sacrifice. Nevertheless, the biblical and Quranic story of Abraham, who so deeply trusted in God that he, without questioning, was willing to sacrifice his only son, points to the religious significance of human sacrifice.

In the materials, the theme of sacrifice is invoked to differentiate between those who prioritize religion and God above worldly goods and those who do not. The theme of sacrifice, for example, is invoked in Mullah Fazlullah's speech to a handful of suicide bombers on their way to fulfil their missions. He presents the option to sacrifice oneself as a special blessing from God and those conducting the sacrifices as especially pious:

He [Allah] wants the bodies of the pious, not of everyone. Because of the faith of the pious, their flesh and bones have become so valuable that Allah himself is purchasing it . . . This is the special blessing of Allah upon you people. Accept the favour of Allah, thank Him and turn your bones and flesh into weapons and target the kafir government [referring to the Pakistani government].[61]

Another example from the same material stresses how the willingness to die—sacrifice oneself—is interpreted as evidence of true devotion: Mullah Fazlullah, for instance, holds that 'if at the age of 80 they [the clerics and the intellectuals] are not ready for death, it means that their love for Allah is artificial and not real.'[62]

The link between the willingness to sacrifice oneself and devotion to religion is also established in the jihadi anthems. Here is an illustrative example:

They are sacrificing themselves on their wish,
They are the friends of the religion Islam,
They are attacking in their turn,
They are friends of religion,
They are in love with all the verses of the Holy Quran,
The fidayeen are on their way,
And they are beautiful youth.[63]

The TTP spokesman Azam Tariq describes martyrdom as a 'new' form of sacrifice that is required in the fight against satanic powers and unbelief. Human sacrifices through the use of suicide tactics are regarded as more powerful than the enemies' use of 'weaponry, tanks, missile launchers, helicopters, jet aircrafts, drones and long-range missiles'—precisely because they are made in God's name and thus sanctioned by God.[64] The Taliban materials hence stress the virtue of sacrifice, and the practice of sacrificing one's life for a higher cause is distinguished from suicide in order to circumvent the religious injunctions against taking one's own life.

A second image invoked in the narratives is that of a divine test (the framing of the Taliban as being tested by God), which again strengthens the image of the Taliban as especially pious and as the chosen ones. The image of a divine test is linked to the narrative that hardship and adversity are God's way of testing His strongest believers. In Muslim tradition, hardship that tests believers is most typically regarded as coming from God. According to one interpretational discourse, hardship from God is to test the patience [sabr] of believers, and patience in the face of hardship, in turn, is seen as the requirement for heavenly rewards. In the Taliban material, this theme is especially invoked in convincing suicide bombers that God is on their side though the mission seems hard. In his speech to the suicide bombers, Mullah Fazlullah states that 'hardship erases sins', thus providing a religious motivation for their actions.[65]

However, the Pakistani Taliban also uses hardship—such as the earthquakes and floods that struck Pakistan in the early years of this century—to strengthen another type of discourse. In this, hardship is framed as a punishment from God for not living according to His/the Taliban's vision of sharia, and for not having implemented the Taliban perception of good public morality. In the communication material aimed at the adherents of the Taliban, the discourse that hardships are signs that God is with those who are tested, is, however, dominant. The following quote, also from Mullah Fazlullah's speech to the suicide bombers, illustrates the way this theme is invoked: 'You people are believers; that is why you are under examination. You people have dignity; there are a lot of races in the world and in Pakistan, but you people and those from the tribal areas are suffering because you are all believers.'[66]

In the shabnamen, traditional poetry is quoted for the same purpose. In one of his statements, Azam Tariq recites a poem by the most famous national poet of Pakistan, Allama Iqbal: 'The offspring of Abraham [the Muslims] are surrounded by fire and enemies. Again someone is testing someone.'[67]

If God sends exacting tests to the faithful and harsh punishments to the unbelievers, He can also send evidence of His support in the struggle. From the communication materials, it is clear that the Taliban are convinced that they are acting for God and with His support. A statement from the TTP encourages followers to draw confidence from revelations of the divine will:

> The bullet which is written for me will hit my body, not anyone else. Allah told me three times: I will take your life at the required time. *Malak al-Maut* [the angel who takes the soul away after death] came and told me not to worry. He said that he will not come before the due time, and if he has not arrived, no one can kill you. So listen: no one can kill you before your time is due.[68]

A third theme that is related to the use of dreams is that of the expectation of an approaching apocalypse. In the narratives, the extraordinary circumstances are conditioned not only by the constitution of an external threat to religion, but also through the constitution of the idea that the jihad undertaken is part of an apocalyptic struggle. God is, therefore, currently active in earthly matters (most significantly through night dreams). The battle itself is also described in terms of a cosmic war, again giving jihad a specific spiritual significance, since it then becomes constituted as a battle between the forces of good and the forces of evil: God versus Satan.

A fourth way in which religious imagery appears is through the use of analogies to important symbolic battles that have gone down in Islamic mythic history as battles with special spiritual significance due to the intervention of God. These include the Battle of Badr, the Battle of Karbala, and the encounter between Moses and Pharaoh.

The Battle of Badr (624) has been passed down in Islamic history as a decisive victory for Muslims attributable to divine intervention and as a symbol of the battle between truth and falsehood. The Prophet Muhammad and his companions expected to meet 40 unarmed men but instead met a well-prepared army three times the size of their own. This was the first battle the Muslims ever engaged in and is also the most famous and renowned because of the religious narratives about several extraordinary events that occurred during it. References to the Battle of Badr are made when it comes to defining the Taliban self, the enemy, and the nature and significance of jihad—but most importantly also when it comes to providing a promise of ultimate victory.

Abu Sufyan, a leader of the Quraysh tribe in Mecca, was a staunch opponent of the Prophet Muhammad before accepting Islam later in his life. According to Islamic myth, the conflict was seeded when the Quraysh confiscated the belongings of Muhammad and his followers after they migrated to Medina in 622 to seek refuge from hostile attacks. The Battle of Badr took place when Muhammad and his followers saw a passing caravan led by Abu Sufyan and went to stop him and reclaim their belongings. At this point, most Muslims believe, God revealed to Muhammad that his people were now permitted to defend themselves, rather than to continue to suffer persecution. In this context, the following verse is frequently quoted by the militants: 'O Prophet, urge the believers to battle. If there are among you twenty [who are] steadfast, they will overcome two hundred. And if there are among you one hundred [who are] steadfast, they will overcome a thousand of those who have disbelieved because they are a people who do not understand' (Al-Anfal 8:65).[69]

References to the Battle of Badr, both implicit and explicit, frequently appear in Taliban communication and recruitment materials. For instance, in Azam Tariq's biography of Baitullah Mehsud, the battles led by Mehsud against the Pakistani security forces are described as similarly unequal conflicts, with 'tanks, missiles, helicopters, drones and heavy military artillery' on one side, and the mujahedeen, armed only with 'high spirits' and guns on their shoulders, on the other. The mujahedeen are portrayed as winning miraculous victories.[70]

Besides the Battle of Badr, images of the Battle of Karbala (685) between the supporters and relatives of the Prophet Muhammad's grandson Hussain ibn Ali on one side, and the forces of the Umayyad caliph Yazid ibn Muawiya on the other, are also invoked. In Islamic myth, this battle has spiritual significance, not because it led to the victory of Hussain and his followers, but, on the contrary, because it led to his death and paved the way for subsequent revolutions against the unjust Umayyad dynasty. Thus this reference also plays into the theme of sacrifice and hardship. In the will written by Abdul Rashid Ghazi before he died in the besieged Red Mosque, he describes the siege of the mosque by hostile (Pakistani government) forces as 'no different from that of Karbala'. He describes 'suffering' and 'martyrdom' as prerequisites for an 'Islamic revolution' ('We are confident that our blood will plant the seeds of a revolution'), and draws an explicit analogy to the suffering that Hussain endured.[71]

Another historical encounter that is frequently mentioned in the communication and recruitment materials is the one between Moses and Pharaoh. The following statement is illustrative: 'The pharaoh of the past did not have jet fighters, tanks, drones or modern weapons. But our determination is the same as that of Prophet Moses. So by the grace of Allah, we will eliminate these by the stick of Prophet Moses.' The same imagery is also drawn upon in several leaflets, framing the Taliban as Moses and the US as Pharaoh.[72]

Polarized rhetoric pitting good at war with evil and the faithful at war with unbelievers is common. According to Fazlullah, 'In every era the fight between good and bad has taken place, and this is also happening today'.[73] A TTP video proclaims: 'There are two open fronts in this world today: the first is the battle array of the mujahedeen and *ansar al-muhajireen* [the helpers of the refugees]. The second is the battle formation of the kuffar and the *munafiqeen*.'[74] And Hakimullah Mehsud declared in a speech: 'Today a war between Muslims and the unbelievers is going on; this is not a fight between the Taliban and the USA. This war is the war between the Muslim *ummah* and the unbelievers.'[75]

A fifth type of religious imagery invoked in these communications involves the afterlife. This type of rhetoric both urges patience in waging jihad and encourages those engaged in jihad to expect rewards not in this life but in the next. One of Mullah Fazlullah's speeches is again a good example:

> People and clerics of some communities say about me that I deceive the boys [the suicide bombers] by giving them expectations of heaven. Well it is true, I tell them of heaven, give them hope and expectations of heaven, because I have nothing, and I cannot repay them. Allah will repay them, and Allah has said that the repayment for this is paradise.[76]

Enabling others, even the current enemy, is also sometimes constructed as an objective of jihad: 'We want all of them [the enemies] to embrace Islam and save themselves from hell and enter into Heaven.'[77] In some of the shabnamen distributed to local villagers, the Taliban imperatives are framed as a means of escaping damnation in the next world, and the willingness to sacrifice one's life for the sake of Allah is framed as the path to salvation (*rahe nijat*).[78]

An expanded timeline into the afterlife makes death and human sacrifice necessary in order to obtain the ultimate reward for the struggle, namely paradise. Thus the purpose of jihad cannot only be explained by the constitution of religion as an object to be defended or the more aggressive discourse of establishing sharia on earth, but also through the parallel struggle for salvation in the hereafter. This expanded timeline that moves into the afterlife both promotes patience in relation to the effects of jihad and adjusts the expectations of those engaged in jihad so that they do not take payoff in this life to be a criterion of success for their activities.

A final tendency in the material is that the Taliban and mujahedeen are often identified as God's chosen ones, a vanguard:
'Allah has selected those He likes most for this work [to establish His rule on earth]. So who are these people whom Allah
selects and raises for this work? Allah selected those people who
are near to Him.'[79] Hence the mujahedeen are also described
in terms that indicate that they are close to God, such as the
'friends of the holy Prophet',[80] the 'children of Prophet Jacob',[81]
the 'servants of Muhammad', or 'Allah's lions'.[82] The application
of these designations frames them as special and their actions
as especially noble. The following quote from the recruitment
materials is a good illustration:

> The mujahedeen of Tehrike Taliban Pakistan are Allah's slaves,
> Muhammad's agents; we are servants of Muhammad, a mercy to the
> worlds, peace be upon him. If hideous jokes and cartoons are made
> about my Prophet, then your Taliban brothers are the only ones
> who bring honour through retaliation, who risk their lives and are
> martyred to show their love for Muhammad, peace be upon him,
> whereas other people engage in demonstrations, protests, boycotts,
> and give political statements.[83]

The special closeness to Allah and his prophets is also established
by addressing the prophets with family titles, such as Uncle
(for Moses and Jesus), Grandfather (for Noah), and Father (for
Abraham).[84] Comparisons are sometimes made between the missions of the prophets and that of the Taliban. A speech by Mullah
Fazlullah invokes many of these comparisons and justifications:

> Prophet Noah stood against the whole world, but he never sur-
> rendered and continued his work till the end. Allah eliminated the
> evil, and good flourished then. Similarly, Prophet Abraham stood
> alone in the battle against the kingdom of the whole world, and
> he did not surrender either. He left the country but never stepped
> back from his mission or religion. Prophet Moses and his brother
> faced Pharaoh, who had a strong force of seven million. They didn't
> withdraw but continued their mission. They and their nation suf-
> fered great hardships in this mission. We should also get used to

such sufferings. If this path was not good, then Allah would have stopped His prophets. Because of them, their whole nation suffered, but Allah praised them.[85]

Implicitly, such comparisons cast the Taliban as an important force in the history of Islam. According to a text by Abdullah Mehsud, the Taliban is represented as the first generation to promote unity since the 'four rightly guided caliphs' who succeeded the Prophet Muhammad.[86] Furthermore, such comparisons imply a place for the Taliban and its leaders among the Islamic prophets.

Similarly, praise of the Taliban leaders and commanders echoes the biographical literature (*sirat*) about the Prophet Muhammad, which praises both his outward beauty and his inner qualities. For instance, Tariq's biography of Baitullah Mehsud describes the Taliban leader as follows:

> He was neither short nor tall. He had a whitish complexion, smiling face, long black beard, thick hair, and big black eyes. He had strong health and nerves. Furthermore Allah had blessed him with a strange set of praiseworthy traits. He had a humble nature, adventurous attitude, and eagerness for jihad; he was good at making important decisions, was a good orator, and was endowed with leadership qualities.

Biographies like this are used on par with the prophetic examples—as 'a model for the Muslim ummah', a 'glowing chapter in the history of Islam' that encourages Muslims 'to follow in the footsteps of Amir Baitullah'.[87]

Adherents of the Taliban often stress the movement's sense of justice by generating heroic narratives about the low crime rate or the socio-economic justice during the Taliban rule in Afghanistan, as was especially clear from the interviews I have conducted. These narratives are, however, used by the Taliban supporters as religious references to an idealized and morally superior society on par with the ideals traditionally derived from the Quran and the Hadith (narrations about the Prophet Muhammad's life and words). Whereas the example of Medina under the prophetic reign is the typical or 'orthodox' reference for a politically just society among Muslims, the Taliban reign in Afghanistan takes on a similar role for Taliban adherents. Hence religion and religious imagery are drawn upon in unorthodox ways and the particularity of these is important to understand in order to take the role of religion seriously. The challenge in any study of religious violence is precisely to understand the particular ways religion is applied in the justifying claims, and to avoid treating religion as a general and inflexible category.[88]

∽

Notes and References

1. See, for example, Michael K. Jerryson and Mark Juergensmeyer (eds), *Buddhist Warfare* (Oxford: Oxford University Press, 2010); Mark Juergensmeyer, *Terror in the Mind of God: The Global Rise of Religious Violence* (Berkeley: University of California Press, 2000); Martin E. Marty and R. Scott Appleby (eds), *The Fundamentalism Project: Fundamentalisms Comprehended*, Vol. 5 (Chicago: University of Chicago Press, 1995).

2. See also my summary of the roles religion plays in the Taliban material in Mona K. Sheikh, 2012, 'Sacred Pillars of Violence: Findings from a Study of the Pakistani Taliban', *Politics, Religion & Ideology*, 13(4): 439–54.

3. Tim Foxley, 'The Taliban's Propaganda Activities: How Well Is the Afghan Insurgency Communicating and What Is It Saying?', SIPRI Project Paper (Sweden: Stockholm International Peace Research Institute, 2007), available at www.sipri.org/research/conflict/publications/foxley (accessed on 25 January 2011); Muhammad A. Rana (ed.), *Understanding the Militants' Media in Pakistan: Outreach and Impact* (Islamabad: Pak Institute for Peace Studies, 2010).

4. International Crisis Group, *Taliban Propaganda: Winning the War of Words?*, Asia Report 158 (Kabul/Brussels: International Crisis Group, 2008), p. 24. See also Brian G. Williams, 2007, 'The Taliban

Fedayeen: The World's Worst Suicide Bombers?', *Terrorism Monitor*, 5(14), available at www.jamestown.org/single/?no_cache=1andtx_ttnews %5Btt_news %5D=4285 (accessed on 1 June 2011).

5. International Crisis Group, *Taliban Propaganda*, p. 14.

6. Rana, *Understanding the Militants' Media*, p. 102. Rana's account does not, however, include a systematic overview of Pakistani Taliban publications or their distributors.

7. This refers to an agreement signed in February 2011 between leaders of the Sunni and Shia communities of Kurram Agency. The agreement guaranteed safe passage of Shias on the Thall–Parachinar Road, lifting the almost four-year blockade of the Shias of Parachinar.

8. Fazal Sayed Haqqani, the leader of the Tehrike Taliban, Kurram Agency, 'Message from TTP Kurram Agency', distributed on 10 May 2011 in Kurram Agency.

9. One of the few publications on this is Muhammad A. Rana's *Understanding the Militants' Media in Pakistan*. On the Pakistani Taliban's use of the media, see Christopher Anzalone, 'The Pakistani Taliban's Media Jihad', *Foreign Policy*, 17 June 2011, available at http://afpak.foreignpolicy.com/posts/2011/06/17/the_pakistani_talibans_media_jihad (accessed on 1 October 2015). For a comprehensive overview of Al-Qaeda-related media, see Daniel Kimmage, 'Al-Qaeda Central and the Internet', Counterterrorism Strategy Initiative Policy Paper (Washington, DC: New America Foundation, March 2010); Daniel Kimmage, *The Al-Qaeda Media Nexus: The Virtual Network behind the Global Message* (Washington: Radio Free Europe/Radio Liberty, 2008), available at http://docs.rferl.org/en-US/AQ_Media_Nexus.pdf (accessed on 1 October 2015).

10. Anzalone, 'Pakistani Taliban's Media Jihad'.

11. Anzalone, 'Pakistani Taliban's Media Jihad'. The few available details about its productions indicate that it has close connections with the TTP in the tribal areas, most likely the local Darra Adam Khel faction of the Taliban. A search on the SITE Intelligence Group website showed only a single production by Ummat Studio. The production included here was collected physically in the KPP. SITE is a monitoring service that provides numerous daily translations of propaganda and multimedia from 'terrorist' websites. See http://news.siteintelgroup.com (accessed on 17 July 2011).

12. This relationship is confirmed by the descriptions found on SITE.
13. Links to these productions are posted not only on forums that are visited by those who have similar ideological inclinations but also on news sites aimed at a broader audience. For instance, many videos by the Swati Taliban are available on the news website Zamaswat.com (accessed on 7 July 2011).
14. See Rana, *Understanding the Militants' Media*, for a description of the characteristics of the shabnamen.
15. Ninian Smart's *Dimensions of the Sacred* is operational in understanding what aspects of religion are in play and defended by religious–political activists like the Taliban. See Ninian Smart, *Dimensions of the Sacred: An Anatomy of the World's Beliefs* (Berkeley: University of California Press, 1996). This framework can be applied to the study of religious violence by using a discourse–analytical framework in order to clarify exactly what is meant by religion. See Mona Kanwal Sheikh, 2014, 'The Religious Challenge to Securitisation Theory', *Millennium: Journal of International Studies*, 43(1): 252–72.
16. 'Jamia Hafsa-Sisters Biyaan', video recording of a speech by Hamna Abdullah and prayer by Umm Hasaan, retrieved from www.youtube.com/watch?v=tc5Tg8eVIcU (accessed on 11 January 2011). Translation by the Middle East Media Research Institute (MEMRI), available at www.memritv.org/report/en/print2282.htm#_edn1 (accessed on 11 January 2011).
17. 'Jamia Hafsa-Sisters Biyaan'.
18. 'Tehrike Taliban Dara Adam Khel', video issued by TTP Darra Adam Khel, Ummat Studio, distributed by al-Moqatel, released 6 January 2011, collected from the KPP, winter 2010–11.
19. 'Tehrike Taliban Dara Adam Khel'.
20. 'Message from Hakimullah Mehsud and Wali al-Rahman Mehsud', video issued by TTP headquarters, Al-Sahab Media Production, released October 2009, retrieved from www.archive.org/details/AMEF_Message-Hakimullah-Wali-ur-Rahman-Mehsud_English (accessed on 11 January 2011). Translation from Ansar al-Mujahideen, available at http://ansar1.info/ (accessed on 11 January 2011).
21. 'Fazlullah Speech to Suicide Bombers', video issued by the Swati Taliban, Fateh Studio, collected from the KPP, winter 2010–11.

22. 'Tehrike Taliban Dara Adam Khel'.

23. Examples include 'Message to the Three Mehsud Tribes', video issued by the Mehsud Faction, South Waziristan, n.d.; Azam Tariq, 'Statement by TTP's Central Spokesman from South Waziristan', issued by the TTP, South Waziristan, n.d.; Saif-ul-Islam, spokesman of the TNSM, Malakand Division, including Kohistan and Hazara, 'Organization of TNSM, Malakand Division Pakistan' (13 January 2011).

24. Tariq, 'Statement by TTP's Central Spokesman'.

25. Azam Tariq, 'Biography of Baitullah Mehsud', *Hitteen*, 2009. Translation titled 'The Life of Baitullah Masood', available at https://ent.siteintelgroup.com/Jihadist-News/10-29-10-gimf-baitullah-mehsud-bio.html (accessed on 1 March 2011).

26. For example, 'Important Announcement from the Shura of Waziristan', issued by the leader and Mujahideen Shura of North Waziristan, distributed 24 October 2010.

27. 'Fazlullah Speech to Suicide Bombers'.

28. For example, Tariq, 'Biography of Baitullah Mehsud'.

29. Tariq, 'Biography of Baitullah Mehsud'.

30. 'Maulana Fazlullah New Video 4', video recording of a speech by Mullah Fazlullah (Swati Taliban), retrieved from YouTube/Zamaswat.com, www.youtube.com/watch?v=vwpYawdgNtE (accessed on 11 January 2011).

31. 'Maulana Fazlullah New Video 4'.

32. For example, 'Message from Hakimullah Mehsud and Wali al-Rahman Mehsud'. Statements from 'Maulana Fazlullah New Video 4' are also illustrative: 'Look, the children of the same father have become each other's enemies because of the different parties taking part in the election. The grandsons of the same grandfather, the people praying at the same mosque, and the clerics of the same sect have become enemies because of democracy, which is the system of the Christians.' Another statement is: 'This [democracy] is the biggest idol in the present era and is pushing people to hell.'

33. 'Message from Hakimullah Mehsud and Wali al-Rahman Mehsud'. The video 'Bloodshed and Revenge' contains a similarly illustrative statement: 'Tehrike Taliban's jihad in Pakistan is targeted at the kufr constitution, laws, and system in the region. It is against the guardians of this unjust system. We are neither the enemies

of Pakistan nor are we the enemies of the soldiers, police, and the leaders.' 'Bloodshed and Revenge', video released by the TTP head-quarters, Umar Studio, July 2009, retrieved from www.2shared. com/file/7370960/8370331e/TTPENGDVD.html (accessed on 11 January 2011). Translation released by the producers, available at www.alqimmah.net/showthread.php?t=9318 (accessed on 11 January 2011).

34. 'Message from Hakimullah Mehsud and Wali al-Rahman Mehsud'.

35. For example, Tariq, 'Statement by TTP's Central Spokesman'; 'Lashkare Jhangvi (International)', issued by the organization of Lashkare Jhangvi, 12 December 2010; 'Shura Ittihad al-Mujahi-deen', issued by Hafiz Gul Bahadur, Baitullah Mehsud, and Mullah Nazir, 19 February 2009.

36. 'Message from TTP Kurram Agency'.

37. Ibn Taymiyya's *Mardin fatwa*, which distinguishes between the 'house of peace' (*dar al-Islam*) and the 'house of war' (*dar al-harb*), is a popular reference for militants who interpret the distinction as a green light to denounce other Muslims as infidels and wage war on them. It is also a critical text for the determination of legitimate versus prohibited targets.

38. The main text cited by the Taliban is the *Kitab al-Tawhid*. Regardless of how his writings are applied to justify militant jihad, Ibn Abd Al-Wahhab was a prominent reformer. He believed that Muslims had increasingly betrayed the original Islam (typified by the first generations of Muslims, the *salaf*) through harmful inno-vations (*bida*) and shirk. His criticism was initially aimed at Sufi rituals and interpretations of the intercession between the indi-vidual and God. See Natana DeLong-Bas, *Wahhabi Islam: From Revival and Reform to Global Jihad* (Oxford: Oxford University Press, 2004).

39. See, for example, Abdullah Mehsud, n.d., 'Is There Also Another Side of the Picture?', North Waziristan.

40. The two main classical categories of Islamic jurisprudence are *muamalaat* (the domain of interpersonal/social/political relations) and ibadaat (the domain of worship denoting the individual–God relationship).

41. 'Maulana Fazlullah New Video 2', video recording of a speech by Mullah Fazlullah (Swati Taliban), retrieved from YouTube/

Zamaswat.com, www.youtube.com/watch?v=zaRLaEGrxh4 (accessed on 11 January 2011).

42. 'Maulana Fazlullah New Video 2'.

43. 'Bloodshed and Revenge'.

44. 'Fazlullah Speech to Suicide Bombers'. In the same speech, he intones: 'This is our slogan: Land of Allah, la ilaha illallah, people of Allah on this land, la ilaha illallah, Allah's sky over this land, la ilaha illallah, we want the rule of one God over this land, la ilaha illallah, we don't obey PATA or civil law, la ilaha illallah.'

45. Tariq, 'Biography of Baitullah Mehsud'.

46. Tariq, 'Biography of Baitullah Mehsud'.

47. 'Jamia Hafsa-Sisters Biyaan'.

48. Iain Edgar, 2008, 'The Inspirational Night Dream in the Motivation and Justification of Jihad', *Left Curve*, 32: 27–34.

49. Iain Edgar, 2008, 'The "True Dream" in Contemporary Islamic/Jihadist Dreamwork: A Case Study of the Dreams of Mullah Omar', *Dreamtime*, 25(1): 4–6, 34–6.

50. 'Tehrike Taliban Dara Adam Khel'.

51. 'Fazlullah Speech to Suicide Bombers'.

52. 'Fazlullah Speech to Suicide Bombers'.

53. 'Kidnapping' (original heading illegible), issued by the leader of the Mujahideen Shura of North Waziristan, 2009.

54. Mehsud, 'Is There Also Another Side of the Picture?'

55. John Kelsay, *Arguing the Just War in Islam* (Cambridge: Harvard University Press, 2007).

56. 'Fazlullah Speech to Suicide Bombers'.

57. 'Fazlullah Speech to Suicide Bombers'.

58. 'Fazlullah Speech to Suicide Bombers'.

59. According to the account provided by the US embassy in Islamabad, Davis saw that one of them had a gun. Apparently fearing that he was about to be robbed, he opened fire on the youths, killing both. When US officials arrived to rescue him from a growing mob, they ran over a bystander, resulting in a third death. Rob Crilly, 'Raymond Davis Incident: What Sort of Diplomat Carries a Loaded Gun?', *The Telegraph*, 1 February 2011, available at www.telegraph.co.uk/news/worldnews/asia/pakistan/8295780/Raymond-Davis-incident-What-sort-of-diplomat-carries-a-loaded-gun.html (accessed on 1 October 2015).

60. For example, 'Manifesto', issued by Zafar Khan, Shura Ittihade Mujahideen, Wana, South Waziristan, n.d.
61. 'Fazlullah Speech to Suicide Bombers'.
62. 'Maulana Fazlullah New Video 2'.
63. 'Tehrike Taliban Dara Adam Khel'.
64. Tariq, 'Biography of Baitullah Mehsud'.
65. 'Fazlullah Speech to Suicide Bombers'.
66. 'Fazlullah Speech to Suicide Bombers'.
67. Tariq, 'Statement by TTP's Central Spokesman'.
68. 'Maulana Fazlullah New Video 2'.
69. Quotations from the Quran are from the Saheeh International version, available at www.quran.com (accessed on 1 October 2015).
70. Tariq, 'Biography of Baitullah Mehsud'.
71. Abdul Rashid Ghazi, 'Will of Abdul Rashid Ghazi', written before his death in the Red Mosque and published online on 8 July 2007, copy obtained through the administration of the Red Mosque.
72. See, for example, Tariq, 'Statement by TTP's Central Spokesman'.
73. 'Fazlullah Speech to Suicide Bombers'.
74. 'Bloodshed and Revenge'.
75. 'Operation Rah-e-Nijat and the Actual Facts', video recording of a speech by TTP chief Hakimullah Mehsud, Part 1 of 3, retrieved from www.youtube.com/watch?v=P6holdOJTdY (accessed on 11 January 2011).
76. Fazlullah Speech to Suicide Bombers'.
77. 'Fazlullah Speech to Suicide Bombers'. This point is also related to the theme of sacrifice, where the afterlife is prized over life on earth. Later in his speech, Fazlullah advises the young suicide bombers: 'Don't destroy your eternal life for a mere profit in this short life.'
78. For example, Tariq, 'Statement by TTP's Central Spokesman'.
79. 'Maulana Fazlullah New Video 2'.
80. 'Maulana Fazlullah New Video 4'.
81. 'Maulana Fazlullah New Video 1', video recording of a speech by Mullah Fazlullah (Swati Taliban), retrieved from YouTube/Zamaswat.com, http://www.youtube.com/watch?v=bC-CDUKJCiU (accessed on 11 January 2011).
82. 'Bloodshed and Revenge'.

83. 'Bloodshed and Revenge'.
84. For example, see 'Maulana Fazlullah New Video 1'.
85. 'Fazlullah Speech to Suicide Bombers'.
86. Mehsud, 'Is There Also Another Side of the Picture?'
87. Tariq, 'Biography of Baitullah Mehsud'.
88. For a theoretical and methodological discussion on how to approach religion in international relations, see Mona K. Sheikh, 2011, 'How Does Religion Matter? Pathways to Religion in International Relations', *Review of International Studies*, 38(2): 365–92; Sheikh, 'The Religious Challenge to Securitisation Theory'.

ᐍ

6

The Justice of Violence

In this chapter, I look at the conceptual and normative implications of the venture into Taliban narratives. It appears that the Taliban framings of jihad resemble just war discourses that justify conventional warfare. Yet in political and public discussions about terrorism, key hegemonic Western concepts of political authority, justice, and rationality often function as the measures by which religious violence is diagnosed and categorized as terrorism. The fact that the Taliban activists' framings of jihad resemble discourses known from the Western just war tradition poses a challenge for observers looking for neat categories to define the character of Taliban violence. As a part of the endeavour to cast critical light on the measures by which religious violence is typically diagnosed, this chapter also seeks to clarify that religious and secular discourses are not only interrelated (defined against each other) in the Taliban narratives but also coexist simultaneously, providing legitimacy to the same narrative.

From the religious justifications for violence given by the Pakistani Taliban, it appears that they have to strike a delicate balance between, on the one hand, the claims of exceptionalism—justifying the use of violent means against an extraordinary threat to religion—and, on the other hand, the claims to the legacy of Islamic theology and jurisprudence, which place limitations on the conduct of jihad. Attempting to balance or reconcile these two different discourses engenders logical paradoxes, such as the claim that an omnipotent God requires the protection of the Taliban, or condemning the brutality of the enemy, while simultaneously arguing that such conduct warrants equally harsh actions in response.

Ultimately, in the articulation of the rules and means by which the Pakistani Taliban conduct jihad, the defensive discourse, based on the claims of exceptionalism, outweighs the religious discourse. It, therefore, does not deepen our understanding of fundamentalist movements like the Taliban to assume that they reflect religious orthodoxy or authenticity. Furthermore, their religious justifications are interwoven with secular rationales, and their views of how to act in times of crisis are strongly influenced by political circumstances.

Balancing the Sacred and the Secular

Before I elaborate on their concepts of authority, rationality, and just violence, I will briefly show how the religious and secular discourses can coexist. We are confronted with the fact that Taliban activists regularly employ a secular political language—whether they would normatively wish it or not—vis-à-vis their religious mode of justification. While both the religious discourses of the Taliban and the hegemonic Western discourses on religion/secularism try to establish a radical difference between the religious and the secular, these domains can nevertheless melt together. Despite the merits of the Enlightenment project, the way it discursively unfolded ruled out the multiplicity of the self and nature by categorizing multiplicity as unreason.

As I have sought to show in the previous chapters, in the Taliban rhetoric, competing justifications, sacred and secular, are typically in play at the same time. Mundane justifications coexist with religious ones, and individual fighters' personal justifications and explanations can vary widely. Yet the Taliban movement reproduces certain narratives of defence that are the strongest recurrent element in my conversations with Taliban activists and affiliates.

Since religion and secularism are not static categories with a fixed content but are labels that bear with them specific connotations in particular contexts, they are best understood as discourses.[1] The religious discourse of the Taliban imposes limits on the practice of jihad, since it must stay within the boundaries of orthodox religious jurisprudence to retain its legitimacy as a battle for Islam. In the secular discourse based on the claims of exceptionalism and emergency, the rules governing the practice of jihad are constituted in more fluid terms, based on the perceived magnitude of the threat and the importance of the defended object, namely religion. The communication materials and the actors I have interviewed move in and out of the two discourses. This is why some of the narratives appear to be inconsistent or contradictory: their embrace of militant jihad is justified by reference to both an external threat and a religious imperative.

The duality of this reasoning is important in addressing the thesis that religion creates a special proclivity for violence. As my study shows, references to cosmic war between good and evil and other types of religious imagery do infuse a special significance into the duty to act, but such rhetoric does not automatically prove that religion is especially likely to incite violence or that religious justifications for violence are easier to make than secular ones. On the contrary, the logic that God is existentially threatened would seem to be hard to sell to an audience who believes in an all-powerful God. The apparent strategic advantage of the religious justification is its potential to consolidate a double rationality for Taliban actions, and thus target a wider audience: both those who are merely fed up with the aggressive policies and interventions of the West and those who agree with the Taliban interpretation of religious imperatives.

The audience of the Taliban message determines which discourse is more salient: the religious justifications are invoked for co-religionists and the secular ones for a broader audience that includes non-Muslims. But does this mean that the Taliban activists are acting and communicating strategically or are hiding their real religious agenda when speaking to Western audiences? The approach to language and the mind presented in the introduction holds that humans are not dominated by a single overarching identity or language only, but by multiple ones. Those who argue that the Taliban application of secular reason is strategic rely on a Kantian notion of an autonomous individual acting according to its will, which in turn is seen as fully independent from the social dynamics surrounding it. This study challenges the centred and unitary concept of the subject as a single and internally consistent psychic entity, a concept that has been upheld by the exclusionary logic of the Enlightenment discourse. The notions of the unity of the subject and of nature deny the multiplicity inherent in both. Observers who call for a neat definition of religious actors find themselves embedded in this sort of idea, demanding a simple diagnosis of actors as either religious or secular.[2]

On the one hand, it makes sense for analysts to differentiate between the religious and the secular, because, theoretically, doing so can get us intellectually closer to understanding the particular way religion works, and because empirically these labels are widely applied in the real world. Rejecting their existence would be to reject the world views of those who uphold such distinctions. On the other hand, a rigid distinction between religious and secular motives risks falsely attributing to religion a special proclivity to incite violence. As long as actors succeed in framing their cause as greater than the lives of individuals, both religious and secular discourses can provide ideological fuel for violent action. This is important to note in order to avoid giving religion an overly explanatory power.

The three sections ahead delve deeper into three concepts, namely political authority, rationality, and just violence. These are discussed since they make differences and similarities between the secular and religious discourses of the Taliban stand out particularly. Taken together, these sections also feed into the conclusion that it is challenging to provide a simple diagnosis of Taliban violence as driven by evil or archaic religious imagery only.

Political Authority

From the analysis in chapters 2–5, it becomes clear that the Taliban narratives create equivalence between political and religious authority by claims that equate worldly government with divine sovereignty. One premise behind the claims is the belief that ultimate authority—in this world and the world hereafter—belongs to God. Another normative premise is that the 'political' is a main channel through which God's sovereignty should be established. Although any difference between political authority and religious authority is, in principle, eliminated in the dominant Taliban narratives, the main premise of their battle for more religion in politics is, in fact, that 'the political' is contested. This means that their claims are based on the realization that the authority of God in this realm has to be fought for. Thus it seems paradoxical that their move to eliminate the difference between religious and political authority and represent the former as the natural state is conditioned by some degree of acceptance of the political as a space of contestation.

The battle that the religio-political activists of the Pakistani Taliban are part of is thus also normative: it is about defining the true content of political authority, and to that end, extraordinary means are considered appropriate. In the battle for God's authority on earth, the narratives analysed have shown that the Taliban activists create an epistemic authority for themselves that minimizes the difference between them and God:

they portray themselves as God's guardians. And yet, herein lies another discursive paradox as I have already pointed out: that God, who is almighty and sovereign, needs the Taliban's help to establish His authority on earth. These sorts of paradoxes exist precisely because their battle has a normative character: it attempts to affirm a certain relationship between the realm of the sacred and that of the profane, engaging with ideas where another relationship is seen as the natural one. The inconsistencies or paradoxes reflect the difficult task of striking a meaningful balance between a secular discourse, where the political is constructed as independent of religion (and thus open to different authority claims), and a religious discourse establishing God as the natural sovereign. Hence, the inconsistencies or paradoxes are the result of the fact that the Pakistani Taliban reflects both discourses at the same time.

The battle over the definition of political authority is important because it is fundamentally about defining criteria of legitimate action. The Taliban are challenging the natural link between the secular state on the one hand, and security, justice, and order on the other, instead articulating a narrative that they seek to put on the political agenda: it creates a link between the political authority of God on the one side, and security, justice, and order on the other. As a consequence, they are also challenging foundational ideas about political authority and the state that were constituted at the same moment the Westphalian system of sovereign states appeared in the seventeenth century. One of the significant privileges that came with the constitution of the state was the monopoly over the use of legitimate violence, as Max Weber defined it in 1918.[3] Especially in Europe, the memory of the devastating sectarian wars between Christian groups stripped religion of this privilege, and the post-Westphalian order that led primarily to a 'territorialization' of religion (where religion was allowed to flourish domestically but not as a legitimate dogma in relations *between* states) came to be seen as a bulwark against sectarian wars.

Talal Asad's works *Formations of the Secular* (2003) and *Genealogies of Religion* (1993) have pointed to the politics and power practices involved in the construction and application of concepts like religion and secularism. Asad links the constitution of religion regarded as a disembodied, personal experience to the rise of the nation state. The understanding of religion as private and cognitive—as religious *belief*—is tied to the process whereby the state consolidated its power and insulated it from alternative bastions of power. The drawn-out struggles between the church and state were ended, and, more urgently, the civil and international wars of the sixteenth and seventeenth centuries were to be stopped only if faith was removed as a legitimate reason for violence, which in some instances meant creating a political sphere disconnected from questions of religion: internalizing conscience, making it private and spiritual but no longer public and political.[4]

A few scholars who studied the religion–violence link have considered this conceptual context to be relevant in explaining religious revival as a challenge to the post-Westphalian order.[5] The sociologist of religion Mark Juergensmeyer has very precisely described the global resurgence of religion as its reclaiming of some of the authoritative functions now controlled by the state, thus challenging the state's hegemonic position as the provider of what can be regarded as society's fundamental needs: order, justice, and security.[6] Even though such authority is *legally* attributed to the state and the international system of states, religion, as advocated by the Pakistani Taliban, is forcefully claiming the *legitimacy* to act as this kind of authority.

Religion, like the state, provides an assertive system of rules and law. In the narratives of the Pakistani Taliban, religion is a more fundamental authority than the state since the former comes from the creator of the world Himself, while the state is subjected to God's authority. Thus while the Taliban narratives do not establish the state as an illegitimate institution as such (in contrast to other Islamist movements striving for the caliphate, there is indeed an implicit recognition of the state as the proper channel through which political authority is exercised), the hierarchy is obvious: if state law/authority violates religious law, religious law/authority has the upper hand. The continuation of this logic implies that if politicians and the state law enforcement fail to do their job properly, the duty to act becomes incumbent on the religious class of society, which the Taliban consider themselves part of.

Rationality

The Taliban narratives draw upon imagery, dreams, and myths that represent other sources of epistemic authority than Western academia, as I have shown in Chapter 5.[7] This does not mean 'rational academic' categories cannot be applied to understand people who have a religious world as their reference. I point this out in order to rebut the logic which maintains that the differences many would intuitively feel between the two types of rationalities (the academic and the religious) make the attempt to analyse the religious impossible.

Religious rationality is not to be regarded as an oxymoron. On the contrary, its particular characteristics backlight the contingency of the way hegemonic Western discourses have constructed rationality as religion-free knowledge and as a particular mode of thinking. Social scientists, especially, are having difficulties moving beyond the deep-rooted notion that religion is a dying vestige of our primitive, pre-scientific past. Though there is a slow turn towards a new paradigm for the study of religion in the social sciences that takes the insider approach—faith, doctrines, and imagery—more seriously,[8] politically and scientifically, there is still a dominant tendency in the US and Western Europe to understand religious commitment as largely antithetical to the rational calculus.[9]

The way rationality has been constructed in contrast to religion in hegemonic Western discourses is closely related to the story about the constitution of political authority, the state, and politics. As described by Stephen Toulmin, the idea that the nature of politics is rational and that society is run by pure human reason and the autonomous, self-referential logic of politics (raison d'état) was a vision of society originally modelled on a Newtonian view of nature.[10] In the US and Western Europe, this idea was transformed by democratization and brought in its wake an increased emphasis on rational dialogue, stressing the irrational nature of religious convictions and thus their unsuitability for inclusion in politics. This in turn served to define the nature of modern politics, because a view of religion as 'superstitious belief' made politics identical to reason.[11] Ultimately, science became the touchstone of this arrangement—and, therefore, we as academics are not neutral observers of this dynamics but are implied in the order of secularism—because dividing religion and politics demanded that one could separate faith and science, belief and knowledge, revelation and discovery. Only thus—according to this narrative—could the social order be based on the rational decision of humans, independent of religious sanction, and religion could be relegated to private life.[12]

The rationality that can be traced in the Taliban narratives draws on other forms of knowledge than these discourses on scientific knowledge. According to social psychologist Arie Kruglanski, a main component of knowledge is that it provides evidence. However, it need not necessarily be provided in the sense prescribed, for instance, by logical positivists (through verification or falsification) because '*evidence* refers to information *relevant* to a conclusion'. In the case of the Pakistani Taliban, the references to religious myths and dreams, to the Quran, the Hadith, and jurisprudential literature based on the interpretations of revelation and the will of God have the same status: they are used as evidence to justify the directions given for action, and thus qualify as a form of knowledge following the criteria provided by Kruglanski.[13]

At the same time, there is a strong emotional dimension to the rationality that conditions Taliban jihad: a dimension that is cultivated through the use of jihadi anthems and the invocation of images of a cosmic war and religious mythology, elevating and enlarging to a spiritual level the dimensions of the conflict they are part of. This amounts to what Vendulka Kubálková calls abductive reasoning: explaining the circumstances religiously with the idea that they are part of a larger divine plan or apocalyptic battle.[14] So overall, the evidence for the necessity of jihad is found not only in the Taliban activists' religious references and interpretations but also within feelings, which is to say that the emotional dimension of the activists' faith also establishes religious evidence. In the Taliban discourses, feelings and emotions are not part of the irrational but, on the contrary, are central to defining those with real knowledge (knowledge of the Divine). Receiving orders from God through nocturnal dreams is an element that gives the individual epistemic authority in this discourse, because he or she is thereby seen as having been gifted with special insight. The implications of this competing source of knowledge and manner of constituting rationality are that religion can shape a distinct form of rationality and knowledge that is on par with how rational choice utility calculations can, for example, shape political action. More attention to these forms of knowledge, not least the relevance of the emotional and spiritual dimension of faith for power and political action, is warranted in order to understand the dynamics behind religious violence.

Just Violence

The question of political authority is closely related to the definition of legitimate violence, that is, the *causes* that are considered important enough to mobilize extraordinary *measures* and *means* are regarded as just. The 'just war' theories, developed in the crossover between law, international relations, and theology are part of the hegemonic Western discourses that define what is considered to be the legitimate and illegitimate use of violence.

The core proposition of the corpus of just war theories is that sometimes states can have moral justifications for resorting to armed force.[15] Rather than descriptive templates, the just war theories represent discourses in which having a just cause has conventionally been related to questions of territorial sovereignty, thus defending principles of strong sovereign immunity from foreign aggression and intervention. This means that within this body of discourses, it is a central claim that just wars are wars of self-defence waged for the cause of resisting aggression. However, today the types of war that fall under the just war category have expanded to include the deployment of military forces beyond mere self-defence, such as a right to humanitarian intervention, which overrides the conventional immunities of state sovereignty; a preventive right to wage wars against rogue states that might support hostile sub-state groups; and a liberal cosmopolitan right to engage in interstate wars of forced democratic regime change.[16] In the intellectual constitution of just wars and in political practice, the evaluation of the just causes of war (besides looking at its wider purpose) is carried out by examining criteria such as whether going to war is the last resort (necessity), whether the state possesses the right motive (intentionality), whether it has a reasonable chance of success (sufficiency), whether the decision is made and announced by proper authorities (legitimacy), and whether the end is proportional to the means used (efficiency).

From the analysis of the Taliban narratives, it appears that similar criteria are applied in their justifications of violence. In their narratives, arguments of necessity, intentionality, sufficiency, legitimacy, and efficiency are also applied, yet most distinctively the question of intentionality is linked to the higher purpose of religion. In terms of just causes of war, the parallel defensive and offensive discourses resemble the justifications that can also be found in the just war discourse: legitimating wars of self-defence waged for the cause of resisting aggression, and the more offensive wars of regime change waged for the cause of humanitarian rights. However, while the defensive/resistance aspect (for example, the defence against foreign invasion in Afghanistan) is clear in the case of the Pakistani Taliban, the regime change that is fought for is not democratic—as in the just war discourse— but religious, and the main argument is the restoration of order, justice, and security rather than humanitarian rights. The empty signifiers of order, justice, and security are in turn connected to their particular notion of sharia and the punishment system derived from their interpretation of it.

While there are obvious structural similarities in the way violence is argued for, the main difference lies in the way the two discourses—the Taliban and the hegemonic Western just war discourses—are sanctioned according to their own logics. The just war discourse developed in Western academia constitutes itself as a set of universal rules that are often applied as objective and valid for state actors on the international scene. Although Christian religio-ethical roots are part of its genealogy, this heritage is sometimes left out of its self-depiction as an objective and universal set of criteria for just violence.[17]

By contrast, in the Taliban narratives, Islam sanctions the just causes and violence through the concept of jihad. Thus the Taliban references invoke ethical discourses that have been formulated by Muslim jurists since the nineteenth century. In this, the legitimacy of jihad has also been constituted with reference to defensive (waged to resist aggression), preventive (as a means of preventive war against hostile states), and system-transforming (a right to spread Islam and force regime change) purposes.[18] However, in contrast to the just war discourses, the jihad discourses are constituted as valid for Muslims only. This lack of a common frame of reference and source of justification arguably also explains why the counterpart can be depicted as being without legitimate ethical standards. This in turn locks the

conflict into two parties with competing justifications of violence, though there are many similarities in the two normative
traditions on just violence.

There might be many convincing arguments for cultivating a
global ethos; certainly, my errand is not to promote relativism.
Rather, I seek to unfold how the just war theories/discourses also
provide many of the images that underlie the distinction between
state war as justifiable and contemporary religious terrorism—
seen in terms of unjustified violence—as acts without any further
motivation than evildoing and the production of fear.[19] Since
closer scrutiny of the case of the Pakistani Taliban shows that
even acts of suicide bombing can fall under the broad categories
of just war reasoning, for example, as acts of last resort, this constitutes an ethical and intellectual challenge. The challenge that
becomes visible with this is an inconsistency and asymmetry in
the way post-Westphalian concepts of political authority and just
violence make scholars prone to adopting the perspective of the
secular state, thus rarely including the valuable insight the epistemic world view of religious actors would provide. This asymmetry, I believe, is due to the lack of recognition of religion as a
forceful and competing provider of key functions that are typically related solely to the state (order, security, and justice), and
also a lack of attentiveness to the viewpoints of religio-political
activists. In this regard, international relations as a discipline is
fundamentally partial, since its raison d'être is the state system.

While the motivations or causes of violence are important
criteria by which distinctions between legitimate and illegitimate violence are typically made, both in just war discourses
and in the Taliban constitution of jihad, the question of means
(for example, the use of suicide bombings) is equally decisive
for diagnosing the justice of violence. The assumption behind
approaching state-driven wars and security politics as something
completely different from the war and security politics of terrorists is that—as Talal Asad has noted—there is a moral distinction between secular warfare, defined as a state function, and

religious terrorism, defined as disruptive activity forcing chaos upon order.[20]

In his book *On Suicide Bombing* (2007), Asad examines some of the inconsistent arguments produced to distinguish between the moral constraints to which state war is subjected on the one hand, and the 'absolute evil of terrorism', especially suicide terrorism, on the other. Since the evil of terrorism is often described in terms of the 'killing of innocent people, the intrusion of fear into everyday life, the deliberate violation of private purposes, the insecurity of public spaces, and the endless coerciveness of precaution', it must be admitted, argues Asad, that secular state war does the same.[21] This proposition is controversial since it eliminates the difference between what is popularly regarded as terrorism on the one hand and secular state war on the other, when the criteria used for making this distinction are the means and effects of violence. The crux of the matter is that when we measure by the parameters that are embedded in the definitions of terrorism (the killing of innocent people, the intrusion of fear into everyday life, and so on), there remains no self-evident difference.[22]

Within the just war tradition in Western academia, there are heated discussions about the rules of just conduct (*jus in bello*).[23] The discrimination between civil and military targets has been at the centre of *jus in bello* concerns and evolved around issues related to the foreseeable breaches of immunities. One of the questions raised by just war scholars is whether there is a real difference in terms of *effects* between the unintended but predictable indiscriminate killing involved in conventional warfare and deliberate attacks on innocent non-combatants.[24] One can, of course, intuitively claim an ethical difference between predicted civilian losses and intentional attacks on civilians like those committed by some militant Taliban factions. But this evaluation presupposes that we know or have access to the real intentions and motivations of a military commander vis-à-vis a terrorist warrior.

There can be a large gap between normative discourse and practice when it comes to the conduct of the Taliban. In traditional Islamic jurisprudence, there are codified laws on appropriate behaviour in jihad, where, for example, it is made imperative to avoid harming civilians, women, children, trees and buildings, and so on.[25] In many instances, the Taliban apply means that violate these laws, though they are still applied as an ethical frame of reference.

Illuminating the complexity of the issue of discrimination, Virginia Held has argued that it is difficult in principle to discriminate between legitimate and illegitimate targets when the enemy is a democratic polity where citizens elect their leaders and are ultimately responsible for their government's policies.[26] This is not to justify indiscriminate violence, but to add complexity to neat differentiations between the character of secular state violence and 'religious terrorism' on the basis of the principle of discrimination, which is open to flexible interpretations. Similar to the principle of discrimination, the *jus in bello* principle of proportionality (concerning debates about how much force is morally appropriate) is also dependent on fluctuating political discourses. The determination of appropriate means to avert an identified danger depends on how the enemy is perceived or portrayed both publicly and politically. If the enemy is portrayed as the incarnation of evil, it easily legitimizes elimination 'by any means necessary'. It depends on how much suffering and danger the opponent is claimed to have inflicted upon the referent object, as well as the character of the threat.

Adding to this, the question of war ethics has on several occasions haunted the US in media coverage about the treatment of war prisoners, especially during the era of the last Bush presidency. So, quite evidently, there is a problem of a normative gap between just war ideals and war situations on the ground. The paradox of the matter is that the public and academic reflections on just war represent clear standards, even though they are, and can easily be, compromised and bent when the character of the enemy is represented as being morally inferior. The influential American philosopher Michael Walzer has also justified this standard differentiation through his description of 'emergency ethics'. Explaining the term, he argues that unethical behaviour by morally strong leaders can be justified against an unjust enemy as long as there is an accompanying moral realization that both 'the evil we oppose and the evil we do' are essentially wrong.[27] This means that in facing serious threats, even extraordinary war acts and the suspension of normal ethical standards can be justified, including acts such as mass surveillance, torture, pre-emptive strikes, and targeted assassinations. The targeted killing of Osama bin Laden by American Special Forces in Pakistan in May 2011 illustrates this point. It illuminates that the claims of defence can be a stronger explanation than the ethical claims of just war, both for Western countries as well as movements like the Taliban. However, tensions within them are resolved by developing concepts like emergency ethics or, in the Taliban case, emergency jihad. In both cases, the terms highlight attempts to prioritize some ethical needs ahead of others, rather than ruling them out completely.

Even though investigating the motives of warriors is a methodological grey area, it nevertheless remains central to arguments about the distinction between the conduct of state armies and that of non-state activists fighting a state. But terrorist acts can also be categorized as security politics and acts of self-defence on par with 'our own', if analysed on a discursive/performative level. Doing so opens up far more complicated questions, such as why just causes behind state war are sometimes important enough in themselves that we need not take too seriously matters of just conduct on 'our' side. If states can invoke emergency ethics in situations of war, why can't religio-political activists be expected to do the same?

The uncomfortable answer to such questions points to the necessity of shifting the centre of gravity of ethical concern towards the evaluation of conduct. This not only means looking more substantially at how ideas such as discrimination, sufficiency, and efficiency are conceptually filled out and practised, but also scrutinizing claims of defensive action, applying the analysis equally to institutionalized and non-institutionalized acts of violence.

The reasons for this are twofold. First, motivation analysis does not take us very far, because in the end our judgements about motivations will always be based on whose security narratives we believe in and who we grant the authority to have legitimate security–political concerns in the first place. From the analysis of the Taliban narratives, it appears that their violence can be challenged when it is inconsistent with respect to the normative jihad discourses they recognize as authoritative. The Taliban narratives emphasize justifying *the state of exception* rather than stressing the *religious rules of war.* The second reason is that as long as there is no symmetry in our views on the qualities and attributes of state and religion (not least the recognition that religion is a strong provider of ethical justification for violence), there will be no consistency in our judgements either. This does not mean that particular interpretations of religion (like those of the Taliban) should necessarily be considered as valid as the international system and laws, but it does mean including the viewpoints of those who have other frames of reference. With the rise of religious activists declaring war on states, there is a danger that observers of religious violence will miss the boat if they do not take seriously the competing force of religious authority vis-à-vis state authority regarding claims to the monopoly over the legitimate use of force.

⌀

Notes and References

1. Mona K. Sheikh and Ole Wæver, 'Western Secularisms: Variation in a Doctrine and its Practice', in Arlene B. Tickner and David L. Blaney (eds), *Thinking International Relations Differently* (London: Routledge, 2012).

2. The existence of a natural boundary between the religious and the secular has been intensely challenged in scholarly debates across academic disciplines during the past decades. See, for example, Sheikh and Wæver, 'Western Secularisms'. The works of Talal Asad have been highly influential in focusing scholarly attention on the concepts of religion and secularism from historical, philosophical, political, sociological, and anthropological perspectives. See, for example, Talal Asad, 'Reflections on Blasphemy and Secular Criticism', in Hent de Vries (ed.), *Religion: Beyond a Concept* (New York: Fordham University Press, 2008); *Formations of the Secular: Christianity, Islam, Modernity* (Stanford: Stanford University Press, 2003); and *Genealogies of Religion: Discipline and Reasons of Power in Christianity and Islam* (Baltimore: Johns Hopkins University Press, 1993). For a recent volume addressing the challenges of boundary-making, see Craig Calhoun, Mark Juergensmeyer, and Jonathan VanAntwerpen (eds), *Rethinking Secularism* (Oxford: Oxford University Press, 2011).

3. In fact, the sociological approach of Weber (1918) was clear in his definition of the state as *a human community that successfully claims the monopoly of the legitimate use of physical force within a given territory*. See Hans H. Gerth and C. Wright Mills, *From Max Weber: Essays in Sociology* (New York: Oxford University Press, 1946).

4. Sheikh and Wæver, 'Western Secularisms'.

5. For example, Daniel Philpott, 2002, 'The Challenge of September 11 to Secularism in International Relations', *World Politics*, 55(1): 66–95; Elizabeth Hurd, *The Politics of Secularism in International Relations* (Princeton: Princeton University Press, 2007); Jeffrey Haynes, *An Introduction to International Relations and Religion* (Harlow: Pearson Education, 2007).

6. Mark Juergensmeyer, *Global Rebellion: Religious Challenges to the Secular State, from Christian Militias to Al Qaeda* (Berkeley: University of California Press, 2008).

7. Mona K. Sheikh, 2012, 'Sacred Pillars of Violence: Findings from a Study of the Pakistani Taliban', *Politics, Religion & Ideology*, 13(4): 439–54.

8. Mark Juergensmeyer and Mona Kanwal Sheikh. 'A Sociotheological Approach to Understanding Religious Violence', in Michael Jerryson, Mark Juergensmeyer, and Margo Kitts (eds), *The Oxford*

Handbook of Religion and Violence (Oxford: Oxford University Press, 2013).

9. Sheikh and Wæver, 'Western Secularisms'.

10. Stephen E. Toulmin, *Cosmopolis: The Hidden Agenda of Modernity* (New York: Free Press, 1990).

11. Charles Taylor, *Modern Social Imaginaries* (Durham: Duke University Press, 2004); William Connolly, *Why I Am Not a Secularist* (Minneapolis: University of Minnesota Press, 1999); Sheikh and Wæver, 'Western Secularisms'.

12. Sheikh and Wæver, 'Western Secularisms'.

13. Arie W. Kruglanski, *Lay Epistemics and Human Knowledge: Cognitive and Motivational Bases* (New York: Plenum, 1989).

14. Vendulka Kubálková, 2000, 'Towards an International Political Theology', *Millennium: Journal of International Studies*, 29(3): 675–704.

15. In the just war (*justum bellum*) tradition, theorists distinguish between the rules that govern the justice of war (*jus ad bellum*) and those that govern just and fair conduct in war (*jus in bello*). In other words, the tradition covers discussions concerning ethical grounds for going into war on the one hand, and ethical conduct in the course of battle on the other. Furthermore, the just war tradition also engages with rules of post-conflict settlements.

16. Nicholas Rengger, 2002, 'On the Just War Tradition in the Twenty-first Century', *International Affairs*, 78(2): 353–63; Mark Rigstad, 2007, 'Jus Ad Bellum after 9/11: A State of the Art Report', *The IPT Beacon*, 6(3): 1–30, available at http://international-political-theory.net/3/rigstad.pdf (accessed on 1 June 2011).

17. Rengger, 'On the Just War Tradition in the Twenty-first Century', p. 362.

18. While the first cause is commonly agreed upon, the second cause is often seen as the jihad of the early Muslims in the seventh century. The third cause is the most disputed among Muslims, just as there is great debate about the interventionist policies of forced democratic regime change. Historically, one of the strongest justifications for engaging in militancy has been attributed to the resistance against colonial rule in the part of Islamic scholarship dealing with just causes and just conducts in jihad. Originally, the concept of militant jihad was linked to political authority, and legitimate

jihad was to be declared by the ruler of the country. Since the Taliban do not have political authority, their jihad is constituted as an 'emergency' jihad in which the condition that jihad should be announced by proper political authorities is annulled. For example, David Cook, *Understanding Jihad* (Berkeley: University of California Press, 2005); John Kelsay, *Arguing the Just War in Islam* (Harvard: Harvard University Press, 2007).

19. Talal Asad, *On Suicide Bombing* (New York: Columbia University Press, 2007).
20. Asad, *On Suicide Bombing.*
21. Asad, *On Suicide Bombing*, p. 16.
22. Asad, *On Suicide Bombing.*
23. *Jus in bello* falls under the two broad principles of discrimination and proportionality. The principle of discrimination concerns debates about who are legitimate targets in war and who is to be viewed as a combatant in war (and thus also who is guilty/innocent, responsible/non-responsible). The principle of proportionality concerns debates about how much force is morally appropriate.
24. The radical position taken in this debate is that there is no moral distinction in targeting an armed combatant or a civilian involved in arming or feeding the combatant. This debate also covers the question of collective versus individual responsibility. See, for instance, David Rodin, 2004, 'Terrorism without Intention', *Ethics*, 114(4): 752–71 and Ted Honderich, *After the Terror* (Edinburgh: Edinburgh University Press, 2002).
25. Kelsay, *Arguing the Just War in Islam.*
26. Virginia Held, 2004, 'Terrorism and War', *The Journal of Ethics*, 8(1): 59–75.
27. Cited in Asad, *On Suicide Bombing*, p. 18.

Conclusion:
A Rational Enemy?

The greatest menace to our civilization today is the conflict between giant organized systems of self-righteousness—each system only too delighted to find that the other is wicked—each only too glad that the sins give it the pretext for still deeper hatred and animosity.

—Herbert Butterfield[1]

Enemies are often those whose stories we have not yet heard. Understanding the Taliban grievances and justifications for violence is the first step towards finding ways to deal with the phenomenon. My analysis has shown that the Taliban acts of violence are just as much about the fear of the elimination of Islam as about a missionary zeal to spread the true faith. This notion challenges common understandings of Islamism as an aggressive and expansive movement interpreted as analogous to the Christian crusades. For policymakers in the West, such an analysis can offer a self-critical examination of how the other party feels threatened, and how Western policies contribute to sustaining the Taliban's fears.

The foregoing is not to argue that the Pakistani Taliban act only in a defensive, crisis-response mode, but rather to cast light on this crucial aspect of their motivation. It is essential to study what makes militant activists successful in mobilizing adherents and what claims are powerful enough to move individuals to extraordinary action such as suicide attacks. To arrive at such an understanding, we must expand the conventional view of security politics as the province only of the state and views of militant Islamism as driven solely by faith and doctrines. These approaches pay too little attention to the powerful security and political dynamics shaping violence.

In Taliban rhetoric, acts of violence are explained by the defence of the sacred. Yet the Taliban concept of the sacred also encompasses worldly concerns such as social justice, peace, and political order—elements that Western discourses generally assign to the sphere of secular politics—which, in their view, can be advanced by the implementation of sharia.

Such nuances call for more sensitivity towards the implications of our opponents' concepts, world views, and narratives. Although the point seems banal at first glance, in war the motivation of the enemy is often represented as being illogical and irrational, reduced to a dark wish for destruction and chaos. The Taliban activists have a rationale for their actions that we might find odd, but that does not make it irrelevant. To assume that they are devoid of rationality and reason is itself an irrational view.

There are certainly fundamental and perhaps irreconcilable differences between the Taliban vision of political authority and that which is dominant in the West—not least in the concepts of justice and punishment. However, to understand the fateful logic that leads us from normative disagreement to war, we must examine the processes that lead to hardened normative doctrines and remove them from the sphere of security politics, where negotiation or conversation is no longer an option. Such analytical interventions illuminate the differences between the conflicting sides and enable us to reach a better understanding of what the conflict is about from the other side's point of view. Talking to the Taliban has strengthened my belief that rigorous efforts to understand the logic, rationality, and world view of our opponents are fundamental to effective conflict containment.

This also means that academia has a role to play and is not detached from world politics.

Understanding difference by focusing on common dynamics that we as humans react to—in this case, the mechanism of security and the perception of being under attack—holds the potential for moving away from the sort of radical othering that leads to the justification of violence, including emergency interpretations of jihad in conflict. It is also true that justifications of violence vary in different cultures and societies. Political and religious definitions of legitimate and illegitimate violence are based on forms of moral reasoning that can be particular to given cultures. However, in situations of conflict, we need to be aware that the criteria and moral reasoning used by one side to justify its violence do not necessarily apply to the violence committed by its adversaries. Acknowledging this can enable each side to move away from dismissing the other's stories as unworthy of attention or portraying their adversaries as irrational actors with no just intention or purpose.

Since the defence claims of the Pakistani Taliban are arguably part of macro-level conflict discourses between 'Islam' and 'the West', resolution also demands changes in broader conceptual structures.[2] In a globalized world, the West and Islam are not purely geographical, cultural, or religious labels. Due to the low level of global consensus, they are, in a sense, empty categories and thus liable to being hijacked by extremist groups. In conflict, they function as opposing value spaces and meta-references containing different doctrines of governance and public order, based on diverse concepts about the relationship of religion, politics, and law. Relaxing tensions will require focusing on the mechanisms of these labelling processes. I hope my book will contribute to this awareness.

The findings of this project also call upon us to examine and understand the dynamic structure of the conflict that the Pakistani Taliban is part of. The conflict is driven not just by one party's aggressive behaviour but by (at least) two parties responding to each other. The implication of this insight is that if we want to effect change in their patterns of behaviour, we should change our own pattern of behaviour. This point is valid for Western observers and policymakers, for the Pakistani government and military, and also for the Taliban activists with whom I talked and who hoped to convince the world that their actions are just and rational.

A security dilemma in the context of international relations typically refers to a situation wherein states are drawn into conflict over security concerns, even though none of the states actually desire conflict.[3] It occurs when states fear for their security in relation to other states. As each state acts to make itself more secure, the other state interprets its actions as threatening. A cycle of unintended provocations ends up escalating the conflict. The British historian Herbert Butterfield described such self-reinforcing conflicts with reference to the classical Greek tragedies, in which the conflict is driven not by either of the contending parties in the story but by the situation itself. Neither party recognizes the dynamics of the conflict or their own role in keeping it alive. Instead both parties frame their own actions as rational reactions to the threats from the other, seeing 'only the sins of the enemy' and failing 'to reflect on those predicaments and dilemmas which so often develop and which underlie the great conflicts between masses of human beings'.[4]

Regardless of the differences in political opinion about how the conflict with the Taliban ought to be contained or solved (for example, whether to pursue compromise initiatives such as negotiations or peace deals), the prerequisite for any effective political strategy is to understand the character and dynamics of the conflict. According to Western discourses, the conflict with the Taliban began with 9/11, but according to the Pakistani Taliban and their sympathizers, it has been caused by a long history of Western antagonism towards the religious–political autonomy of Muslims. A call for a better understanding of the motivations of Taliban violence does not imply that such violence should be accepted by the international community.

Rather, immersing into the world view of the Taliban adherents and a more self-critical stance in relation to the policies of the West and how these feed into the dynamics of the conflict can help us design better strategies to deal with the challenging overlap between religious movements, millennialism, and acts of terrorism. There is little to lose from such an undertaking. The history of the Taliban movement in Pakistan shows that the militaristic strategy to encounter the movement has only led to the multiplication of Taliban movements in the area.

When conflicts are cast in transhistorical terms and presented as detached from material issues, diplomatic efforts of reconciliation appear more complicated. The present age, tormented by violence associated with both religious and secular doctrines and non-state security dilemmas, calls for new approaches to diplomacy and conflict resolution. These dilemmas are upheld simultaneously by fear and by the assertion of hardened doctrines.[5]

Transforming the Taliban

The future direction of the Pakistani Taliban remains an open question. It appears to me that the movement has come to stay, even if its particular interpretation of sharia and religion is unlikely to gain a foothold all over Pakistan. When I spoke to Taliban representatives in 2008–9, they clearly stated that once the US withdrew from Afghanistan, their battle would be over and they would 'go to sleep peacefully', as one of the TTP spokesmen put it. Today despite the withdrawal of combat troops from Afghanistan, the Pakistani Taliban shows no signs of going to sleep. But whether it will ever become part of the mainstream political conversation in Pakistan will depend on how the movement is able to define itself in the future and on the policies implemented to deal with it.

Given the escalation of violence during the past decade, it might seem utopian or simply bizarre to imagine the Pakistani Taliban movement as part of the political conversation in

Pakistan. Nevertheless, there are signs pointing to that possibility. First, although the Taliban movements oppose the concept of democracy, that was never their primary objective. The main justification for targeting the Pakistani government and its security forces was the government's cooperation with the US in the invasion of Afghanistan. Taliban violence in Pakistan began when Afghanistan was invaded and the Pakistani army began their military operations in FATA.

Second, the Pakistani Taliban has shown itself to be flexible and pragmatic, willing to change its alliances and modes of operation in order to achieve its aims. Although it originated in the tribal areas as a movement purporting to represent Pashtun interests, it has expanded its activities to overlap with those of interest groups in other parts of the country. For example, the Pakistani Taliban contains elements of the SSP as I have described, and the SSP has been part of Pakistan's political system since decades. The TTP's supporters also include supporters of Fazlur Rehman from the JUI, one of the largest Islamist parliamentary parties that have embraced democracy. Some of the TTP supporters were also supporters of the MMA coalition that participated in democratic elections. These alliances suggest the possibility that adherents of the Pakistani Taliban may be willing to engage in more mainstream forms of political activity, directly or indirectly.

There are precedents for such a change: other Islamist movements have changed their ideological stances in order to engage with the political process. Even though the Taliban regime in Afghanistan was not democratic, it did invite members of other parties to join the administration in Kabul, and in a short time, it went from being a revolutionary movement to a political movement in charge of a country. The Al-Nour party and the Muslim Brotherhood in Egypt, the Islamic Salvation Front in Algeria, and Hezbollah in Lebanon offer evidence that movements can transform themselves from violent to non-violent, from militant to democratic (or vice versa). More research on the factors that catalyze such change is clearly warranted. Although it is difficult to envision the highly fragmented Pakistani Taliban turning into a unified political party in the near future, it is certainly conceivable that elements of the movement will support political candidates working through mainstream channels to promote sharia in Pakistan.

There are reasons to regard such potential developments as positive. Without change, the TTP could be expected to continue its violent battle to implement a particular interpretation of sharia in areas of Pakistan where it might obtain significant popular support. These efforts will continue unless the movement is transformed, and helped with its transformation process, in the years to come.

Talking to Terrorists

One step towards transforming the Pakistani Taliban movement was taken when the government of Pakistan, led by Nawaz Sharif, appointed a negotiation team to talk with the TTP in early 2014. The TTP appointed clerics from both the JI and the JUI, along with the imam of the Red Mosque, to represent them in the negotiations. It was the first time the TTP had entered into talks with the central government, even through intermediaries.

The talks were suspended shortly after they began because of a Taliban attack on the Frontier Corps in northwest Pakistan and retaliatory surgical strikes by the army into the troubled area of North Waziristan. Then the launch of a large-scale ground offensive in North Waziristan in June 2014 revived the widespread scepticism about the success of any negotiations. The indirect representation of both the government and the Taliban in the negotiation teams, the failure of a handful of previous peace deals with the militants, and the continued violence have all been invoked as evidence of the futility of pursuing peace talks. Recent attempts to approach the Taliban have been condemned by some as showing weakness and giving into terrorist demands. Yet despite these failures and the likelihood of more failures

in the future, there are good reasons for the Pakistani government to keep engaging in peace talks. In particular, the Pakistani
government's push for negotiations with the TTP was helpful in
delegitimizing the 'last-resort' argument often used by Taliban
spokesmen to justify violence: that violence is their only option
because nobody will listen to their grievances.

The leadership of the TTP has often represented the most
hardened attitude within the movement. However, fragmentation
within the movement may create opportunities for negotiation.
Some Taliban-affiliated groups will always oppose peace deals;
identifying and negotiating with the more peaceably disposed
factions will increase the chances of success. The TTP has been
divided since its former leader Hakimullah Mehsud was killed in
a drone attack. The subsequent leader Fazlullah was mistrusted
because he did not come from the tribal areas. The question
of whether to negotiate with the government already divides
the movement; another divisive issue is whether it is religiously
legitimate to target the Pakistani army and declare its troops
infidel or apostate Muslims.

The case of Ireland demonstrates that differentiating between
factions and groups can prove helpful in the advancement of
peace negotiations and in reducing terrorist activities in the
long run. Before a peace treaty was negotiated with the Irish
Republican Army (IRA), the British prime minister consistently
referred to the entire IRA as a 'murder gang'. A subsequent
policy of differentiation enabled a strategy of separating the
intransigent spoilers from those who were ready to negotiate a
peace deal.[6] Counter-insurgency strategists stand to gain from
even partial peace deals that isolate more extreme factions,
because they reduce the size of the battleground.[7]

A serious impediment to peace negotiations is to frame
them as a form of surrender. The very point of negotiating a
peace deal is to enter into a give-and-take situation, and with
a wise strategy, it is possible for negotiators to take more than
they give and even to transform hardened attitudes into more

tractable positions. Pushing for peace talks does not necessarily reflect a naive approach to the Taliban movement, their edgy demands, or their potentially shady strategies. It can also entail taking advantage of momentum to transform the conflict dynamics. The indirect representation of the Taliban through religious figures active in the parliamentary system may be an advantage in this regard, since these clerics are in a unique position to convince the Taliban to fight their ideological battles and channel their aspirations for sharia through the institutions of democratic politics.

The most frequently proposed alternative to pursuing talks is a large-scale military operation to eliminate the leadership of the Pakistani Taliban movement. Yet the notion that continued military operations in Waziristan will flush out the Taliban seems like a mission impossible and disregards some of the main reasons why the Pakistani Taliban gained ground in the first place. Army aggression would probably make things worse, as happened after the military intrusion into the tribal areas in 2002–4 and the 2007 siege of the Red Mosque in Islamabad. These incidents gave rise to so many new Taliban-affiliated movements that observers today have a hard time keeping count.[8]

At the same time, the ongoing violence is not a complete barrier to successful peace talks. Examples from other countries show that peace negotiations with insurgent groups often take place simultaneously with ongoing violence, and that it is rare that the beginning of peace talks brings an immediate ceasefire.[9] Nepal's bloody, decade-long civil war which claimed 14,000 lives ended in 2006 with the signing of a peace deal between the government of Nepal and Maoist guerrillas. The guerrillas did not disarm immediately, but a new Maoist party arose to contest elections, leading to a gradual shift in the dynamics of the situation. The same is true for the peace deal between the Moro Islamic Liberation Front and the Philippine government that was signed in January 2014. The final peace deal was many years in the making: it came after many failures and decades of war that cost more than 100,000 lives. Nobody is saying that the road to a stable peace deal will be clear of rocks.

The fragmented nature of the Taliban movement in Pakistan, its many factions, and complex hierarchy may provide strategic advantages for peace negotiations, but the challenge is to choose a conversation partner who would actually be able to convince most insurgents to abide by any peace agreement. However, the talks in the beginning of 2014 represented the first-ever approach to the TTP as such and were, therefore, an important milestone in the history of negotiation attempts. Earlier peace talks with the Taliban took place either before the TTP was established as an umbrella movement or with isolated local commanders, and with provincial government representatives or army representatives as conversation partners.[10]

Not all previous attempts to negotiate with the Pakistani Taliban have failed, though most have been short-lived. Some informal peace agreements have been more successful than the formal ones. One of these has been with the North Waziristan-based commander Hafiz Gul Bahadur, who is mainly focused on the battle in Afghanistan. Bahadur's faction has basically agreed that in exchange for their not attacking Pakistani interests, Islamabad will not target them. The Pakistani army has also reportedly made peace deals with factions in the Bajaur and Khyber agencies. Sometimes peace efforts are more successful if they are kept out of the media limelight, because they avoid drawing attention from spoilers.

In the debate on whether to pursue talks with the Taliban, there is a tendency to forget that their militant activities are not primarily directed towards implementing their harsh version of sharia in Pakistan, as observers often mistakenly assume. In the first instance, the Taliban loyalists on Pakistani territory, led by Nek Mohammad, reacted against the invasion of Afghanistan, and in the second instance, they reacted against the Pakistani army's military operations in the tribal areas. Some of those who support the Taliban and offer to fight among their ranks admire clerics such as Sami ul Haq or Fazlur Rehman from the JUI, who support democracy along with a religiously guided rule of law. So while religion does play a role in the rhetoric that justifies Taliban violence, it is not necessarily the case that their ideological intransigence will preclude any peace deal or their support to particular parliamentarians in the long run.

It is critical to understand in a better way the grievances and mindset of the Pakistani Taliban in order to find a solution to tackle the spread of Taliban movements, their narratives, and violence across Pakistan. This, I believe, goes for the Pakistani Taliban as well as other terrorist movements that are currently on the rise across the world. At the same time, a self-critical evaluation of the policies embraced by the US and parts of Europe is important, if we sincerely want to break with the dynamics that uphold the threat of terrorist acts not only in countries like Pakistan and Afghanistan but also in the West.

⌒⌁⌒

Notes and References

1. Herbert Butterfield, *The Whig Interpretation of History* (London: G. Bell, 1931).
2. On macro-level conflict structures, see Barry Buzan and Ole Wæver, 2009, 'Macrosecuritization and Security Constellations: Reconsidering Scale in Securitization Theory', *Review of International Studies*, 35(2): 253–76.
3. John H. Herz, 1950, 'Idealist Internationalism and the Security Dilemma', *World Politics*, 2(2): 157–80.
4. Herbert Butterfield, 1950, 'The Tragic Element in Modern International Conflict', *The Review of Politics*, 12(2): 147–64.
5. See Mona K. Sheikh, 2014, 'Doctrinal War', *e-International Relations*, available at http://www.e-ir.info/2014/01/15/doctrinal-war (accessed on 1 October 2015).

6. Audrey Kurth Cronin, *How Terrorism Ends: Understanding the Decline and Demise of Terrorist Campaigns* (Princeton: Princeton University Press, 2009).

7. See Mona K. Sheikh, 'Disaggregating the Pakistani Taliban: Does the Good, the Bad and the Ugly Taliban Distinction Represent a Failed Policy?', Policy Brief (Copenhagen: Danish Institute for International Studies, 2009), available at http://en.diis.dk/files/publications/Briefs2009/Disaggregating_Pakistani_Taliban.pdf (accessed on 1 October 2015).

8. The estimate here is based on my interview in 2012 of Ashraf Ali, the director of the FATA Research Centre that closely monitors the development of the Taliban movements in Pakistan.

9. Cronin, *How Terrorism Ends*.

10. Some of the known peace deals with factions of the Taliban include the Shakai Agreement, April 2004 (Nek Mohammad, South Waziristan); truce with the Ahmedzai Waziris, October 2004; Sra Rogah peace deal, February 2005 (Baitullah Mehsud, South Waziristan); Miranshah agreement, September 2006 (Hafiz Gul Bahadur and Maulvi Sadiq Noor, North Waziristan); peace deal with Sufi Muhammad, April 2007 (TNSM, Swat); the Swat peace agreement I, May 2007 (Mullah Fazlullah, Swat); the Swat peace agreement II, May 2008 (Mullah Fazlullah, Swat); and peace deal with Sufi Muhammad, February 2009 (TNSM, Swat). See Shabana Fayyaz, 'Towards Durable Peace in Waziristan', Pakistan Security Research Unit, Brief no. 10, Peace Studies (West Yorkshire: University of Bradford, 2007); Mona K. Sheikh, 'Where Are We Now? Reintegration, Reconciliation and Negotiation with the Taliban', in Mona K. Sheikh and Maja Greenwood (eds), *Taliban Talks: Past, Present and Prospects for the US, Afghanistan and Pakistan* (Copenhagen: Danish Institute for International Studies, 2013), pp. 7–22, available at http://diis.inforce.dk/graphics/Publications/Reports2013/RP2013-06-Taliban-Talks_web.jpg.pdf (accessed on 10 August 2015).

ﷺ

Glossary

ahkam al-jihad	Jurisprudential rulings
ahl al-bayt	Followers of the house, that is, the family of the Prophet Muhammad
al-jihad al-akbar	Greater jihad
al-jihad al-asghar	Lesser jihad
Amir ul Momineen	Commander/leader of the faithful
arkan	Members
bakra	Headwear resembling a turban
bidaat	Innovation
dar al-harb	House of war
dar al-Islam	House of peace
dawa	Proselytizing jihad
deen	Faith
fard	Religious obligation
fard al-ayn	Individual duty
fard al-kifaya	Collective duty
fatwa	Jurisprudential ruling/opinion
fidayeen	Those willing to sacrifice themselves for a religious cause
fiqh	Islamic jurisprudence
fuqaha	Jurists
Hadith	Narrations about the deeds and sayings of Prophet Muhammad
hajj	Pilgrimage

hamdard	Sympathizers
haram	Unlawful according to Islamic jurisprudence
ibadaat	Domain of worship
imam	Muslim prayer leader
imam al-adil	Just imam
iman	Faith
jirga	Council of elders
kafir (pl. kuffar)	Unbeliever, infidel
kalma	Declaration of faith
kufr	Act of unbelief
madhab	Schools of jurisprudence
madrassa	Religious seminary
mujahedeen	Those who conduct jihad
munafiq	Hypocrite
murtad	Apostate Muslim
mushrik (pl. mushrikeen)	Idolater
mutaffiq	Affiliates
namaz	Practice of ritualistic prayer in Islam
napak	Impure
nifaz	Enforcement
niyat	Intention
pashtunwali	Ethical code of the Pashtun population
pir	Holy personage
qanun	Law
qital	Fighting
rahe nijat	Path to salvation
roza	Fasting
ruya	Night dreams
sahaba karam	Early honourable followers of the Prophet Muhammad
shabnama (pl. shabnamen)	Night letter
shahadat	Declaration of faith
shaheed	Martyr/martyred
shirk	Idolatry
shura	Consultative council

sirat	Biographical literature (about the Prophet Muhammad)
siyasat	Politics
sulta	Sovereignty
sunnah	Tradition of Prophet Muhammad
tagruth	Idolatory
taqlid	Adherence to prior legal rulings
tassawuf	God-consciousness
tawhid	Doctrine of the oneness and unity of God
ulama	Religious scholars; clerics
ummah	Transnational Muslim community

Taliban Communication Materials

Recorded materials intended for distribution and texts of printed matter are part of the Taliban Communications Archive at the library of the Danish Institute for International Studies (http://www.diis.dk/en/diis/kommunikation/library). Interview transcripts are not available publicly.

Cited Interviews

Asia, anonymous Jamia Hafsa student, Islamabad, 14 June 2008.

Hamna Abdullah, the daughter of Umm Hasaan and Abdul Aziz Ghazi, student of Jamia Hafsa, Islamabad, 14 June 2008.

Mubeen, anonymous Jamia Hafsa student, Islamabad, 14 June 2008.

Umm Hasaan, the principal of Jamia Hafsa and wife of Abdul Aziz Ghazi, the imam of the Red Mosque, Islamabad, 14 June 2008.

Khalifa Abdul Qayum, the vice president of the SSP, Dera Ismail Khan, 16 June 2008.

Matiul Haq, TTP, Malakand, 16 June 2008.

Muslim Khan, the leader and spokesman of the TTP, Swat, 16 June 2008.

Sami ul Haq, the principal of Darul Uloom Haqqania, leader of JUI (S), Akora Khattak, 16 June 2008.

Muhammad Yahya Mujahid, spokesman JuD/LeT, Muzaffarabad, 21 June 2008.

Taliban Speeches and Videos

'Bloodshed and Revenge', video released by the TTP headquarters, Umar Studio, July 2009, retrieved from http://www.2shared. com/file/7370960/8370331e/TTPENGDVD.html (accessed on 11 January 2011). Translation released by the producers, available at www.alqimmah.net/showthread.php?t=9318 (accessed on 11 January 2011).

'Fazlullah Speech to Suicide Bombers', video issued by the Swati Taliban, Fateh Studio, collected from the KPP, winter 2010–11.

'Ittehade Mujahideen Khurasan', video issued by the TTP-affiliated movement Ittehade Mujahideen Khurasan, Studio Intiqam, collected from the KPP, winter 2010–11.

'Jamia Hafsa-Sisters Biyaan', video recording of a speech by Hamna Abdullah and prayer by Umm Hasaan, retrieved from www.youtube.com/watch?v=tc5Tg8eVIcU (accessed on 11 January 2011). Translation by the Middle East Media Research Institute (MEMRI), available at www.memritv.org/report/en/print2282.htm#_edn1 (accessed on 11 January 2011).

'Maulana Fazlullah New Video 1', video recording of a speech by Mullah Fazlullah (Swati Taliban), retrieved from YouTube/Zamaswat. com, http://www.youtube.com/watch?v=bC-CDUKJCiU (accessed on 11 January 2011).

'Maulana Fazlullah New Video 2', video recording of a speech by Mullah Fazlullah (Swati Taliban), retrieved from YouTube/Zamaswat.com, http://www.youtube.com/watch?v=zaRLaEGrxh4 (accessed on 11 January 2011).

'Maulana Fazlullah New Video 3', video recording of a speech by Mullah Fazlullah (Swati Taliban), retrieved from YouTube/Zamaswat.com, http://www.youtube.com/watch?v=IxSeugcSsXI (accessed on 11 January 2011).

'Maulana Fazlullah New Video 4', video recording of a speech by Mullah Fazlullah (Swati Taliban), retrieved from YouTube/Zamaswat. com, www.youtube.com/watch?v=vwpYawdgNtE (accessed on 11 January 2011).

'Message from Hakimullah Mehsud and Wali al-Rahman Mehsud', video issued by TTP headquarters, Al-Sahab Media Production,

released October 2009, retrieved from www.archive.org/details/
AMEF_Message-Hakimullah-Wali-ur-Rahman-Mehsud_English
(accessed on 11 January 2011). Translation available from Ansar
al-Mujahideen, available at at http://ansar1.info/ (accessed on 11
January 2011).

'Operation Rah-e-Nijat and the Actual Facts', video recording of a
speech by TTP chief Hakimullah Mehsud, retrieved from YouTube,
Part 1: www.youtube.com/watch?v=P6holdOJTdY; Part 2: www.
youtube.com/watch?v=_aU-_d4wOug&feature=related; Part 3:
www.youtube.com/watch?v=MR4nvRuC3ls&feature=related (all
accessed on 11 January 2011).

'Tehrike Taliban Dara Adam Khel', video issued by TTP Darra Adam
Khel, Ummat Studio, distributed by al-Moqatel, released 6 January
2011, collected from the KPP, winter 2010–11.

'TTP video', video released by TTP headquarters, Umar Studio, collected from the KPP, winter 2010–11.

Night Letters, Leaflets, and Other Communications

Abdullah Mehsud, 'Is There Also Another Side of the Picture?'
[بے کیا تصویر کا دوسرا رخ بھی موجود], North Waziristan (n.d.).

Abdul Rashid Ghazi, 'Will of Abdul Rashid Ghazi' [عبدالرشید غازی
وصیت نامہ مولانہ], written before his death in the Red Mosque and
published online on 8 July 2007. Copy received through the administration of the Red Mosque.

'Announcement' [اعلان], issued by Tehrike Taliban Tank Faction (press
release dated 9 June 2009).

Azam Tariq, 'Biography of Baitullah Mehsud', *Hitteen*, 2009.
Translation titled 'The Life of Baitullah Masood', available
at https://ent.siteintelgroup.com/Jihadist-News/10-29-10-gimf-
baitullah-mehsud-bio.html (accessed on 1 March 2011).

Azam Tariq, 'Statement by TTP's Central Spokesman from South
Waziristan' [کے مرکزی ترجمان کا جنوبی وزیرستان سے جاری بیان تحریک طالبان
پاکستان], issued by the TTP, South Waziristan (n.d.).

'General Announcement' [اطلاع عام], issued by the Pakistani army to
the inhabitants of North Waziristan, dropped from helicopters in
Miranshah (1 July 2009).

'Important Announcement I' [ضروری اعلان], issued by the leader of the Mujahideen Shura, North Waziristan (distributed in Miranshah Bazaar on 16 January 2011).

'Important Announcement II' [ضروری اعلان], issued by the leader of the North Waziristan Shura (Hafiz Gul Bahadur) (distributed on 31 January 2011).

'Important Announcement from the Shura of Waziristan' [باشندگان اوزیرستان کے لئے ضروری اعلان شوره وزیرستان کی طرف سے تمام], issued by the leader and Mujahideen Shura of North Waziristan (distributed on 24 October 2010).

'Kidnapping' (original heading illegible), issued by the leader of the Mujahideen Shura, North Waziristan Agency (2009).

'Lashkare Jhangvi (International)' [الشکر جهنگوی العالمی], issued by the organization of Lashkare Jhangvi (dated 12 December 2010).

'Manifesto' [اعلامیه], issued by Zafar Khan, Shura Ittihade Mujahideen, Wana, South Waziristan (n.d.).

'Message from Fidayeene Islam', issued by Fidayeene Islam Tehrike Taliban Pakistan (distributed in Miranshah on 23 May 2011).

'Message from Hakimullah Mehsud' [حکیم الله محسود], issued by the Mehsud Faction, South Waziristan (n.d.).

'Message from TTP Kurram Agency', issued by Fazal Sayed Haqqani, leader of the Tehrike Taliban, Kurram Agency (distributed in Kurram Agency on 10 May 2011).

'Message to the Three Mehsud Tribes' [پیغام بنام قوم درے محسود], issued by the Mehsud Faction, South Waziristan (n.d.).

'Notice' [اطلاع], issued by the leader of the Mujahideen Shura, North Waziristan Agency (n.d.).

'Organization of TNSM, Malakand Division Pakistan' [محمدی ملاکنڈ ڈویژن پاکستان تنظیم تحریک نفاظ شریعت], written by Saif-ul-Islam, spokesman of TNSM Malakand Division including Kohistan and Hazara (dated 13 January 2011).

'Phone Call from TTP Spokesman Azam Tariq', message from TTP Miranshah, North Waziristan (26 January 2011).

'Phone Call Taking Responsibility for a Suicide Attack', statement to the *News International* in Peshawar by Amir Muawiya, Taliban commander and spokesperson of the Abdullah Azzam Shaheed Brigade (n.d.).

'Press Release from Miranshah', issued by anonymous Mujahedeen Islam, Miranshah, North Waziristan (3 April 2009).

'Shura Ittihad al-Mujahideen' [شوره اتحاد المجاهدين], issued by Hafiz Gul Bahadur, Baitullah Mehsud, and Mullah Nazir (collected on 19 February 2009).

'Statement by Amir Baitullah Mehsud' [امير بيت الله محسود كا فرمان], issued by members of the Shura Tehrike Taliban Pakistan, Mehsud Faction, South Waziristan (n.d.).

'Warning I' [خبردار], issued by the leader of the Mujahedeen Shura, North Waziristan (dated 2 May 2009).

'Warning II' [خبردار], issued by the leader of Mujahedeen Shura, North Waziristan (distributed on 30 June 2009).

∽

Index

About the Author

Mona Kanwal Sheikh is a senior researcher at the Danish Institute for International Studies, Copenhagen, Denmark. A leading expert on the Pakistani Taliban, she holds a PhD in International Relations (IR) from the University of Copenhagen, Denmark. She has been a visiting research scholar at the Orfalea Center for Global and International Studies, University of California, Santa Barbara, and the Institute for South Asia Studies, University of California, Berkeley. During her research period, she was also hosted by the Kroc Institute for International Peace Studies, University of Notre Dame, Indiana, USA. She has been awarded prestigious research prizes for her work on the Pakistani Taliban by the Danish Ministry of Science.

Sheikh has published in leading IR journals on the concepts of religion, violence, secularism, and evil. She has also published a significant number of policy briefs and reports relating to Pakistan and the Taliban movement. As a public speaker and former columnist, she frequently participates in debates on Islam and the West, religion and secularism, and terrorism and political violence.

✣